EUROPE THROUGH THE BACK DOOR

At last, a different Europe guidebook — one that deals with the day-to-day techniques of independent, budget travel. Most books only discuss what to see, where to stop, and so on. *Europe Through the Back Door* goes beyond these whats and wheres to also include the vital how-to's of traveling. Thumb through the book. You'll find chapters on basic problems you had never considered before — and probably wouldn't consider until you had to face them in Europe.

Rick Steves is one of the few travel writers with actual experience traveling the same way you will. Never having traveled as a "guest" of the travel industry, he has had to travel on a budget, learning from thousands of mistakes made along the way. His hard-earned experience will save you (literally) hundreds of dollars and dozens of headaches.

The success of the first three editions of this book was due as much to its wit and readability as to its practical information. John Muir Publications is excited to bring you his updated and expanded fourth edition which is sure to make you a seasoned traveler — on your first trip.

Lisa Cron
Editor

Europe Through the Back Door

Fifth Edition

---

by Rick Steves

cover by Jennifer Dewey

illustrated by Melissa Meier

maps by David C. Hoerlein

The updated and expanded do-it-yourself guide to budget travel, with practical information on all aspects of European travel.

John Muir Publications
Santa Fe, NM

THANKS TO:

Maps: David C. Hoerlein

Photography: Rick Steves

Nice-ites: Patty Price

A geyser of bright ideas: Gene Openshaw

Thanks to Carl, Ruth, Gene, Greg, Patty, Dave, Anne, the mini-bus tours and my parents for sharing with me the excitement of European travel.

Special thanks to all those with nuclear bombs for not using them.

Rick Steves' lecture and travel seminar schedules are available from EUROPE THROUGH THE BACK DOOR, 111 4th North, Edmonds, WA 98020.
Telephone: 206-771-8303

Library of Congress Cataloging in Publication Data

Steves, Rick, 1955-
  Europe Through the Back Door

    Includes Index.
      1. Europe — Description and Travel — 1971   — Guide
Books. I. Title
D909.F93854   1984   914'.04558   84-2117

ISBN 0-912528-40-0

Printing history:
  First edition, 1980
  Second edition, 1981
  Third edition, 1982
  Fourth edition, 1984
  Fifth edition, 1985
Distributed to the trade by W. W. Norton & Co., New York

To
The People of Europe

**Also
to those
who further the
myths that inhibit
independent travel —
in hopes that their
eyes will be
opened.**

Contents

THE BACK DOOR PHILOSOPHY 9

1 PLANNING AND PREPARATION 11

Tour vs. Independent Travel 11
Alone or With a Friend? 12
Information Sources 15
Itinerary Planning 21
Jet Lag and the First Day of Your Trip.......30
PACK LIGHT PACK LIGHT PACK LIGHT. 32
Backpackademia — What to Bring? 33

2 TRANSPORTATION 39

Flying to Europe 39
Flights within Europe 41
Cars 41
Driving Miscellany 43
Hitchhiking — Rules of Thumb 44
Walking (and Dodging)....................47
Hiking 47
Trains 48

3 THE BUDGET — EATING AND
SLEEPING ON $20 A DAY 64

Sleeping Cheap...........................66
Finding a Hotel 66
Hostels 73
Pensions, Zimmers, B & Bs...............78
Camping — European Style...............79
Sleeping Free............................83

Eating Cheap 87
   Restaurants 87
   Morsels — One Country at a Time 91
   Picnic — Spend Like a Pauper,
      Eat like a Prince 98
   Eating and Sleeping —
      The Five Commandments 103

4 FINANCES AND MONEY 106
   Travelers Checks 106
   Changing Money in Europe 107
   Keys to Successful Bargaining 110
   Theft and the Tourist 113
   Soft Currency and the Black Market 116

**5 HURDLING THE LANGUAGE
BARRIER** 120
   Communicating in a Language
      You Don't Speak 120
   International Words 126
   A Yankee-English Phrase Book 127
   Practical Phrases in French, German, Greek,
      Italian, Portuguese, Serbo-Croatian,
      Spanish, Flemish-Dutch and Swedish 131
   Insults in Five Languages 139

6 HEALTH 143
   Before Your Trip 143
   Health in Europe 145
   Traveler's Toilet Trauma 149

**7 THE WOMAN TRAVELING
ALONE** 152

8 TRAVEL PHOTOGRAPHY 157

9 MUSEUMS 164
   Culture for the Uncultured 164
   Open Air Folk Museums 166
   The Louvre — A Talk with a Guide 170

10   COPING ABROAD 173
    City Survival 173
    Bus Tour Self-Defense 177
    Telephoning in Europe 181
    Avoiding Some Avoidable Problems 184

11   ATTITUDE ADJUSTMENT —
FOR A BETTER TRIP 186
    The Ugly American 186
    Be Open Minded 189
    Don't Be a Creative Worrier 190
    The KISS Rule —
        "Keep It Simple, Stupid" 190
    Be Miltantly Humble —
        Attila Had a Lousy Trip 191
    Swallow Pride, Ask Questions, Be Crazy 192
    The Travel Industry 195
    Know Thy Travel Agent — A Quiz 196

12   MISCELLANEOUS TIPS AND
TRICKS 199
    Terrorism and Tourism 199
    Geriatric Globe-Trotting 202
    Travel Laundry 204
    Souvenir Strategy 206

13   EUROPE —
THE WHIRLWIND TOUR 209
    The Whirlwind Tour Itinerary —
        Some Specifics 212
    High Speed Town-Hopping 217
    The Home-Base Strategy 218

PART TWO —
THIRTY-FOUR BACK DOORS 220
    Hilltowns of Tuscany and Umbria 225
    Civita de Bagnoregio 228

Italy's Cinqueterre 231
Palermo 235
Dingle Peninsula — A Gaelic Bike Ride 238
North Ireland — A Terrible Beauty 241
London — A Warm Look at a Cold City 245
The Moors of England 252
Bath, England — Elegant and Frivolous 254
York Castle Museum —
    A Walk With Dickens 256
The Romantic Road 259
Castle Day...............................263
Kleine Scheidegg and Gimmelwald —
    The Heart of Switzerland 267
From France to Italy — Over Mt. Blanc.....274
Alsace — The French-Teutonic
    Land of Wine 278
Brittany 283
Carcassonne — Europe's Greatest
    Medieval Fortress City 286
Versailles — Europe's Palace of Palaces 289
France by Car............................292
French Cuisine 295
Oslo 298
Stalking Stockholm 301
Eastern Europe..........................304
Ignored Bulgaria.........................307
Moscow After Dark......................310
South Spain.............................312
A Day in Lisbon.........................317
Morocco — Plunge Deep 321
Yugoslavia 326
The Gorge of Samaria on
    The Isle of Crete....................330
The Best Way From Athens to Turkey 333
Eastern Turkey 337
The Treasures of Luxor...................342
Bad Towns..............................348

EUROPE
THROUGH THE BACK DOOR

Most people enter Europe through the front door. In fact, seeing Europe in this way has become common-place — almost blasé.

Make your trip special. Come with me . . . through the back door. A warm, relaxed, personable Europe will greet us as an intimate friend. We can become temporary Europeans, part of the family — approaching Europe on its level, accepting its way of life, appreciating its different ways. We will demand nothing — nothing except that no fuss be made over us. We will feel its fjords and caress its castles.

Spending money has very little to do with enjoying your trip. In fact, spending less money brings you closer to Europe. A lot of money forces you through Europe's grand front entrance. You will receive the formal, polite (and often stuffy) treatment. But through the back door . . . well, that's a different story — a story I'd like to tell. The most important decision you will make is which door to enter.

The first half of this book is devoted to the skills of European travel. In the last half, I will give you the keys to some of Europe's most exciting back doors, places where you can see Europe — not just other tourists.

Rick Steves

The Back-Door Travel Philosophy

Travel is intensified living — maximum thrills per minute. It's one of the last great sources of legal adventure.

Affording travel is a matter of priorities. Many people who "can't afford a trip" could sell their car and travel for two years. A friend marvels at my ability to come up with the money to travel as we sit on $2000 worth of living room furniture. I read my journal on a $20 sofa and spend my free time and money roaming the world.

Experiencing the real thing requires candid informality. A "Sound and Light" show at the Acropolis with six bus-loads of tourists is OK, but you'll find the real Greece down the street playing Backgammon in an Athens tea house. Luxor has plenty of monuments to the dead. After touring the tombs, liven things up with a bicycle ride through Village Egypt. These nearby towns are a cultural carnival — and a perfect example of how some of the best things in travel are free.

Traditional travel writing gives its readers an eloquent void — a thousand column inches wide. This book will fill that hole with a foundation in travel skills that will prepare and encourage you to experience Europe — as well as the world — from Walla Walla to Bora Bora. You'll see Europe with the eyes of a temporary local person — a living Europe, not just a quick appraisal from the roof garden of the Inter-Continental hotel and cultural cliches kept alive only for tourists.

I will discuss problems and offer solutions, bolstered b' cocky optimism. Too much travel writing comes from trips. A guest of a country's tourist industry gains exp' that is helpful only to other guests of the industry. I travel the way you will. My job is to make mistakes so you can learn from them.

This book will dispel myths and conquer the fears and apprehensions that inhibit travelers. Here are a few of my beliefs:

You can travel anywhere in Europe (and the world) for $20 a day plus transportation costs. Money has little to do with enjoying your trip. In fact, spending more money builds a thicker wall between you and what you came to see. If you spend enough, you can surround yourself with other Americans and talk baseball. A tight budget forces you to travel "close to the ground," meeting and communicating with the people, not relying on service with a purchased smile. I'll never sacrifice sleep, nutrition, safety or cleanliness in the name of budget. I enjoy — and prefer — the alternatives to expensive hotels and restaurants.

I have found that if I don't enjoy a place it's often because I don't know enough about it. Seek out the truth. Recognize tourist traps.

A culture is legitimized by its existence. Give a people the benefit of your open mind. We really have no right to ridicule a starving Hindu for his fat cow. It's natural — but incorrect — to measure the world by America's yardstick of cultural values. I try to understand and accept without judging.

Of course, travel, like the world, is a series of hills and valleys. Be fanatically positive. Remember, that Lisbon traffic jam is so much more fun than those back home. Optimism is a mental discipline — a requirement for "dream-travel."

Travel is addictive. It can make you a happier American as well as a citizen of the world. Our Earth is home to five billion equally important people. That's wonderfully humbling. Globe-trotting destroys ethno-centricity and encourages the understanding and appreciation of various cultures. Travel changes people, and I like the results. Many travelers assimilate the best points of different cultures into their own character. Europe is a cultural garden and "Back Door travelers" are fixing the ultimate salad — won't you join us?

1
Planning and Preparation

The more you plan and prepare, the better trip you'll have. A European adventure is a huge investment of time and money. Those who invest wisely enjoy fabulous returns.

Tour vs. Independent Travel

One of the first big decisions to make is whether to travel alone or with a group. Consider the pros and cons of each. The proper decision requires some introspection: do you want the security of knowing that all your rooms are reserved and that a trained guide will take you smoothly from one hotel to the next? Do you require good hotels and restaurant meals, wishing at the same time to be as economical as possible? Will you forego adventure, independence and the challenge of doing it on your own in order to take the worry and bother out of your travels? Is sitting on a bus with the same group of tourists an acceptable way to spend your vacation? If the answer to these questions is "yes," then you need a good European tour company to show you Europe. Your travel agent can help you.

For many people, tours are the most economical way to see Europe. Without a tour, three restaurant meals a day and a big modern hotel are very expensive. Large tour companies book thousands of rooms and meals year-round and can, with their tremendous economic clout, get prices that no individual tourist could even come close to. For instance, on a recent "Cosmos" tour (one of the largest and cheapest tour companies in Europe), I spent $40 per day for three weeks, getting fine rooms (with private bath), three hot meals a day, bus transportation and the services of a European guide. Considering that each hotel room alone would have cost the tourist off the street at least $50, that all-inclusive tour price of $40 per day was great. Such comfort these days is very expensive without a tour. (To get the most out of your tour, read the chapter on "Bus Tour Self-Defense.")

A tour, however, is not the most inexpensive way to see Europe. The cheapest and, for me, the best way to see Europe is to travel independently. If you've read this far you have what it takes mentally to handle Europe on your own. To the independent traveler, Europe can be a rewarding challenge and adventure as well as an enjoyable vacation. While the tour groups that unload on Europe's quaintest towns are treated as an entity, a mob to be fed, shown around and moved out, the individual traveler enjoys the personal side of international travel. From this point on, this book will focus mainly on the skills of do-it-yourself European travel.

If you're destined for a tour, read on. Even on a bus with 50 other people, you can and should be in control—thinking as an independent tourist—not a meek sheep in vagabondage.

Alone or With a Friend?

The independent traveler must weigh the advantages and disadvantages of traveling alone or with a friend.

Traveling alone gives you complete freedom and independence. You never have to wait for your partner to pack up; you never need to consider what the partner wants to see, where he wants to go, how fast he wants to travel, when he's tired, how much he wants to spend; you go where you want to, when you want to. You will meet more people when you travel alone for two reasons: you are more accessible in the eyes of a European, and loneliness will drive you to reach out and make friends. When you are traveling with someone it is just too easy to focus on your partner and forget about meeting Europeans.

Solo travel is intensely personal. Without the comfortable crutch of a friend, you're more likely to know the joys of self-discovery and the pleasures found in the kindness of strangers. You will be exploring yourself as well as a new city or country.

Traveling alone can be very lonely. Hotel rooms become silent cells and meals are served in a puddle of silence. Big cities can be cold and ugly when the only person you have to talk to is yourself. Being sick alone in a country where no one even knows you exist is an experience you will try unsuccessfully to forget.

Traveling with a partner overcomes many of these problems. Shared experiences are more fun, and for the rest of your life, there will be a special bond between you and the friend that you shared Europe with. When I travel with a partner it's easier for me to be "wild and crazy." The confident, uninhibited extrovert is more likely to run into exciting and memorable events on his trip.

Traveling with a partner is cheaper. Rarely does a double room cost as much as two singles. If a single room costs $10, a double room will generally be around $14, a savings of $3 per night per person. Picnicking is cheaper and easier when you aren't eating alone. Those traveling in pairs are able to split the cost of travel guides, maps, magazines, taxis, storage lockers and much more. Besides expenses, they can share the burden of time-consuming hassles. For example, only one person has to stand in ticket or bank lines.

Remember, traveling together greatly accelerates a relationship — especially a romantic one. You see each other constantly, making endless decisions, and the niceties go out the window. Everything becomes very real, and you are in an adventure — and a struggle — together. You can jam the experiences of years into one summer (I think that is one thing that keeps me returning to Europe).

I'd be scared to death to marry someone I hadn't traveled with. A mutual travel experience is unreasonably stressful on a relationship — revealing its ultimate course. It's the greatest way to get to know somebody in every conceivable sense.

Your choice of a travel partner is crucial. It can make or break a trip. My favorite formula is to travel with a well-matched partner. Traveling with the wrong partner can be like a two-month computer date. I would much rather travel alone. Analyse your travel styles and goals for compatibility. Consider a trial weekend together before merging your dream trips.

I went to Europe once to dive into as many cultures and experience as many adventures as possible. The trip was a challenge, and I planned to rest when I got home. My partner wanted to get away from it all, to relax and escape the pressures of the business world. Our ideas of acceptable hotels and good meals were quite different. The trip was a near-disaster. Choose a partner carefully.

Many people have no choice — for better or worse — they have their partner. In the case of married couples, remember to minimize the stress of traveling together by recognizing each others' needs for independence. There's absolutely nothing dangerous, insulting or wrong with taking time alone to exercise your independence, but it's a freedom too few travel partnerships exercise. After you do your own thing for a few hours — or even days — your togetherness will be fun again.

Traveling in a threesome or foursome is usually troublesome. The "split and be independent" strategy is particularly valuable here, especially if each person is strong-willed.

Another way to minimize travel partnership stress is to go communal with your money. Separate checks, double bank charges, and long lists of petty IOU's in six different currencies are a pain. Pool your resources, noting how much each person contributes, and just assume everything equals out in the long run. Keep track of major individual expenses, but don't worry who got an extra postcard or "gelati." Enjoy treating each other to taxis and dinner out of your "kitty" and after the trip, divvy up the remains. If one person consumed $25 or $30 more, that's a small price to pay for the convenience of communal money.

Information Sources

Books

Too many people spend their vacations stranded on a Paris street corner. They thought they could manage without a guidebook — or maybe they didn't think at all. You need a good directory-type guidebook. You can't fake it in Europe. Those who get the best trip for the least expense and with minimal headaches not only have a good guidebook — they *use* it. I can step off the plane for my first time in Bangkok and travel like an old pro by taking full advantage of a good guidebook.

Before buying a book, study it; how old is the information? The cheapest books are often the oldest — no bargain. Who wrote it? What's his experience? Is it readable? Many guidebooks are practical only as a powerful sedative. It should be fun but not wordy. Don't believe everything you read. The power of the printed word is scary. Most books are peppered with information that is simply wrong. Incredibly enough, even this book may have an error (but I could be wrong). Many "writers" succumb to the temptation to write guidebooks based on hearsay, travel brochures and other books.

A comprehensive review of all the Europe guides is beyond the scope of this book. I'll just mention a few books that I've found very helpful.

Let's Go: Europe   Aptly subtitled "The Bible of the Budget Traveler," I wouldn't travel without it. "Let's Go" covers the big cities, towns and countryside of all European countries as well as North Africa and the USSR. You'll find listings of budget accommodations and restaurants, info on public transportation, capsule social, political and historic run-downs and a refreshingly opinionated look at sights and tourist activities. It doesn't teach "Ugly Americanism" like many prominent Europe guidebooks.

Written by Harvard students for young travelers, it's the best book available for anyone wanting to travel as a temporary European in search of cultural intimacy on a budget. It is updated each year and not available in Europe. (Always use the most recent edition — I've bought the last twelve.)

"Let's Go's" problem is that so many people use it. If all you've read is "Let's Go" it's hard to tell someone an anecdote they haven't already heard.

Let's Go: Britain and Ireland

Let's Go: France

Let's Go: Italy

Let's Go: Spain, Portugal and Morocco

Let's Go: Greece

Let's Go: Israel and Egypt

If you'll be spending two weeks in any of these areas and like "Let's Go's" style these editions are for you. Offering ten times the coverage of "Let's Go: Europe" and giving you some elite info (very few people use these compared to "Europe"), these are easily the best guides available for these countries. The new Morocco, Israel and Egypt coverage really filled a void.

Europe on $25 a Day, by Arthur Frommer This standard guide is good for the big cities but totally ignores everything else (and there's so much more!). Reliable and handy listings of budget hotels, restaurants, and sightseeing ideas. I would buy it and take along only the chapters on the cities I plan to visit as supplemental information.

Frommer Books on Specific Countries These books offer a much more thorough coverage of each country — regions, towns and villages as well as cities. Some of these are "wordy" at the expense of practical help and most over-emphasize hotel and restaurant listings, neglecting sights and culture. I hate to see 80% of a book's pages spent listing places to eat and sleep when any B & B will do. This conditions readers to think that

80% of their concern will be on finding room and board. Not true. *Scandinavia on $25 a Day* is the best book available on that region.

Discovery Trips in Europe   This Sunset guide is great pre-trip reading offering "Discovery Trips" (their "Back Doors") to every corner of Europe rather than attempting a comprehensive coverage. It will give you some unique ideas for your itinerary. Well written and worth studying and taking applicable photocopies or notes with you.

The Whole World Handbook   By CIEE, this is, without any doubt, the greatest sourcebook for those interested in working or studying in Europe. CIEE is the biggest and most energetic student travel service in the USA — well worth taking advantage of.

Michelin Green Guides   These famous, tall, green books are packed with solid "meat and potatoes" info on the sights and culture of different parts of Europe. They ignore hotels and eating but are a gold mine of data on what to see and how. These $7.95 guides to Paris, London, Italy, Spain, Portugal, Germany, Austria, Switzerland, The Loire Valley and most regions of France offer practical and concise information on all major sights plus comprehensive general chapters on history, lifestyles, art, culture, customs, economy and so on. My favorite feature is the large map with places listed according to their touristic importance rather than their population. For instance, an exciting village appears bolder on the map than a big, dull city. Many tour guides really impress their groups — by reading Michelin. Michelin guides are available in English all over Europe so don't pack them along.

Michelin guides have some problems, however. Many towns are judged simply by the magnificence of their cathedrals and nothing else. Natural beauty is rated relative to the country it's found in. A gorge, cave, mountain or forest in Portugal may be great if all you've ever seen is Portugal, but an American or Canadian would hardly be impressed. We visit

Portugal for other reasons. Several Michelin guides have not been updated since the early seventies, so prices quoted can be ridiculously low.

Blue Guides   This series of books (which has nothing to do with European brothels) takes a very dry and scholarly approach to the countries of Europe. Blue Guides are ideal if you want to learn as much as you possibly can about each country (architecture or art history, for instance). With the Blue Guide to Greece I had all the information I would ever need about any sight in Greece. There was no need ever to hire or buy a guide.

Europe 101: History, Art and Culture for the Traveler by Rick Steves.   1st edition, 528 pages, April 1984. This is the first and only travelers' guide to Europe's history and art. Full of boiled down, practical information to make your sightseeing more meaningful and enjoyable. The perfect companion to all the "survival guides," *Europe 101* is your "passport to culture" in a fun and easy-to-read manual. See catalog, p. 366.

There are many other handy books. Find a bookstore that specializes in travel books and browse — books are a traveler's most valuable tool.

While adequate travel information is what keeps your ship afloat, be careful not to go overboard. You can always find good travel books in English in Europe. I rip my books up, bringing with me only the chapters that will be needed on my trip. There is no point in carrying around 120 pages of information on the British Isles if you're not going there. When I finish seeing a country, I throw away my stapled-together chapter on that area or give it to another traveler.

Your public library has a lifetime of valuable reading on European culture. Look under Dewey Decimal #914 for plenty of books on your destination. Versailles came to life after I read a Newsweek book on the court of Louis XIV. If you have a travel partner, specialize in your studying so you can take turns being "guide" and do a thorough job.

Talk to Other Travelers

Both in Europe and here at home, travelers love to share their mental souvenirs and the lessons they've learned. Grab every opportunity you can to learn from other tourists. First-hand, fresh information is the best kind anywhere, and it just waits to be harvested. Keep in mind, however, that all assessments of a place's touristic merit (including my own) are a product of that person's time there and his personality. It could have rained, he could have met the meanest people or he may have been sick in "that lousy, overrated city." Or, he may have fallen in love in that "wonderful" village. All opinions are just that — opinions.

Many of the best guidebooks are not sold in the USA. Take advantage of every opportunity (train or bus rides, etc.) to swap information with travelers from other parts of the English-speaking world. This is particularly important when traveling beyond Europe.

Classes

If you are now a student or can enroll part-time to prepare for your trip, there are plenty of worthwhile classes. While you can get by with English, a foreign language — even a few phrases — can only add to your enjoyment of Europe. History makes Europe come alive. A basic modern European history course turns a dull museum into a highlight. Eastern Europe is a demographic nightmare. An Eastern European studies class will bring a little order to that chaos. Art history is probably the most valuable course for the prospective tourist. With no background on the subject, art is difficult to appreciate. Please don't go to Europe — especially Italy or Greece — without at least having read something on art and architecture.

National Tourist Offices

Tourism is an important part of Europe's economy. Each country has a National Tourist Office with a healthy promotional budget. They are happy to send you a free package of information on their country. Just send them a postcard. Mention your specific interests (e.g., hiking in Austria, castles in Germany, maps, calendar of festivals, etc.) to get exactly what you need along with the general packet.

Austrian National Tourist Office
545 Fifth Avenue
New York, NY 10017
212/697-0651

British Tourist Authority
680 5th Ave.
New York, NY 10019
212/581-4700

Belgian National Tourist Office
745 Fifth Avenue
New York, NY 10151
212/758-8130

Bulgarian Tourist Office
50 East 42nd Street
New York, NY 10017
212/722-1110

Czechoslovakia Travel Bureau
10 East 40th Street
New York, NY 10016
212/689-9720

Finland National Tourist Office
75 Rockefeller Plaza
New York, NY 10019
212/582-2802
(Use same address and phone for the other Scandinavian countries as well.)

French Tourist Office
610 Fifth Avenue
New York, NY 10020
212/757-1125

German National Tourist Office
747 Third Avenue
New York, NY 10017
212/308-3300

Greek National Tourist Organization
645 Fifth Avenue
New York, NY 10022
212/421-5777

Hungarian Travel Bureau IBUSZ
630 Fifth Avenue
New York, NY 10111
212/582-7412

Icelandic Tourist Office
(same address and phone as Finland, above)

Irish Tourist Board
590 Fifth Avenue
New York, NY 10036
212/869-5500

Italian Government Travel Office
630 Fifth Avenue
New York, NY 10111
212/245-4822

Luxembourg National Tourist Office
801 Second Avenue
New York, NY 10017
212/370-9850

Netherlands National Tourist Office
576 Fifth Avenue
New York, NY 10036
212/245-5320

Norwegian National Tourist Office
(same as Finland)

Polish National Tourist Office
500 Fifth Avenue
New York, NY 10110
212/391-0844

Portuguese National Tourist Office
548 Fifth Avenue
New York, NY 10036
212/354-4403

Rumanian National Tourist Office
573 Third Avenue
New York, NY 10016
212/697-6971

or 444 So. Flower St.
Los Angeles, CA 90071
213-688-7332

Spanish National Tourist Office
665 Fifth Avenue
New York, NY 10022
212/759-8822

Swedish National Tourist Office
(same as Finland)

Swiss National Tourist Office
608 Fifth Avenue
New York, NY 10020
212/757-5944

Turkish Tourism Office
821 United Nations Plaza
New York, NY 10017
212/687-2194

U.S.S.R.: Intourist
630 Fifth Avenue
New York, NY 10111
212/757-3884

Yugoslavia National Tourist Office
630 Fifth Avenue
New York, NY 10111
212/757-2801

Middle East and North Africa
Egyptian Tourist Office
630 Fifth Avenue
New York, NY 10111
212/246-6960

Israel Government Tourist Office
350 Fifth Avenue
New York, NY 10118
212/560-0650

Jordan Information Bureau
1701 K Street, N.W.
Washington, D.C. 20006
202/659-3322

Moroccan National Tourist Office
521 Fifth Avenue
New York, NY 10017
212/557-2520

Itinerary Planning

If you have any goals at all for your trip, make an itinerary. I never start a trip without having every day planned out. Your reaction may be, "That shackles him to a rigid plan at the expense of spontaneity and freedom!" While I have always begun a trip with a well thought out plan, I maintain my flexibility and make plenty of changes. An itinerary forces you to see the consequences of any spontaneous change you make while in Europe. For instance, if you spend two extra days in the sunny Alps, you'll see that you won't make it to, say, the Greek Isles. With the help of an itinerary, you can lay out your goals, maximize their potential and avoid regrettable changes.

The success of your trip may depend on how well you deal with the problems of weather, tourist crowds, fatigue and inefficient transportation when you plan your itinerary.

To design an efficient plan:

1. Establish a logical general travel plan   Eliminate needless travel time and expense. The most efficient plan is the "open-jaws" trip. Airlines have "open-jaws" tickets that allow you to fly into one port and out of another at no extra expense. You just pay half the round-trip fare for each port. A good example would be fly into Oslo, travel south through whatever interests you in Europe, and fly home from Lisbon, eliminating the costly and time-consuming return to Oslo. Your travel agent will know which fares allow "open-jaws".

2. Make the most of the weather conditions you'll encounter
Match the coolest month of your trip with the warmest area, and vice versa. For example, if you visit Europe in the spring and early summer, start in the southern countries and work your way north. If possible, avoid the mid-summer Mediterranean heat. Spend those weeks in Scandinavia or the Alps. (See climate charts, p. 363 and 364.)

3. Avoid tourist crowds   Crowds during peak season (July through the middle of August) can be a major problem. Many people do not enjoy popular cities like Venice or Florence simply because of the mass of tourists flooding the narrow streets. (I have a theory that Venice is sinking because of the many thousands of tons of tourists it must support each summer. It wasn't built for that.) Make a special effort to avoid these crowds. Hit the most touristy places (Italy, France, Eng-

land, Germany) in the least crowded weeks of your trip. Try to spend peak season in relatively untouristed areas (East Europe, Iberia, Finland, untraveled areas in crowded countries), hiking in the mountains or visiting friends or relatives. When I land in Europe on June 1st, I know that fairies flee when tourists trample and I have about twenty days to enjoy Europe's top tourist attractions before the crowds invade. The popular places are most enjoyable during "shoulder" season (travel industry jargon for May, June, late August and September, when the crowds are thinner and the European weather is still good).

4. Save your good health   If you plan to visit countries that may be "hazardous to your health" (North Africa or the Middle East), do so at the end of your trip so you won't needlessly jeopardize your healthy enjoyment of the safer countries. If you are going to get sick, it's best to do it at the end of your trip so you can recover at home missing work, not vacation.

5. Punctuate a long trip with rest periods   Constant sightseeing is grueling. I try to schedule a peaceful period every two weeks. If your trip is six weeks or longer, schedule a vacation from your vacation in the middle of it. Most people need several days in a place where they couldn't see a museum or take a tour even if they wanted to. A stop in the mountains or on an island, in a friendly rural town, or a visit with a relative is a great way to revitalize your tourist spirit. Alternate intense big cities with villages and countryside.

6. Leave some slack in your itinerary Don't schedule yourself too tight (a common tendency). Everyday chores, small business matters, transportation problems and planning mistakes deserve about one day of slack per week in your itinerary.

7. Do not overestimate your powers of absorption Especially on your first trip, European travel can be very intense, bombarding your senses from all sides day after day. Each day is packed with experiences and memories. It may be fantastic, but your body can only take so much. You have a saturation point. Rare is the tourist who doesn't become somewhat jaded after six or eight weeks of travel. At the start of my trip, I will seek out every great painting and cathedral I can. After two months, I often "see" cathedrals with a sweep of my head from the doorway, and I probably wouldn't even cross the street for a Rembrandt. Don't burn out on mediocre castles, palaces and museums. Save your energy for the biggies.

Assume you will return This Douglas MacArthur approach is a key to touristic happiness. You will never satisfy your thirst for Europe with one trip. Don't try to. Enjoy what you're seeing. Forget what you won't get to on this trip. If you worry about things that are just out of reach, you won't appreciate what's in your hand. I'm planning my 14th three-month European vacation, and I still need more time. I'm happy about what I can't get to. It is a blessing that we can never see all of Europe. The day when there is no more to see will be a sad one. I cherish the places I haven't seen as endangered species.

The seven factors listed above must be weighed and

thoughtfully juggled until you arrive at a plan that gives you the optimal mix. There are several trade-offs, and you can't have the best of each point. Design the trip that best fits your needs.

Your Best Itinerary — In Eight Steps

1. Read up on Europe, talk to travelers, study. What you want to see now is determined by what you know (or don't know) — which is not necessarily what you would enjoy the most.

2. List all the places you want to see. Minimize clutter and redundancy. (A so-so sight breaking a convenient night train into two half-day journeys is clutter. On a quick trip, focus on only one part of the Alps. Oxford and Cambridge are redundant — choose one.) Have a reason for every stop. Don't go to places just because they're famous.

3. Determine your length of stay, mode of transportation in Europe, and how you'll fly. Research flights for the cheapest dates and ports.

4. List your sights in a logical order, considering: efficient transportation (minimizing miles), an "open-jaws" flight plan, your mode of transportation, weather and crowds.

5. Write in number of days you'd like to stay in each place, considering transportation time. Eurailers use night trains (N/T) whenever possible.

6. Add up days. Adjust by cutting, streamlining or adding to fit or fill your time limitations. Consider economizing on car rental or Eurailpass. (Try to manage a 23 day trip on a 15 day train pass by doing London, Paris and Amsterdam outside of its validity.)

7. Fine tune. Study guidebooks. Be sure crucial sights are open the day you're in town. Maximize festival and market days. Ask your travel agent which flight departure days are cheapest. Fill out a day by day itinerary.

8. Resist the temptation to clutter your itinerary with additional sights. Be satisfied with your efficient plan and focus any more study and preparation on those places only.

Sample Itinerary Worksheet:

Step 1. Study notes.

Step 2. Places I want to see:

London	Rome
Amsterdam	Florence
Alps	Venice
Rhine	Paris
Bavaria	Greece

Step 3. I can escape for 23 days.   Train travel is my choice. Cheapest places to fly to: London, Frankfurt, Amsterdam.

**Steps 4 and 5. Logical order, and
             desired time in each place:**

3 days London

1   English channel crossing

5   Paris

3   Alps

2   Florence

3   Rome

2   Venice

3   Munich/Bavaria

3	Romantic Road/Rhine Cruise
<u>4</u>	Amsterdam
29	Eliminated Greece and still need to cut 6 days. "Open-jaws" into London and out of Amsterdam is economical.

Step 6. Itinerary adjusted to time limitations:

4 days London N/T

3   Paris N/T

3   Alps N/T

1   Florence

2   Rome N/T

2   Venice N/T

3   Munich/Bavaria

2   Romantic Road/Rhine Cruise

<u>3</u>   Amsterdam

23 days with a 15 day Eurailpass

Step 7. Day-by-Day Fine Tuned Plan

F   1 Leave Home

S   2 Arrive next day in London. Buy train ticket to Paris and a Monday eve play ticket. Take orientation bus tour.

S   3 Sightsee all day London. Speaker's Corner Sunday AM.

M   4 Sightsee all day London. Leave bags at station. See play. N/T

T   5 Arrive early in Paris. Find hotel. Museums closed

on Tuesdays. Explore Latin Quarter, Champs Elysees, take bus orientation tour.

W   6   Sightsee all day Paris. Louvre, Notre Dame, eve — Montmartre.

T   7   Early side trip to Versailles. Afternoon in Paris. N/T

F   8   Arrive early in Interlaken. All day Alps hike — (Back Door).

S   9   Free in Alps, Lauterbrunnen, Gimmelwald, Schilthorn.

S   10   Cruise Swiss lakes, afternoon and evening in city. N/T

M   11   Florence. Check museum hours carefully. David closes at 1:00, Uffizi open all day.

T   12   Early train to Rome. Set up near station. Explore classical Rome.

W   13   Visit Vatican, St. Peter's, Famous night spots. N/T

T   14   Arrive early in Venice. Slow boat (#1) down Grand Canal to St. Marks. All day free.

F   15   All day free in Venice. N/T

S   16   Arrive early in Munich. Reserve Romantic Road bus tour at station. Sightsee all day. Evening beerhall.

S   17   All-day side trip to Neuschwaustein. (Castle Day Back Door).

M   18   Most of day in Salzburg (90 minute train from Munich).

T   19   Romantic Road bus tour from Munich to Weisbaden stopping at Rothenburg and Dinkels- buhl. Short train to Bingen. Check boat schedule.

W	20	Cruise the Rhine, Bingen to Koblenz (10:30-1:20) for the best castles.
T	21	Early train to Amsterdam. Call to reconfirm flight home. Orientation canal tour, nightlife.
F	22	All day free in Amsterdam for museums, shopping, or bike ride into countryside.
S	23	Catch plane, Amsterdam-USA.
S	24	Relax at home, put on a fresh set of clothes, enjoy your own bed, fridge, shower, stereo and try not to think about work tomorrow.

Itinerary Miscellany

Carefully consider travel time. The roads, except super-freeways, are generally slower than American roads. Borrow a Thomas Cook Continental Timetable from your travel agent and get an idea of how long various train journeys will take. Know which trains are fast and avoid minor lines in countries with less-than-good railroad systems (Spain and Portugal).

Take advantage of the "Home-base City approach" and the "High-speed Town-hopping strategy." (see the *Whirlwind Tour chapter.*)

Remember that most cities close many of their major tourist attractions for one day during the week. It would be a shame to be in Milan only on a Monday, for instance, when it is not possible to see Leonardo da Vinci's "Last Supper." Mondays are closed days for many cities, including Brussels, Munich, Vienna, Lisbon, Florence, Milan, Rome and Naples. Paris closes the Louvre and most other sights on Tuesdays.

Minimize "mail stops." Arrange mail pickups before you leave. Some American Express offices offer a free clients' mail service for those who have an AmExCo card or travelers' checks. Friends or relatives (unless they live in Eastern Europe) are fine for mail stops. Every city has a general delivery service. Pick a small town where there is only one post office and no crowds. Have letters sent to you in care of "General Delivery" (or "Poste Restante" in French speaking cities). Tell your friends to print your surname in capitals and omit your middle name. If possible, avoid the Italian mail.

Mail pickup commitments are a pain. Don't design your trip around stale mail. Every year my mail stops are farther apart. Once a month is comfortable. If you get homesick, mail just teases you, stirring those emotions and aggravating the problem. The best remedy for homesickness is to think of Europe as your home. Until you return to the United States, your home is right where you are.

Hit as many festivals, national holidays and arts seasons as you can. This takes some study. Ask the national tourist office of each country you'll visit for a calendar of events. (See the festival listing, Appendix II.) An effort to hit the right places at the right time will reward you with some real highlights.

A wise and efficient itinerary is a key element in the success of your trip.

Jet Lag and the First Day of Your Trip

Start your trip on a happy note by leaving home rested and by minimizing the symptoms of jet lag.

Flying half way around the world is stressful. If you leave frazzled after a hectic last night and a wild bon voyage party there's a good chance you won't be healthy for the first part of your trip. Just a hint of a cold coupled with the stress of a long flight will mean a sniffly first week. Once you're on the road it's pretty hard to slow down enough to fight that cold properly.

An early trip cold used to be a regular part of my vacation until I learned a very important trick. Plan as if you're leaving two days before you really are. Keep that last 48-hour period sacred even if it means being hectic before your false departure date. Then you have two orderly peaceful days after you're packed and physically ready to fly. Mentally, you'll be comfortable about leaving home and starting this adventure. You'll fly away well-rested and 100% capable of enjoying the cultural bombardment of your senses that will follow.

Jet lag is the next hurdle to handle for a happy holiday. Anyone who flies through time zones has to grapple with this bioryth-mic confusion. When you switch your wristwatch eight hours forward your body is saying, "Hey, what's going on?" Body clocks don't reset so easily. All your life you've done things in a twenty-four hour cycle. Now, after crossing the Atlantic your body wants to eat when you tell it to sleep and sleep when you tell it to enjoy a museum. You can't avoid jet lag but with a few tips you can minimize the symptoms.

Leave home well-rested. You dehydrate during a long flight so drink plenty of liquids. The flight attendant learns to keep me well supplied with orange juice. Alcohol is stressful to your body and will aggravate jet lag. The in-flight movie is good for one thing — nap time. With three hours of sleep during the trans-oceanic flight you will be functional the day you land. Upon arrival make yourself stay awake until an early *local* bedtime. Your body may beg for sleep but refuse. You must force your body's transition to the local time. After a solid ten hours of sleep you should wake up feeling like "super-tourist."

Too many people assume their first day will be made worthless by jet lag. Don't prematurely condemn yourself to zombie-dom. Most people, of all ages, that I've traveled with have enjoyed very productive — even hyper — first days. Jet lag is a joke to some and a major problem to others. It's hard to predict just how serious your jet-lag will be. Those who keep strict twenty-four hour schedules will probably feel more jet-lag than those who work swing shift or keep crazy hours.

You'll read about many jet-lag "cures." Most are not worth the trouble. Just leave un-frazzled, minimize jet lag's symptoms and give yourself a chance to enjoy your trip from the moment you step off the plane. Remember, this is the first day of the rest of your trip.

Pack Light Pack Light Pack Light Pack Light

The importance of packing light cannot be overemphasized — but for your own good, I'll try. It's Heaven or Hell — and the choice is yours. The measure of a good traveler is how light he travels. In Europe there are two kinds of travelers — those who pack light and those who wish they did. You can't travel heavy, happy, and cheap.

Limit yourself to twenty pounds in a "carry-on" sized bag (9" x 22" x 14" fits under the airplane seat). You're probably muttering, "impossible," but believe me it can be done and after you enjoy that sweet mobility and freedom you'll never go any other way. (I've taken several hundred people of all ages and most styles to Europe in mini-groups. Only one carry-on bag was allowed and now these former non-believers are the fanatic nucleus of my pack-light cult.)

You'll walk with your luggage more than you think. Before leaving home, give yourself a test. Pack up completely, go into your hometown and be a tourist for an hour. Fully loaded, you should enjoy window shopping — if you can't, go home and thin out.

When you carry your own luggage, it's less likely to get lost, broken, or stolen. It sits on your lap or under your seat on the bus, taxi and airplane. You don't have to worry about it, and when you arrive, you leave — immediately. It's a good feeling. When I land in London, I am virtually downtown before anyone else on the plane even knows if their bags made it.

Too much luggage will dictate your style of travel. The "Back Door" is slammed shut and changing locations becomes a major operation. Porters are only a problem to those who need them. One bag hanging on your back is nearly forgotten. Take this advice seriously. Don't be one of the thousands of tourists who return home cursing their luggage and vowing never again to travel with so much stuff.

Backpackademia — What to Bring?

How do you fit a whole trip's worth of luggage into a small suitcase or rucksack? The answer is simple — bring very little. Spread out everything you think you'll need on the living room floor. Pick up each item and scrutinize it critically. Ask yourself, "Will I really use this snorkle and fins enough to justify carrying it around all summer?" Not "will you use it" but "will you use it *enough?*" I'd buy them in Greece before I'd carry that extra weight through the Alps.

Think in terms of what you can do without — not what will be handy on your trip. The key rule of thumb is, "When in doubt, leave it out." I've seen people pack a whole summer's supply of deodorant, nylons or razors, thinking you can't get it there. Europeans are civil. The world's getting awfully small — I bought Herbal Essence shampoo in Afghanistan a few years ago. You can get anything in Europe. Tourist shops in major international hotels are a sure bet whenever you have difficulty finding some personal item. Remember, trying a strange brand of Bulgarian toothpaste can be as memorable as a Swiss fondue. Live off the land with relish.

With this "live off the land" approach, I pack exactly the same for a 3-week or a 3-month trip.

Packsack, Rucksack or Suitcase?

Whether you take a small suitcase with a shoulder strap (wheels are silly) or a rucksack is up to you. This chapter applies equally to suitcase or rucksack travelers. Most young travelers go the rucksack route. If you are a "suitcase" person who would like the ease of a rucksack without foregoing the "respectability" of a suitcase, look into the popular convertible, suitcase/rucksacks with zip-away shoulder straps. These carry-on sized bags give you the best of both worlds. (See Back Door catalog, page 366.)

I used to carry a frame pack because I had a sleeping bag. Unless you plan to camp or sleep out a lot, a sleeping bag is a bulky security blanket. Even on a low budget, bedding will be provided. I would rather risk being cold one or two nights out of the summer than carry my sleeping bag for ten weeks — just in case I might need it.

Without a sleeping bag, a medium sized rucksack is plenty big. Start your trip with it only two-thirds full to leave room for picnic food and things travelers always tend to pick up. Also, remember, bags don't pack so compact and orderly once you actually start living out of them. Sturdy stitching, front and side pouches, padded shoulder straps and a low-profile color are rucksack virtues. There's no point in spending over $50 or $60 for your bag.

Clothing

The bulk of your luggage is clothing. Minimize by bringing less and washing more often. There is no need for more than three pairs of socks (unless you enjoy carrying a bag full of dirty laundry). Every night you will spend two minutes doing a little washing. This does not mean more washing, it just means doing a little washing as you go along.

Recommended Clothing (for summer travel):

    One pair long pants

    Walking shorts with plenty of pockets — doubles as a swimsuit

    Two T-shirts or short-sleeved shirts

    Long-sleeved shirt

    Dark, warm sweater — for warmth and for dressing up; it never looks wrinkled and is always dark — no matter how dirty it is.

Light, waterproofed windbreaker jacket — folds up into
   pocket

Underwear and socks — three sets, quick dry

One pair of shoes — sturdy vibram-type sole, good trac-
   tion, well-broken in, light, cool

Women's extras — summer dress or skirt, swimsuit,
   sandals

For winter travel, I pack just as light. The only difference
is a down coat, long johns, mittens, and an extra pair of socks
and underwear since things dry slower. Pack with the help of a
climate chart.

Europe is casual. I have never felt out of place at sympho-
nies, operas, plays, etc. wearing a new pair of jeans and a
good-looking sweater. Obviously, there are situations where
more formal attire would be in order, but the casual tourist
rarely encounters these. Older travelers may have different
tastes in clothing.

Bring dark clothes that wash and dry quickly and easily.
You should have no trouble drying clothing overnight in your
hotel room. I know this sounds barbaric, but my body dries out
a damp pair of socks or shirt in a jiffy.

It is always fun to buy clothes as you travel. This is just
another reason to pack only a minimal amount of clothing.
Last summer I put away my Yankee-style wide-legged jeans
and enjoyed the European-style comfort of a light baggy pair
of cotton pants I bought in Amsterdam.

Extras You May Want to Pack

Sleeping bag   Only if you plan on sleeping out. A light blanket
or flannel sheet is a good compromise. I have used my hostel
sheet many times in Mediterranean countries for sleeping out,
or as a beach blanket. It is also handy for overnight train rides.
A sleeping bag is a bulky item. Think twice before your bring
one.

Hostel sheet   Youth Hostels require you to use a sheet. You
can bring your own or rent one there for about a dollar per

night. If you plan to do a lot of hosteling, bring your own regular bed sheet or buy a regulation hostel sheet at the first hostel you visit.

Poncho or Parka   A plastic poncho, large enough to protect you and your pack in a rainstorm, that can open flat to serve as a ground cloth for sleeping on or for a beach or picnic blanket is ideal for the hard core vagabonds. Otherwise, a good weatherproof parka is the best bet.

Rucksack   Small size for day trips. These nylon sacks are great for carrying your sweater, camera, literature, food, etc., while you leave most of your luggage in your larger rucksack or suitcase at the hotel or in the train station. The little rucksack folds into a pocket-size pouch when not in use.

A good paperback   There is plenty of empty time on a trip to either be bored or to enjoy some good reading. Ideally, the novel will relate to your travels. (i.e., *Iberia* for Spain & Portugal, *Trinity* for Ireland.)

European map   A map best suited to your trip's needs. Get maps for specific local areas as you go.

Money belt   Essential for the peace of mind it brings; you could lose everything except your money belt, and the trip could still go on. Lightweight, beige and water-resistant is best. (Back Door catalog.) Use it before your trip to be sure it works.

Cash   Bring American dollars (Europeans get a kick out of seeing George Washington become a mushroom) for situations when you only want to change a few bucks and not a whole travelers check.

Foreign currency   Before you leave, buy one bill worth about thirty dollars for each country you plan to visit. This will cost you no more in the USA than it would in Europe, and it will make arriving in a new country on a weekend or evening easier, because you will have enough money to get by on until the banks open up and you can change money conveniently and at a fair rate.

Picnic supplies A small tablecloth to give your meal some extra class (and to wipe the knife on), a mini-can opener, a corkscrew, salt and pepper, a damp face cloth in a baggie for cleaning up.

Water bottle One-quart size, or sturdy plastic so it will hold boiling water.

Knife For sausage and big loaves of french bread. I'm happy with my Swiss army knife (with corkscrew).

Ear plugs If night noises bother you, you'll grow to love a good set of plugs. Europe has more than it's share of night noises.

Zip-lock baggies 1,001 uses; great for leftover picnic food, containing wetness and bagging potential leaks before they happen.

First-aid kit (See Health chapter.)

Medicine In original containers with legible prescriptions.

Extra glasses, contacts and prescriptions

Toiletries In a small container. Minimal.

Nothing electrical Every year some American plugs his Universal adapter into my hotel and the whole place goes universally black.

Clothesline For hanging up clothes to dry in your hotel room.

Rubber universal sink stopper   Works better than a sock in sinks that have no stopper.

Small towel   Not all hotels provide a towel. Hand towel size is adequate.

Soap   Not all hotels provide soap. A plastic squeeze-bottle of concentrated, multi-purpose liquid soap is handy for laundry and much more.

Sewing kit   Clothes age rapidly while traveling.

Travel information (minimal)   Rip out appropriate chapters, staple them together, store in a zip-lock baggie. When you are done, throw the chapter away or give it to another traveler.

Postcards from your hometown and family pictures   Always a great conversation piece with Europeans you may meet.

Address list   For sending postcards home and collecting new addresses. Taking a whole address book is not packing light.

Journal   If you fill an "empty book" with the experiences of your trip, it will prove to be your most treasured souvenir — I guarantee it. I use a hard bound type designed to last a lifetime rather than a spiral notebook.

Sony Walkman-type recorder   Feasible for couples, jacks for two stereo mini-earphones — great sound, good way to make friends

Mini-note pad and pen   Carry in back pocket, great organizer, reminder, and communication aid.

2
Transportation

Flying to Europe

Flying to Europe is a great travel bargain — for the well-informed. The rules and regulations are confusing and always changing but, when you make the right choice — the price is right.

The key to budget flying is a good travel agent. You'll never beat the price she can get. Put your energy into finding the right agent, not the cheapest flight — you'll save money and headaches. I can't (and don't want to) keep up with the ever-changing world of air tickets. I rely on the experience of my agent who specializes in budget European travel to work with me to come up with the best combination of economy, reliability and convenience.

There is no great secret to getting to Europe for next to nothing. Basically, you get what you pay for — or less. Remember this equation: a dollar saved = more restrictions, less flexiblity or more risk. There is no such thing as a free lunch (or a good lunch, for that matter) in the airline industry.

Your flight options include regular fare, APEX, standby and charter flights. Regular fare is very expensive. You get the ultimate in flexibility — but I've never met anyone spending his own money who flew that way.

The popular Advanced Purchase Excursion Fare (APEX) is the most flexible of the budget fares. You can pick your dates and ports but must pre-purchase your ticket and meet minimum and maximum stay requirements. (In England, it's 7 to

180 days.) APEX allows "open-jaws" plans (flying into one city and home from another) for no financial penalty. The major drawback of APEX is that you can't change your ticket once you buy it. The only way to change your date is to refund your ticket (usually at a $50 loss) and buy a new one (if seats are still available) at the current fare which is usually higher.

Standby fares are the cheapest way to go. Your savings over the APEX fare is a function of the risk you'll incur (busy season — bigger risks, bigger savings. Off season — low risk, low savings). If you have a very tight budget and don't mind the insecurity and possible delays, go standby. Ask your agent about the current situation. Every time I fly I meet someone spending fifty to a hundred dollars less than me on the plane. We're flying just as fast and eating the same food. The difference was I went to bed the night before knowing I'd be on that flight. My friend went to the airport — and stoodby. Obviously, in the case of an air controllers strike, or something similar, those "cheapskates who scrounged up unsold seats at rockbottom prices" (standby passengers) are rockbottom in the airlines list of concerns.

The charter scene has its ups and downs. Some years offer exciting charter savings. Do some research. Remember, a charter flight can be cancelled if it doesn't fill. Anyone selling charters promotes an air of confidence but at the last minute any flight can be "rescheduled" if it won't pay off. Those who "saved" by booking onto that charter are left all packed with nowhere to go. Get an explicit answer to what happens if the flight is cancelled. "It won't be cancelled," is not good enough.

Scheduled airlines are very reliable. If for some reason they can't fly you home, they find you a seat on another airline. You won't be stranded in Europe — a risk you take when boarding a "fly by night" company.

If you question the reliability of an airline or charter company ask a travel agent about its track record or write to the CAB (Civil Aeronautics Board) in care of the Bureau of Consumer Protection at 1825 Connecticut Avenue, N.E., Washington, D.C. 20428.

Flights Within Europe

Europe is a small continent with big plane fares. There are a few economical flights available (London-Paris, and to and from Athens) but, unless you have a lot more money than time, you are generally better off on the ground. Special budget fares for inter-European flights are found only in Europe — not in the USA. Remember, extending your flight from the USA deeper into the continent (without stopovers) can be very cheap. Look into "open-jaws" possibilities before purchasing your ticket.

Cars

Car travel in Europe is easier than most people think. Totally free, you go where you want to, when you want to — you're not limited by tracks and schedules. You can carry more luggage (if you didn't like the "Pack Light" chapter, you can even tow a trailer) and it's very economical for groups.

Solo car travel is expensive, but three or four people sharing a car rental travel cheaper than three or four using train passes. The super-mobility of a car will save you time and money in locating budget accommodations — a savings I use to help rationalize the "splurge" of a car rental.

The big American companies offer reasonable rentals in Europe but "Auto Europe" or "Europe by Car" are a bit cheaper. Your travel agent has plenty of information worth studying. Read the brochures completely. Prices will vary up to 40% from country-to-country depending on tax and insurance costs. A weekly rate with unlimited mileage is most economical. Booking from the States, rather than in Europe, is cheaper in some countries and more expensive in others. Personally, I like the luxury of walking into the Marseilles Avis office and finding my name on that envelope with the car prepaid and ready to go.

Spontaneous car rental is easy virtually at any date, any-

_____

where in Europe. Even if you have a Eurailpass, remember, there are places — like the hilltown region of Tuscany and Umbria — where two days in a car is fifty dollars very well spent.

Ask about drop-off privileges and take advantage of a large company's willingness to let you drop the car at their nearest office when your time's up. Avis has about a hundred offices in France alone — a tremendous convenience. If you drop the car where you pick it up, ask for the economy plan. So often discounts are there, but "no takey, no getty."

Gas in Europe is expensive — as much as three dollars a gallon — but their little puddle-jumpers get great mileage. Europe's superhighways are wunderbar but the smaller roads are slow and often congested. You'll make slower time in Europe than in the USA but distances are short and many parts of Europe are remarkably compact.

Car travel is best for a group focusing on one area (seven or eight people do wonderfully in a VW or Ford mini-bus; dirt cheap per person). The British Isles are good for driving — inexpensive rentals, no language barrier, exciting rural areas, fine roads, not covered on Eurail, and, after one near head-on collision scares the bloody heck out of you, you'll have no trouble remembering which side of the road to drive on. (To avoid driving in crazy London, pick and drop your car at Heathrow or Gatwick airports and take a subway or train into the city.) Scandinavia (beware of long waits at ferry crossings), Belgium, Holland and Luxembourg (yield for bikes — you're outnumbered), Germany, Switzerland, and Austria (driving down sunny Alpine valleys with yodelling on the tape deck is auto-ecstasy) and Spain and Portugal (with their exasperating public transportation system, I spell relief — C.A.R.) are all regions that are especially suited to car travel. The whirlwind, see-Europe-from-top-to-bottom-type trip is best by train.

Europe is a continent of frustrated race car drivers. You'll find highly skilled maniac drivers in any country, but the most dangerous creature on the road is the timid American. Be aggressive, observe, fit in, wear your seat belt and pay extra for zero-deductible insurance. (Most included car rental insurance policies come with a $500 deductible clause. One dent could kill your budget and it's hard to drive aggressively — which is safer — with that in mind.)

Horror stories about European traffic abound. They're fun to tell but, really, driving in Europe is only a problem to those who make it one. Any good American driver can cope with European traffic.

Driving Miscellany

Adapt, be observant and try to drive European. After a few minutes on the Auto-bahn you'll learn that you don't cruise in the passing lane. In Rome my cabbie went through three red lights. Curious, I asked "Scuzi, do you see red lights?" He said, "In Rome, red lights are discretionary. When I come to light, I look. If no cars come, red light stupid, I go through. If policeman sees no cars — no problem — red light is stupid." In Rome I exercise as much "discretion" as possible. England's roundabouts work wonderfully if you take advantage of the yield system and don't stop. Stopping before a round-about is as bothersome as stopping on our freeway on-ramps.

International licenses are generally unnecessary. Available, quick, cheap and easy, from the AAA, they are a handy piece of legitimate but disposable photo-identity. Basically a translation of your American driver's license — which makes it much easier for a European cop to write you a ticket. I've never used or needed an International Driver's License.

When interested in transportation, always use the toll roads. The gas and time saved on European super freeways justifies the expense. Small roads can be dreadfully jammed up. Obviously, you miss the sights in between but it's most efficient to zip from A to B and have more time for your primary sight-seeing targets.

Get the best maps possible. European maps are cheaper and better than those you get in the States and they use the local spellings. I buy maps in local bookstores and always ask the person who helps me to suggest the best local drive a visitor could take. That friend will be tickled to plan your itinerary —

and no travel writer could do it better. "Back Doors" are found from local sources — not in guidebooks.

There is no language barrier on the roads of Europe. Even dogs understand Europe's international road symbols. Just use your common sense, a good map and assume it's logical.

City parking is a problem. Basically, find a spot as close to the center as possible, grab it and keep it. For short stops, I park just about anywhere my car will fit without blocking traffic (I've been towed once — a great $30 experience). For overnight stops it's crucial to choose a safe, well-traveled and well-lit spot. Nothing is certain except death, taxes, and vandalism to a car parked overnight in a bad Italian neighborhood. In big cities it's often worth parking in a garage.

Remember, on the continent you'll be dealing with kilometers — cut in half and add ten percent to get miles (90 kms = 45 + 9 miles, 54).

Pumping gas in Europe is not exotic. In fact it's easy as finding a gas station ("self-service" is universal), sticking the nozzle in and pulling the big trigger. A liter is about a quart, "petrol" or "benzine" is gas and "gasoil" is diesel. "Super" is super and "normal" is normal. Freeway stations are more expensive than those in towns but during siesta only freeway stations are open.

Hitchhiking — Rules of Thumb

Hitching, sometimes called "auto-stop" or "tramp," is a popular and acceptable means of getting around in Europe. Without a doubt, hitching is the cheapest means of transportation in Europe. It's also a great way to meet people. Most people who pick you up are genuinely interested in getting to know an American.

After picking up a Rhine river boat captain and running him back to his home port, I realized that hitchhiking doesn't wear the same "hippie hat" in Europe that it does in the USA. The farther away from the militant self-sufficiency pushed by our culture you get, the more volunteerism you'll encounter.

Bumming a ride is a perfect example. In the third world, rural Europe in the extreme, anything rolling with room will let you in. You don't hitch, you just flag the vehicle down.

Hitching has two drawbacks. First, it can be terribly time-consuming. Some places will have twenty or thirty people in a chorus line of thumbs, just waiting their turns. Once, I said what I thought was goodby forever to an Irishman after breakfast. He was heading north. We had dinner together that night, and I learned a lot about wasting a day on the side of a road. Second, of course, there is the ever-present danger involved in hitchhiking. I would say that if you're comfortable hitchhiking in the USA than you should have no problem in Europe.

Your success as a hitchhiker will be determined by how well you follow several rules. The hitchhiking gesture is not always the outstretched thumb. In some countries you ring an imaginary bell. In others you make a downward wave with your hand. Observe and learn. Consider what the driver will want to let into his car. Arrange your luggage so it looks as small and desirable as possible. Those hitching with very little or no luggage enjoy a tremendous advantage.

Look like the Cracker Jack boy or his sister — happy, wholesome and a joy to have aboard. To get the long ride, take a local bus out of town to the open country on the road to your destination and make a cardboard sign with your destination printed big and bold in the local language. Long rides are often advertised on hostel bulletin boards or with ride-finding agencies in many cities. Ask about these at tourist information offices.

Speed and safety are a trade-off when it comes to hitching. A single woman maximizes speed and risk. Two women travel safer and nearly as fast. A man and a woman together are the best combination. A single man, with patience will do fine. Two guys go slow and three or more should split up and rendezvous later. Single men and women are better off traveling together and these alliances are easily made at hostels.

When I'm doing some serious hitchhiking I work to create pity. I walk away from town and find a very lonely stretch of road. In a lot of cases I feel that the more sparse the traffic, the quicker I get a ride. On a busy road, people will assume that I'll manage without their ride. If only one car passes in five minutes, the driver senses that I might starve to death or die of exposure if he doesn't stop. Look clean, safe and respectable. Establish eye contact. Charm the driver. Stand up. Pick a good spot on the road, giving the driver both plenty of time to see you and a safe spot to pull over.

When you're in a hurry, there are two sure-fire methods to getting a ride fast. Find a spot where cars must stop like a toll-booth, border, or, best of all, a ferry ride. Here you have a chance to confront the driver eye to eye, smile and convince him that he needs you in his car or truck. A car's license plate is often a destination label as well. While it is easy to zoom past a hitchhiker at 60 mph and not feel guilty, it is much more difficult to turn down a request for a ride when confronted face to face. A man and a woman traveling together have it easy. If the woman hitches and the guy steps out of view around the corner or into a shop, you should both have a ride in a matter of minutes. (Dirty trick, but it works.)

Discretion makes hitching much safer. Feel good about the situation before you commit yourself to it. Keep your luggage on your lap or at least out of the trunk so if things turn sour you can excuse yourself quickly and easily. Women should not sit in the back seat of a two-door car. A fake wedding ring and modest dress are indications that you're interested only in transportation.

Personally, I don't hitchhike at home and I wouldn't rely solely on my thumb to get me through Europe. But I never sit frustrated in a station for two hours because there's no bus or train to take me 12 or 15 miles down the road. I thumb my way out of train and bus schedule problems, getting to my destination in a flash. You'll find that Germany, Ireland and Great Britain are generally good and southern countries much slower for hitching.

With this "hitch when you can't get a bus or train" approach, you'll find yourself walking down lovely mountain or rural roads out of a village. You get rides from small-town folk — fanatically friendly and super safe. I can recall some "it's great to be alive and healthy" days riding my thumb from tiny town to waterfall to desolate Celtic graveyard to coastal village and remembering each ride as much as the destinations. Some times hitching almost becomes an end in itself. In the British Isles, especially Ireland, I've found so much fun in the front seat that I'd skip my planned destination and carry on with the conversation. In rural Ireland, I'd stand on the most desolate road in Connemara and hitch whichever way the car was coming. As I hopped in, the driver would ask, "Where are you goin'?" I'd say "Ireland."

Walking (and Dodging)

You'll walk a lot in Europe. It's a great way to see cities, towns and countrysides. Walking tours are the most intimate look at a city or town. A walker compliments the place she walks through by her interest and will be received warmly. Many areas, from the mountains to the beaches, are best seen on foot. Be very careful. Pedestrians are run down every day. It is not uncommon for 365 pedestrians to be killed in one year on the streets of Paris. The drivers are crazy, and politeness has no place on the roads of Europe.

If you wait for a break in the traffic, you may never get a chance to cross the street. Look for a pedestrian underpass or, when all else fails, find a heavy-set local person and just follow him or her like a shadow — one busy lane at a time — across that seemingly impassable street.

Hiking

Hiking in Europe is a joy. People explore entire regions on foot.

The Jungfrau is a pin-up girl to those who enjoy it from their hotel's terrace cafe. It's the greatest strip-tease on earth for those who hike the region as the mountain reveals herself in an endless string of powerful poses.

The Alps are especially suited to the walking tourist. The

trails are well kept and carefully marked. Very precise maps (scale 1:25,000) are readily available. You're never more than a day's hike from a mountain village where you can replenish your food supply or enjoy a hotel and restaurant meals. By July most trails are free of snow.

The Alpine countries have hundreds of mountain huts to provide food and shelter to the hiker. I know a family that hiked from France to Yugoslavia spending every night along the way in Alpine huts. The huts are generally spaced four to six hours apart. Most serve hot meals and provide bunk-style lodging. If you plan to use the huts, it's a good idea to join an Alpine club. Membership in one of these European or American clubs entitles you to discounts on the cost of lodging and priority over non-members. The club can provide information about the trails and huts and where reservations are likely to be necessary.

Do some research before you leave. Buy the most appropriate guidebook for your hiking plans. Ask for maps and information from the National Tourist Offices.

Trains

The European train system makes life easy for the American visitor. The great trains of Europe shrink that already small continent making the budget whirl-wind or far-reaching tour an exciting possibility for anyone.

Generally, European trains are fast, frequent and inexpensive (faster and more frequent in the north, less expensive, but not as fast, in the South). By using the train you could easily have dinner in Paris, sleep on the train and have breakfast in Rome, Madrid, Munich, Amsterdam or London.

The Eurailpass

For the average independent first-timer planning to see more than one region of Europe (i.e. Rome to Copenhagen) the

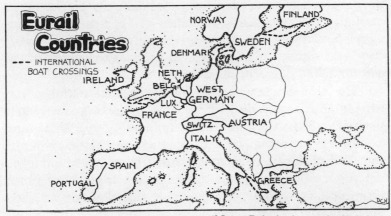

(Note: Britain is not included.)

Eurailpass is probably the best way to go. The Eurailpass is available in these forms (1985) prices:

Eurailpass First-Class: 15 days $260; 21 days $330;
                              1 month $410; 2 months $560;
                              3 months $680

Eurail Youthpass, Second-Class (for those under 26):
                              1 month $290; 2 months $370

The Eurailpass gives you unlimited first-class travel in all the countries named on this map. It's open-dated. You validate it at any train station ticket window just before you catch your first train. The pass must be purchased on this side of the Atlantic. If you are already in Europe a friend at home can buy one for you (your passport number, legal name and money is all it takes) and mail it over. That's as risky as mailing cash. The pass is irreplaceable and, after it's validated, non-refundable. If you never start it you can get a refund less 15%.

While Eurail says the passes are irreplaceable, you can probably, after much delay and hassle, get a replacement pass if you lose yours. The passes have a small receipt tab that will be ripped off and given to you when you validate it in Europe.

Save that tab. If you do lose your pass, take the tab and a good story to the nearest Eurail aid office where, after telegraphing your travel agent to verify your claim to Eurail ownership, they'll generally give you a second lease on Eurail life. If this gets out of hand, Eurail has every right to say "Sorry, Charlie."

Eurail passes must be validated within six months. They increase in price only on January 1st. If you're traveling early in the year, buy in December and save money. They cost the same everywhere (a few mail order companies give a slight discount). Buy your pass from an agent who can help you on your budget-independent Europe plans. Agents who do a lot of Eurail business can issue passes on the spot or within two days. Others take about one week to process an order. (See Back Door catalog.)

The Eurailpass gives you Europe by the tail — you travel virtually anywhere, anytime without reservations. Just step on the proper train, sit in an unreserved seat, and when the uniformed conductor comes, flash your pass.

A few special trains require reservations as do all long runs in Spain and Norway. Otherwise, worrying about reservations on Europe's trains makes as much sense as calling ahead for a Big Mac.

Know your extras. You get much more than just train travel with your Eurailpass. The back of your Eurail map (included) lists all the free and discounted extras that come with a Eurailpass. International boats from Ireland to France, Italy to Greece, Sweden to Finland, cruises on the Rhine, Mosel, Danube and all the Swiss lakes, local buses in countries where they are run by the train companies (the Germanic countries), and more.

Validate your pass thoughtfully. A 21 day pass can usually cover a 30 day trip if you plan carefully. For example, many people start their pass at the French coast between London and Paris to cover the fourteen dollar ride to Paris. Then they spend four days in Paris, not using their pass. At the end of their trip they wish they had four more days of free train travel. To get the most use out of your pass, start it when you're really ready to move (i.e. when you leave Paris). A train pass is not economical in the Low Countries—distances are too short to justify a pass. Have your pass expire when you arrive in Amsterdam.

A Youthrail pass is a second-class Eurailpass available only to those who will be under 26 on the day they validate their pass. Those 26 or over have no choice but a first-class pass — forced luxury. First-class passes are good on second-class and "second-class people" can pay extra to travel with stuffier first-class passengers. If you're under 26 and money matters, go second-class. Virtually all trains have both first and second-class cars (both go the same speed). First-class cars are filled with wealthy "first-class" Europeans and other Eurailers. Second-class cars are where the soldiers and nuns have parties and where your picnic will most likely sprout into a Bruegelian potluck. The major advantage of first-class is it's less crowded than second and this is most important for peak season night travel. Many people complain about over-crowded trains. I've felt like a sardine many times, and spent my share of hours sitting on someone's suitcase in a crowded aisle. But more often than not there is a nearly empty car on the same train that the complainers are suffering on. Complainers are usually too busy being miserable to find answers to their problems. I really enjoy a first-class pass for overnight rides during the summer. Other times, if I'm paying for it, second-class is fine.

(Note: It should be just a little embarrassing to travel first-class. I'll never forget the irate American I met in the Bangkok airport the day before Christmas. He booked first-class to L.A. It wasn't available. He refused to get a four hundred dollar refund to sit "economy" with regular people for 8 hours. Instead, he chose to be very angry, go back downtown and wait two days — missing Christmas at home — so he could fly first-class. What is that Thai lady behind the desk, whose countrymen labor in the fields to support a family on $200 a year, supposed to think about Americans? Incidents like that are commonplace as Americans mingle with the "natives.")

The Eurailpass isn't best for every tourist. In fact, I would estimate that 20% of the people who buy a pass don't travel anywhere near enough to justify its purchase. That's an expensive mistake. Determine what it would cost if you simply buy second-class tickets for each of your expected journeys. If your travel agent can't calculate this for you, get one that knows Europe.

Second-class tickets from Amsterdam to Rome to Madrid to Amsterdam will cost about as much as a two-month Eurail Youthpass ($370). First-class tickets would cost the same as a two-month, first-class Eurailpass. Remember, only those under 26 can buy the second-class Eurailpass but anyone can buy individual second-class train tickets.

If you're traveling just barely enough to justify getting the pass, get one. With the unlimited pass you'll travel more, not worrying about the cost of spontaneous side-trips. The convenience of a train pass is worth a lot. You'll never have to worry about getting the best train ticket deal, no changing extra money to buy tickets and you'll avoid the dreadful ticket lines that exasperate so many travelers. Train stations can be a mess. It's maddening to stand in line beating off all the Spaniards for half an hour and then learn you waited in the wrong line. Many people miss trains because of ticket line frustrations.

There is another train pass, Interail, available only to Europeans under 26. Sold only in Europe, it costs about $170 for one month of second-class travel in all the Eurail countries plus Great Britain, Morocco, Yugoslavia, Romania and Hungary. The European residency requirement is new and those with an American passport must prove residency to get the Interail pass.

Travel Without Eurail

Consider the alternatives to Eurail. If you know where you want to go you can tailor your own personalized train pass at any European station. Just buy a second-class ticket connecting the cities you plan to visit. You'll get one ticket listing your route and up to a year to complete the journey — with unlimited stopovers.

This can be very economical. For instance, if you plan to travel Amsterdam-Brussels-Paris-San Sebastian-Madrid-

Lisbon, you can buy the second-class ticket, with unlimited stopovers for $150 — about half the cost of a 15-day Eurailpass.

You can buy tickets in train stations or at European travel agencies (usually faster, easier, and often cheaper). Buying tickets through your agent at home is unnecessary and probably more expensive. Always ask about special (night, family, senior, round-trip, weekend, etc.) prices.

Most countries have their own mini-version of a Eurailpass. There's the Britrail, Finrail, Swissrail, Scandiarail, and Germrail. I'm still waiting for the Israil. The new Scandiarail pass, given the high cost of train travel up there and the popularity of Scandinavian trips among Americans, is worth a good look. Also worth considering is the Swissrail, which covers endless private mountain lifts as well as the national trains.

Only the Britrail pass, among these single country train passes, is a big seller. England attracts more Americans than any other country and Eurail doesn't cover the British Isles. Worthwhile if you're traveling from London to Edinburgh and back, the Britrail pass has just about the same rules and regulations as the Eurailpass.

The Britrail pass can be purchased in the States or on the Continent — not in England — and is available for from seven to thirty days. This pass differs from the Eurail in that seniors get a discount and people of any age can take advantage of a second-class economy pass. Britrail has some complexities, but everything is adequately explained in its brochure. The Sealink coupon, a discount ticket for the ride from London to the Continent across the Channel confuses many. It's a bargain only for people over 26 who plan to cross the English Channel during the day (youth and night tickets bought at the Sealink office in Victoria Station are cheaper).

To travel from London to the Continent, simply buy a train ticket (at the Sealink office in London's Victoria Station, not in the USA) from London to the European city of your choice. Many people agonize over which English Channel port to use and then worry about missing the boat if their train is late. Relax, don't worry, the boat is part of the train ride. You'll get the most efficient boat and it won't leave until its train butts up against it and all the people file on board. When you dock on the French or Belgium coast, find the train with your destination label and you're home free. Eurail travelers generally buy tickets just to the coast of Europe, validate their pass at that station and Eurail away.

Off the Track — Miscellany

Multi-station Cities Most large European cities and some small ones have more than one train station. Be sure you know which station your train leaves from, even if that means asking what may seem like a stupid question. Stations are easily connected by subway or bus.

Train-splitting Never assume the whole train is going where you are going. Each car is labeled separately, because cars are usually added and dropped here and there all along the journey. Sometimes you'll be left sitting in your car on the track for ten minutes, watching your train fade into the distance, until another train comes along and picks your car up. To survive all of this juggling easily, just check to be sure that the city on your car's nameplate is your destination. The nameplate lists the final stop and some (but not all) of the stops in between.

Baggage Baggage has never been a problem for me on the trains. People complain about the porters of the European train stations. I think they are great — I've never used them. Frankly, I don't feel sorry for anyone who travels with more luggage than he or she can carry. Every car has plenty of room for luggage, so the average tourist never checks baggage through. I've seen Turkish families moving from Germany back to Turkey without checking a thing. They just packed all their worldly belongings into the compartment they reserved, and they were on their way. The only limitation is how long the train is stopped where you're loading or unloading.

Use Train Time Wisely Train travelers, especially Eurailers, spend a lot of time on the train. This time can be dull and unproductive, or you can make a point to make travel time productive. This will free up more leisure time away from the train. Besides, the time spent busy on the train passes faster and more enjoyably. It makes no sense to sit on the train bored and then arrive in Rome only to sit in the station for an hour reading your information and deciding where to go for hotels and what to do next.

Spend train time studying, reading, writing postcards or journal entries, eating, organizing, cleaning, doing anything you can so you don't have to do it after you arrive. Talk to local people or other travelers. There is so much to be learned. Europeans are often less open and forward than Americans. You could sit across from a silent but fascinating and friendly European for an entire train ride, or you could "break the ice" by offering him a cigarette or some candy, showing him your Hometown, USA postcards or by asking him a question. This may start the conversation flowing and the friendship growing.

Station Facilities Europe's train stations can be one of the independent traveler's best and most helpful friends. Take advantage of the assistance they can offer. All stations will have a luggage checking service where, for well under a dollar, you can leave your luggage. People traveling light can usually fit two rucksacks into one storage locker, cutting their storage costs in half.

Most stations have comfortable waiting rooms. The bigger stations are equipped with day hotels for those who want to shower, shave, rest, etc. If you ever, for one reason or another, need a free, warm and safe place to spend the night, a train station (or an airport) is the best place I can think of.

Every station has a train information office that is ready to help you with your scheduling. I usually consult the timetables myself first and write down my plan: for example, Paris-Lyon 14:42, track 6 (using the twenty-four hour clock). I then confirm this with the information desk. Written communication is easiest and safest.

Tourist information and room-booking service is usually either in the station (in the case of major tourist centers) or nearby. This is my first stop after leaving the station. I pick up a map with sightseeing information and, if I need it, advice on where to find budget accommodations. Oftentimes, the station's money-changing office is open long after others have closed for the night. Train stations are major bus stops, so connections from train to bus are generally no more difficult than crossing the street. Busses go from the stations to the nearby towns that lack train service.

When reading the schedules posted in any station, remember that there are always two lists — trains arriving and trains departing. Every train on the schedule is not for you. Some are first-class only, require supplements, require reservations, are sleeping cars only, leave only on certain days, etc. That is why, even after years of reading train schedules, I still confirm my plan with the information desk or with a conductor on the track.

A handy tool that has become my itinerary planning bible is the *Thomas Cook Continental Timetable*. This is a book put out monthly by Thomas Cook Limited, P.O. Box 36, Peterborough PE3 6SB, England. The book has every European train schedule in it, complete with maps. Your travel agent should be able to lend you one, order you one through the Forsyth Travel Library (for their catalog write Box 2975, Shawnee Mission, KS 66201), or even give you an old Cook Timetable. Don't rely on it for the actual train you will take, but use it at home before you leave to familiarize yourself with how to read train schedules and to learn the frequency and duration of train trips you expect to take on your trip. I don't carry a timetable with me. Every station and most trains will be equipped with the same schedule, updated. Those who do carry the "Cook Book" on the train enjoy tremendous popularity.

Managing on the trains is largely a matter of asking questions, letting people help you, assuming things are logical and *thinking*. I always ask someone on the platform if the train is going where I think it is. Uniformed train personnel can answer any question — if you can communicate. Speak slowly, clearly, and with caveman simplicity. Be observant. If the loudspeaker comes on, gauge by the reaction of those around you if the announcement concerns you, and if it's good or bad news. If, after the babble, everyone dashes across the station to track 15, you should assume your train is no longer arriving on track 2.

Luggage is never completely safe. There is a thief on every train (union rules) planning to grab a bag (see chapter on theft). Don't be careless. Before leaving my luggage in a compartment, I establish a relationship with everyone in the room. If they didn't know each other before the ride, I'm safe leaving it among mutual guards rather than a pack of vultures.

Physically I feel completely safe on trains. Women should use discretion in choosing a compartment for an overnight ride. Sleeping in an empty compartment in southern Europe is an open invitation to your own private Casanova. Choose a room with a European grannie or nun in it. That way you'll get a little peace — and he won't even try.

Train Schedules — Breaking the Code

Train schedules are a great help to the traveler — if you can read them. Many Eurail travelers never take the time to figure them out. Here are a few pointers and a sample map and schedule to practice on. Understand it — you'll be glad you did.

Every station is virtually wall-papered with these schedules and maps. Find the trip you want to take on the appropriate train map. Your route will be numbered, referring you to the proper time-table. That table is the schedule of the trains traveling along that line, in both directions (arr. = arrivals, dep. = departures).

As an example, let's go from Venice to Rome (the local spellings are always used, i.e., Venezia, Roma). This is #389 on the map. So refer to table 389. Locate your starting point, Venezia. Reading from left to right, you will see that trains leave Venice for Rome at 6:10, 9:40, 10:25, 11:28 and so on.

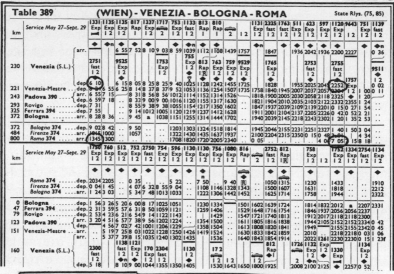

58 TRAINS

TABLE 389

Table 389	(WIEN) - VENEZIA - BOLOGNA - ROMA	State Rlys. (75, 85)

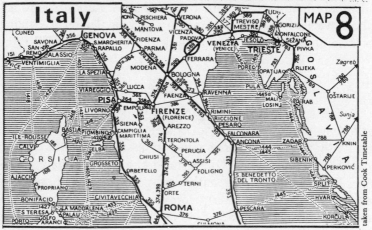

Italy — MAP 8 — taken from Cook Timetable

Those trains will arrive in Rome at 13:45, 17:08, 18:20 and 17:20 respectively. (European schedules use the 24-hour clock.) As you can see, all departures don't go all the way to Rome. For example, the 8:25 train only goes to Bologna, arriving at 10:38. From there the 11:51 train will get you to Rome by 17:08.

This schedule shows overnight trains in both directions. You could leave Venice at 22:52 (10:52 p.m.) and arrive in

Rome by 7:05, just in time for breakfast. Traveling from Rome
to Venice, your trip would start at 0:35 and end at 8:15.
Train schedules are helpful in planning your stopovers.
For instance, this table shows a train leaving Venice at 8:05,
arriving in Florence (Firenze) by 10:57. You could spend the
middle of the day exploring that city and catch the 16:37 train
to Rome (arr. 20:05).
Remember each table shows just some of the trains that
travel along that track. Other tables feed onto the same line and
the only person who knows everything is the one at the train
station information window. Let him help you. He'll fix mistakes and save you many hours. Travelers who buy "The Eurail
Guide" are very often misled in this respect. Each table has
three parts: a schedule for each direction and a section for the
many exceptions to the rules (not shown here). You never
know when one of those confusing exceptions might affect
your train. You should use the tables but always confirm your
plans with the person at the information window. Just show
him your plan on a scrap of paper (i.e., Venezia-Firenze,
8:05-10:57; Firenze-Roma, 16:37-20:05). If your plan is good,
the information person will nod, direct you to your track, and
you're on your way. If there's a problem, he'll solve it.

How to Sleep on the Train

The economy of night travel is tremendous. You slaughter
two birds with one stone. Sleeping while rolling down the
tracks saves time and money, both of which, for most travelers,
are limited resources. The economy of night travel applies to
travel everywhere. The first concern after such a proposal is,
"Aren't you missing a lot of beautiful scenery? You just slept
through half of Sweden!" Well, there are very few train rides
that will have you looking out the windows most of the time.
(Chur to Martigny in Switzerland and Oslo to Bergen in Norway are very scenic.) In other words, nearly every eight-hour
train ride will be a bore unless you spend it sleeping. Obviously,
you will miss a few beautiful sights, but that will be more than

The Economy of Night Travel

The typical traveler:

Friday   Finish sightseeing in Copenhagen.

Friday night   Sleep in Copenhagen. Room costs $20.

Saturday   Spend entire day on train traveling to Stockholm.

Saturday night   Arrive when most rooms are booked. Find acceptable but expensive room for $25.

Sunday   Free for sightseeing in Stockholm.

The clever traveler:

Friday   Finish sightseeing in Copenhagen.

Friday night   22:00-08:00 sleep on the train traveling to Stockholm.

Saturday   Arrive early when plenty of budget beds are available. Get set up in a hotel. Saturday is free for sightseeing in Stockholm!

The efficient traveler saved $45 and a whole day of sightseeing by sleeping on the train.

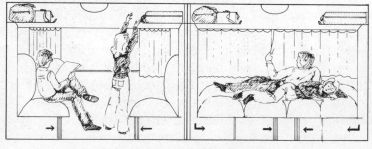

Some train seats make into a bed.

made up for by the whole extra day you gain in your itinerary.

The second concern usually voiced (which should be the first) is, "How do you sleep?" Sleeping on an overnight train ride can be a waking nightmare. One night of endless bouncing of the head, sitting up straight in a dark eternity of steel wheels crashing along rails, trying doggedly — yet hopelessly — to get comfortable, will teach you the importance of finding a spot to stretch out for the night. This is an art that all night travelers will develop. Those with the greatest skill at this game sleep. Those not so talented will spend the night gnashing their teeth and cultivating sore necks and tail bones.

Many trains have seats that pull out or arm rests that lift allowing you to turn your compartment into a bed on wheels. This is only possible if you have more seats than people in your compartment. That compartment can be an overcrowded prison or your own private bedroom — depending on how good

Losers in the "sleep-stakes".

you are at encouraging people to sit elsewhere. There are many ways to play this game (which has few rules and encourages creativity). Here are a few tricks.

The "Big Sleep" Arrive thirty minutes before your train leaves. Walk most of the length of the train, but not to the last car. Choose a car that is going where you want to go and find an empty compartment. Pull out the seats, close the curtains, turn out the lights and pretend you are sound asleep. It's amazing. At 9:00 PM, everyone on that train is snoring away! A car may have ten compartments, each capable of sleeping three or seating six. The first thirty people to get on that car have room to sleep. Number thirty-one will go into any car with the lights on and people sitting up. The most convincing "sleepers" will be the last to be "woken up."

The "Toe-Jam" A crude method of reserving the compartment is to simply jam the door with your foot. This technique works nicely until you find yourself fighting the conductor coming to take tickets.

The "Hare Krishna" Approach A more interesting way that works equally well and is not nearly as rude is to sit cross-legged on the floor and chant religious-sounding, exotically discordant harmonies, with a far-away look on your face. People will open the door, stare in for a few seconds — and leave, determined to sit in the aisle rather than share a compartment with the likes of you. You'll probably sleep alone — or with 5 other religious fanatics who want to chant the night away.

For those snoring, chanting, or jamming their foot on the door, the last minutes are the most tense. There are always a few people wandering around looking for a less crowded part of the train. When the train jolts into motion, you may breathe a sigh of relief, but don't relax for another five or ten minutes. If, by then, you still have your space, you will probably sleep well that night.

Another trick is to use the reservation cards to your advantage. Each compartment will have a reservation board outside the door. Never sit in a seat that is reserved, because you will be "bumped out" just before the train leaves. Few people realize that you can determine how far the people on a train will travel by reading their reservation tags. Each tag explains which segment of the journey that seat is reserved for. Find a compartment with three or four people traveling for just an hour or two, and then for the rest of the night you will probably have that compartment all to yourself.

Most trains are a collection of cars going to several different places. Each car has a destination sign label. Tourists will crowd into the car labeled, say, Munich, sometimes leaving other cars less crowded. Try to find a car that will stay on the Munich-bound train as long as possible, but splits before Munich. Before your car splits (the conductor can always tell you in time), move into a Munich-bound car. This may let you sleep in comfort until 6:00 AM or whenever it splits, while those on the Munich-bound car (due to arrive at 8:30 AM) sit in eternal darkness. Your night was short, but you got to stretch out and sleep.

Remember that trains add and lose cars through the night. A train could be packed with tourists heading for Milan, and at 1:00 AM an empty Milan-bound car could be added. The difference between being packed liked sardines and stretching out in your own fish bowl could be as little as one car away.

For safety, never sleep without your valuables either in a money belt or, at least, securely attached to your body. For good measure, I clip and fasten my rucksack to the luggage rack. If one tug doesn't take the bag, a thief will usually leave it rather than ask you how your luggage is attached.

If you anticipate a very crowded train and must get some sleep, you can usually reserve a "couchette", or sleeping berth, a day in advance at the ticket counter or, if there are any available, from the conductor on the train. These will often cost as much as a hotel, but a good night's sleep is worth a lot.

3
The Budget —
Eating and Sleeping
On $20/Day

In the ten years I've been teaching travel, my notes on budgeting for a European vacation have had to be continuously revised. It looked for awhile like "Europe on the Cheap" was on the road to extinction. We saw Mr. Frommer's book grow from "Europe on $5 a Day" to "Europe on $25 a Day" and many were predicting that "Europe on $25 a Rest Stop" was just around the corner.

Things have changed. Inflation has slowed and, most importantly, the dollar is stronger than ever. Every year since 1980 our dollar has gained in value against the European currencies, giving us a net gain after inflation. In other words, your 1985 travel dollar will go farther now than it did in 1980. That's great news for budget American travelers.

That's not to say the sloppy traveler won't blow a lot of money. You could spend a fortune in a jiffy anywhere in Europe if you let your budgetary guard down. Prices will never be as low as the early 70's and a basic foundation in the skills of budget travel is still necessary to live comfortably in Europe for $20 a day.

Twenty dollars a day for room and board is not far fetched. Civil people have a blast in Europe spending much less than that. (Uncivil people have so much fun, room and board aren't necessary.) This ten dollars a day for food and ten dollars a night for bed is conservative, and the feedback I get from Back Door travelers bolsters my confidence. It can be done — by you.

64

In 1985 I could travel comfortably for eight weeks for $2,200: $1,200 for round-trip plane ticket and a two-month Eurailpass and $1,000 for room and board. This doesn't include souvenirs and personal incidentals. Admissions and sight-seeing costs are very small.

There are two halves to any budget — transportation and room and board. Transportation expenses are rather fixed. Flying to Europe is a bargain. Get a good agent, understand all your options and make the best choice for you. This cost cannot be cut. Transportation in Europe is reasonable if you take advantage of a Eurailpass or split a car rental between three or four people. This is also a fixed cost. Your budget should not dictate how freely you travel in Europe. If I want to go somewhere, I will, taking advantage of whatever moneysaving options I can. I came to travel.

The area that will make or break your budget — where you have the most control — is in your eating and sleeping expenses. People who spend $5,000 for their vacation spend about the same on transportation as the $2,000 tripper. Room and board is the beaver in your bankbook. If you have extra money it's more fun to spend it in Europe, but if your trip will last as long as your money does — figure $20 per day plus transportation.

I traveled for 3 months a year for years on a part-time piano teacher's income. I ate and slept great by learning and using the skills that follow. For the last few years I've been running around Europe with mini-groups (8 to 18 people). By following these same guidelines in 1984 we played it by ear, thriving on a $15 per person per day budget. I bought over 1500 hotel beds last summer — averaging less than $8 per night per person including breakfast. It can be done!

My budget morality is to never sacrifice safety, reasonable cleanliness, sleep or nutrition to save money. I go to safe, central, friendly, local; shunning flakey decadence, TV's, swimming pools, superficial niceties and service with a purchased smile in favor of an opportunity to travel as a temporary European.

Sleeping Cheap . . .

Finding a Hotel With a Price You Can Sleep With

Hotels are the most expensive way to sleep and, of course, the most comfortable. With a reasonable budget, I spend most of my nights in hotels. Hotels, however, can rip through a tight budget like a grenade in a dollhouse.

I always hear people complaining about that "$120 double in Frankfurt" or the "$100 a night room in London." They come back from their vacations with swollen, bruised and pilfered pocket books telling stories that scare their friends out of international travel and back to Florida or Hawaii one more time. True, you can spend $100 for a room — but that's two-weeks accommodations budget for me.

As far as I'm concerned, the more you spend for your hotel, the bigger wall you build between you and what you came to see. If you spend enough — you won't know where you are. Think about it. "In-ter-con-ti-nen-tal" — what does that imply? Uniform sterility, a lobby full of stay-press Americans with wheels on their suitcases, English menus, boiled water, lamps bolted to the tables — and all the warmth of a submarine.

Europe is full of European hotels — dingy, old-fashioned, a bit rundown, central, friendly, safe, and government regulated, offering good-enough-for-the-European-good-enough-for-me beds for $5 to $10 a night. No matter what your favorite newspaper travel writer, or travel agent says, these are hard-core Europe: fun, cheap, and easy to find. Here are a few tips.

Make No Reservations

Reservations are a needless and expensive security blanket. They'll smother your spontaneity. Make reservations

only if you require a specific hotel or location or if you're
hitting a crowded festival or event.

The problems with reservations are three. First, you can't
see what you're getting before accepting. Second, booking
ahead destroys your flexibility. Nobody knows how long
they'll enjoy Paris or what the weather will be like in the Alps.
Being shackled into a rigid calendar of hotel reservations all
summer would be a crushing blow to the spontaneity and
independence that make travel such good living. And finally,
reservations are much more expensive than playing it by ear.
Through my agent, it was impossible to book a room in Madrid for less than $40. I'm sure it would have been a fine room,
but I don't have $40 for a fine room. I went on my own and had
no trouble landing a wonderfully adequate double for $15.
(Your agent is telling you the truth when she says there's
nothing available, or, "This is the cheapest room possible." But
she's been taught to think all of Madrid is listed in her little
book. Not so! Pedro's Pension never made it in any American
travel agency's book of accommodations. You must have the
courage and spirit to go there bedless and find it yourself,
which leads us to the next point — how to find a room.)

Basic Bed-Finding

In over 1000 unreserved nights in Europe, I've been shut
out twice. That's a 99.8% bedding average earned in peak
season and very often in crowded, touristy, or festive places.
(What's so traumatic about a night without a bed anyway? My
survey shows those who have the opportunity to be a refugee
for a night are a little more sensitive to people who make a life
out of being bedless.)

I would rather know the basic bed-finding skills than have
the best hotel listing in existence. With these ideas, finding a
room upon arrival is no problem.

1. Hotel lists Have a good guidebook's basic listing of hotels
and budget alternatives. These lists, while often crowded with
people with the same book, are reliable and work well. Never

expect the prices to be the same. Tourist information services usually have a better list of local hotels and accommodations.

2. Room Finding Services Popular tourist cities usually have a room finding service at the train station or tourist information office. For a dollar or two they'll get you a room in the price range and neighborhood of your choice. They have the complete listing of that town's available accommodations and their service is usually well worth the price when you consider the time and money saved by avoiding the search on foot. Room finding services are not above pushing you into their "favored" hotels and kickbacks are powerful motivators. Room finding services only give dormitory, hostel and "sleep-in" information if you insist. Remember, many popular towns open up hostels for the summer that are not listed in your books.

3. Use the Telephone If you're looking on your own, telephone the places in your list that sound best. Not only will it save the time and money involved in chasing down these places with the risk of finding them full, but you're beating all the other tourists — with the same guidebook — who may be hoofing it as you dial. It's rewarding to arrive at a hotel when people are being turned away and see your name on the reservation list — because you called first. If the room or price isn't what you were led to believe, you have every right to say, "No, thank you." (See chapter on Telephoning, page 181.)

4. Hotel Runners Sometimes you'll be met by hotel runners as you step off the bus or train. My gut reaction is to steer clear, but these people are usually just hard-working entrepreneurs who lack the location or write-up in a popular guidebook that can make life easy for a small hotel owner. If the guy seems OK and you like what he promises, follow him to his hotel. You are obliged only to inspect the hotel. If it's good, take it. If it's not, leave — you're probably near other budget hotels anyway.

5. The Early Bird Gets the Room   If you anticipate crowds, go to great lengths to arrive in the morning — when the most (and best) rooms are available. If the rooms aren't ready until noon, take one anyway; leave your luggage behind the desk, they'll move you in later and you're set up — free to relax and enjoy the city. I would leave Florence at 6:30 a.m. to arrive in Venice (a crowded city) early enough to get a decent choice of rooms. One of the beauties of overnight train rides is that you arrive bright and early. (Your approach to room-finding will be determined by the market situation — if it's a "buyer's market" or a "seller's market." Sometimes you'll grab anything with a pillow and a blanket. Other times you can arrive late, be selective and have no problems.)

6. Leave the Trouble Zone   If the room situation is impossible, don't struggle — just leave. Thirty minutes by car, train or bus from the most miserable hotel situation anywhere in Europe is a town — Dullsdorf or Nothingston — that has the Dullsdorf Inn or the Nothingston Gasthaus just across the street from the station or right on the main square. It's not full — never has been, never will be. There's a guy sleeping behind the reception desk. Drop in at 11:00 p.m., ask for 14 beds and he'll say, "Take the second and third floors, the keys are in the doors." It always works. Octoberfest, Cannes Film Festival, Pampalona bull-run, Easter at Lourdes — your bed is sleeping in nearby Dullsdorf.

7. Taxi-tips   A great way to find a place in a tough situation is to let a cabbie take you to his favorite hotel. They are experts. Cabs are also handy when you're driving lost in a big city. Many times I've hired a cab, showed him that elusive address, and followed him in my car to my hotel.

8. Let Hotel Managers Help   Nobody knows the hotel scene better than local hotel managers. If one hotel is full, ask for help there. Oftentimes they have a list of neighborhood accommodations or will even telephone a friend who rarely fills up just around the corner. If the hotel is too expensive, there's nothing wrong with asking where you could find a "not so good place." I've always found hotel receptionists understanding and helpful. (Remember my experience is based on budget European-style situations. People who specialize in accommodating soft, rich Americans are more interested in your money than your happiness. The staffs of Europe's small hotels, guesthouses and "bed and breakfast" places may have no room-service and offer only a shower down the hall, but they are more interested in seeing pictures of your children than thinning out your wallet.)

To Save Money, Remember . . .

Large hotels, international chains, big city hotels and those in the North are more expensive. Prices usually rise with demand during festivals and in July and August. Off-season, many hotel people will take an offer. If the place is too expensive, tell her your limit, she may meet it.

Many countries regulate hotel prices according to class or rating. To overcome this price ceiling (especially in peak season when demand exceeds supply) hotels often require that you buy dinner and/or lunch there. Breakfast almost always comes with the room. One more meal (demi- or half-pension) or all three meals (full-pension) is usually uneconomical (although not always) since the hotel is skirting the governmental hotel price ceilings to maximize profit. I prefer the freedom to explore, experiment and sample the atmosphere of restaurants in other neighborhoods.

When going door-to-door, rarely is the first place you check the best. It's worth ten minutes of shopping around to find the going rate before you accept a room. You'll be surprised how prices vary as you walk farther from the station or down a street strewn with "B & B's." Never judge a hotel by its exterior or lobby.

Ask to see the room before accepting. Then the reception-ist knows the room must pass your inspection. He'll have to earn your business. Notice the little boy is given two keys. You only asked for one room. He's instructed to show the hard-to-sell room first. If you insist on seeing both rooms, you'll get the best. Check out the rooms, express displeasure at anything that deserves displeasure. The price will come down or they'll show you a better room. Think about heat and noise. It's worth climbing a few stairs to cheaper rooms higher off the noisy road. Some towns never shut up. A room in back may lack a view but it will also lack night noise. If you accept a bedroom without seeing it first and complain to the receptionist, he'll probably look at you and say "tough sheet."

Room prices are determined not by room quality, but by hotel features like: if the reception desk stays open all night, if there's an elevator, how classy the lobby is, shower to room ratio, and age of facilities. If you can climb stairs, use the night key, manage without a TV in the room and find a small old hotel without a modern shower in each room, your budget will smile.

A person staying only one night is bad news to a hotel. If, before telling you whether there's a vacancy, they ask you how long you're staying, be ambiguous. Some hotels offer a special price for a long stay.

Avoid doing business through your hotel. It's much better style to go to the bull ring and get the ticket yourself. You'll learn more, save money, and you won't sit with other tourists who drown your Spanish fire with Yankee-pankee. So often, tourists are herded together by a conspiracy of hotel managers and tour organizers and driven through touristy evenings — 500 flash attachments in a gymnasium drinking cheap sangria and watching flamenco dancing on stage — and leave disappointed. You can't relive your precious Madrid nights; do them right — on your own.

Always, upon arrival, pick up the hotel's business card or address. In the most confusing cities they come with a little map. Even the best pathfinders get lost in a big city and it's scary — not knowing where your hotel is. With the card, you can hop into a cab, and be home in minutes.

Always establish the complete and final price of a hotel

before accepting. Know what is included and what taxes and services will be added on. More than once I've been given a bill that was double what I expected. Dinners were required and I was billed whether I ate them or not, I was told, in very clear Italian.

Showers

Showers are a Yankee fetish. A night without a shower is traumatic to many of us — it can ruin a day. Here are some tips on survival in a world that doesn't start and end with squeaky hair.

First of all, get used to the idea that you won't have a shower every night. The real winners are those who manage with three showers a week and a few sponge baths tossed in when needed.

Many times you'll have a shower — but no pressure or hot water. When you check in, ask when the best time to take a hot shower is. If a shower is important to you, take it while you can. Many have water pressure or hot water only during certain times. Heating water twenty-four hours a day is a luxury many of us take for granted.

Americans are notorious energy gluttons — wasting hot water and leaving lights on like electricity is cheap. What country besides us sings in the shower, or would even dream of using a special nozzle to take a hot water massage? European electric rates are shocking and hotels have had to put meters in their showers to survive. You'll pay about 50¢ for five minutes of hot water. It's a good idea to have an extra token handy to avoid that lathered look. A "navy shower," using the water only to soap up and rinse off, is a wonderfully conservative method, and those who follow will more likely enjoy some warm *wasser*.

I think about half of all the cold showers Americans take in Europe were cold only because they didn't know how to turn the hot on. Study the always different system and before you shiver, ask the receptionist for help. There are some very peculiar tricks. You'll find showers and baths of all kinds. They are part of traveling — an adventure. Nearly every hotel room in Europe comes with a sink and a bidet. Sponge baths are fast, easy and European. A bidet is that mysterious porcelain thing that looks like an oversized bed pan. Tourists use them as anything from a laundromat to a watermelon rind receptacle to a urinal. They are used by locals to clean the parts of the body that rub together when they walk — in lieu of a shower. Give it a whirl.

Europe's budget hotels rarely provide a shower or toilet in your room. Each floor shares a toilet and a shower "down the hall." To such a bathoholic people, this sounds terrible. Imagine the congestion in the morning when the whole floor tries to pile into that bathtub! You must remember, there are only two peoples on earth who believe a bath a day keeps the fleas away — the Japanese and the Americans. Shower-crazy tour groups don't stay in these "local" hotels; therefore, you've got a private bath — down the hall. I spend four months a year in Europe — shower several times — and I never have to wait.

Many budget hotels and most dorm-style accommodations don't provide towels or soap. BYOS. In some Mediterranean countries private baths are very rare. People routinely use public baths. These are a great experience and often come with full service scrubbers and a massage.

If you're vagabonding or sleeping several nights in transit you can buy a shower in train station "day hotels," in public baths or swimming pools, or even, if you don't mind asking, from hostels or small hotels. Most Mediterranean beaches have free, fresh water showers all the time.

Hostels

Europe's cheapest beds are in hostels. Two thousand youth hostels provide beds throughout Europe for two to five dollars a night.

Hostels are not hotels — not by a long shot. Many people hate hostels. Others love hostels and will be hostelers for the

rest of their lives — regardless of their financial status. Hosteling is a spirit. A hosteler trades service and privacy for a chance to live simply and communally with people from around the world.

A youth hostel is not limited to young people   You may be ready to jump to the next chapter because, by every other standard, you're older than young. Well, last year the Youth Hostel Association came out with a new card giving "youths" over the age of 60 a discount. People of any age can youth hostel if they have the membership card (Bavaria is the only exception with a loosely enforced 26 year old age limit), available at your local student travel office or youth hostel office.

A hostel provides "no frills" accommodations in clean dormitories. The sexes are segregated, with four to twenty people per room. A few hostels have doubles for couples and family rooms. The buildings are usually in a good, easily accessible location, and come in all shapes and sizes. There are castles (Bacharach, Germany), cutter ships (Stockholm), Alpine chalets (Gimmelwald, Switzerland), huge modern buildings (Frankfurt), old tunnel-diggers' barracks (Chamonix), bomb shelters (Friburg, Switzerland), and former royal residences (Holland Park, London).

The facilities vary, but most provide more than you would expect. Hearty super-cheap meals are served, often in family-style settings. A typical dinner is meat and potatoes seasoned by conversation with people from Norway, New Zealand, Canada, and Spain. The self-service kitchen complete with utensils, pots and pans, is a great budget aid that comes with most hostels. Larger hostels even have a small grocery store. Many international friendships rise with the bread in hostel kitchens. Very good hot showers (often with meters) are the norm, but many hostels have cold showers or even none at all. The hostel's recreation and living rooms are my favorite. This is where conversational omelettes are made with eggs from all over the world. People gather, play games, tell stories, share information, read, write, and team up for future travels. Solo travelers find a family wherever they go in hostels. Hostels are ideal meeting places for those in search of a travel partner.

And now the drawbacks:

Hostels have strict rules. They lock up during the day (usually from 10:00-5:00) and they have a curfew at night (10:00, 11:00 or 12:00) when the doors are locked and those outside stay there. These curfews are for the greater good — not to make you miserable. In the mountains, the curfew is early because most people are early-rising hikers. In London the curfew is 11:45, giving you ample time to return from the theatre. Amsterdam, where the sun shines at night, has a 1:45 AM curfew. Pillows and blankets are provided, but not the sheets. You can bring a regular single bed sheet (sewn into a sack if you like), rent one each night ($1 each) or buy a regulation hostel sheet-sack at the first hostel you hit (light, ideal design at a bargain price).

Many school groups (especially German) turn hostels into a teeming kindergarten. Try to be understanding (many groups are disadvantaged kids), we were all noisy kids (I hope) at one time. Get to know the teacher and make the best of it.

Hostel rooms can be large and packed. The first half hour after "lights out" reminds me of Boy Scout camp — giggles, burps, jokes, and strange noises in many languages. Snoring is permitted and practiced openly.

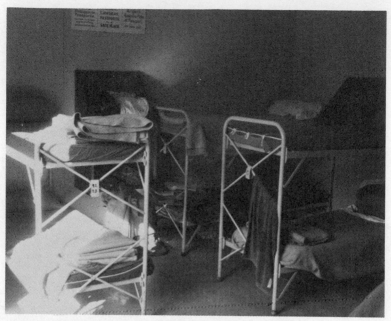

A typical hostel room — for $3 you can't complain.

Theft is a problem in hostels, but the answer is simple — don't leave valuables lying around (no one's going to steal your tennis shoes or journal) and use the storage lockers that are available in most hostels.

Technically, hostels are for hikers, but that can't be enforced these days. It's in your interest to give your car a low profile and arriving by taxi is just plain bad taste. Traditionally, every hosteler does a chore before his card is returned to him. These duties are becoming very rare and most remaining duties are token duties, never taking more than a few minutes.

The hostel is run by a "warden" or "house father." They do their best to strictly enforce no-drinking rules, quiet hours and other regulations. Some are rather loose and laid back, others are like marine sergeants, but all are hostel wardens for the noble purpose of enabling travelers to better appreciate and enjoy that town or region. While they are often over-worked and harried, most wardens are great people who enjoy a quiet cup of coffee with an American and are happy to give you some local travel tips or recommend a special nearby hostel. Be sensitive to the many demands on their time and never treat them like a hotel servant.

Big city hostels are the most crowded and institutional. Rural hostels, far from train lines and famous sites, are usually quiet and frequented by a more mature crowd. If you have a car, use that mobility to enjoy some of Europe's overlooked hostels.

Hostel selectively; there are some hostels that are ends in themselves. Survey other hostelers and hostel wardens for suggestions. I hostel much more in the North where hostels are generally more comfortable and the savings over hotels are more exciting. I rarely hostel in the South, where hostels are less common and two or three people can sleep just as cheaply in a budget hotel.

Getting a hostel bed in peak season can be tricky. The most popular hostels fill up every day. Written reservations are possible but I've never bothered. Telephone reservations work wonderfully where the warden will take them — about 50% of the time. I always call ahead to try to reserve and at least check on the availability of beds. Without a reservation you can count on landing a bed if you arrive in the morning before the hostel closes. If you miss that, line up with the scruffy gang for the 5:00 opening of the office when any remaining beds are doled out. Hostel bed availability is very unpredictable. Some obscure hostels are booked out on certain days two months in advance. But I stumbled into Oberammergau one night during the 1980 Passionplay and found beds for a group of eight.

The latest International Youth Hostel Handbook Vol. I is essential. That small directory, available where you get your card or at any European hostel, lists everything you could ever want to know about each of Europe's 2,000 hostels. In it you'll find which day the hostel is closed, what bus goes there, distance from the station, how many beds, its altitude, phone number with area code, and a great map locating all the hostels.

Pensions, Zimmers, Bed and Breakfast and the Like

Between hotels and youth hostels or campgrounds in price and style are a special class of accommodations. These are small, warm, family run and offer a personal touch at a budget price. They are the next best thing to staying with a local family, and even if hotels weren't more expensive, I'd choose this budget alternative.

Each country has these friendly accommodations in varying degrees of abundance. They have different names and offer slightly different facilities from country to country, but all have one thing in common; they satisfy the need for a place to stay that gives you the privacy of a hotel and the comforts of home at a price you can afford. While information on some of the more established places is available in many budget travel guidebooks, I have always found that the best information is found locally, through tourist information offices, room-finding services or even from the local man waiting for his bus or selling apples. In fact, many times the information is brought to you. I will never forget struggling off the bus upon my arrival in Dubrovnik, Yugoslavia. Fifteen women were begging me to spend the night. Thrilled, I made a snap decision and followed the most attractive offer to a very nice, budget, "Zimmer-type" accommodation.

These places are most commonly known as *Gastehauser, Lager, Zimmer,* or *Fremdenzimmer* in Germany, Switzerland and Austria; *hostalresidencia, pension, casa de huespedes* or *fonda* (in descending order of luxury and price) in Spain; *pensao* or *casa particular* in Portugal; *pension, locanda* or *camera* in Italy; *pension* or *domatio* in Greece, *husrom* in Scandinavia; and *bed and breakfast* in the British Isles.

The bed and breakfast places, very common throughout the British Isles, are a boon to anyone touring England, Scotland, Wales or Ireland. As the name indicates, a breakfast comes with the bed, and this is no ordinary breakfast. Most women "doing B and B" take pride in their breakfasts. Their guests sit down to an elegant and very British tablesetting and feast on cereal, juice, bacon, sausages, eggs, broiled tomatoes, toast, marmalade and coffee or tea, always an impressive meal. While you are finishing your coffee, the landlady (who by this time is probably on very friendly terms with you) will often present you with her guest book, pointing out the other guests from your state that have stayed in her house and inviting you to make an entry.

Your hostess will usually cook you up a simple dinner for a pittance and, if you have time to chat, you'll undoubtedly get tea and biscuits.

When you bid her farewell and thank her for the good sleep and full stomach, it is, more often than not, difficult to get away. Determined to fill you with as much information as food, she wants you to have the best day of sightseeing possible.

The B & B scene is constantly changing and, with a few big city exceptions, the quality is uniformly smashing. Any listing of recommended B & B's is a burden. Find your own. Except in London and a few touristy cities, don't worry about reservations.

Camping — European-Style

Few Americans consider taking advantage of Europe's 10,000-plus campgrounds. Camping is the cheapest way to see Europe and every camper I've talked to gives it rave reviews.

Every town has a campground with enough ground for the average middle class European to pitch his tent or plop his "caravan" (trailer), good showers and washing facilities, a grocery store and restaurant, and a handy bus connection into town, all for three or four dollars per person per night.

"Camping" is the universal word for campground. Unlike the American campground, European camping forbids open fires and you won't find a picturesque riverfront lot with a stove, table and privacy. A "Camping" is more functional — near or in the town — a place to sleep, eat, wash and catch a bus downtown. They rarely fill up and if they do, the "Full" sign usually refers to trailers (most Europeans are trailer campers). A small tent can almost always be squeezed in somewhere. "Campings" are well sign-posted and local tourist information offices have guides and maps listing nearby campgrounds. Every country has good and bad campgrounds. Campgrounds mirror their surroundings. If the region is overcrowded, dusty, dirty, unkempt and generally chaotic, you're unlikely to find an oasis behind the campground's gates. A sleepy Austrian valley will most likely offer a sleepy Austrian campground.

European campgrounds come well equipped. Showers and washing facilities, while often over-crowded, are usually very good. Hot water, as in many hostels and hotels, is metered and you'll learn to carry coins and "douche" European-style, lathering up and scrubbing with the water off then rinsing to abbreviated shower songs.

European tenters appreciate the in-camp grocery store, cafe and restaurant. The store, while higher priced, stays open longer than most, offering late-comers a budget alternative to the restaurant. The restaurant or cafe is a likely camp "hang-out" and Americans enjoy mixing in this easygoing European social scene. I've scuttled many nights on the town so I wouldn't miss the fun right in the camp. Camping, like hosteling, is a great way to meet locals. If the campground doesn't have a place to eat you'll find one nearby.

Silence reigns in European campgrounds after the ten or eleven o'clock curfew. Noisemakers are dealt with strictly. Many places close the gates to cars after 10:00. If you do arrive after the office closes, set up quietly and register in the morning.

Campgrounds are remarkably theft-free. "Campings" are full of basically honest middle-class European families and someone's at the gate all day. I've never heard of a campground with a theft problem (unlike Youth Hostels) and most people just leave their gear zipped inside their tent.

Prices vary from country to country, and within countries according to facilities and style. Expect to spend three to four dollars per night per person . . . about the same as hosteling. You pay by the tent, so four people in one tent sleep cheaper than four individual campers.

Camp registration is easy. As in most hotels, you show your passport, fill out a short form and learn the rules. Check out time is usually noon. English is the second language of "campings" throughout Europe and most managers will understand the monoglot American.

The "International Camping Carnet," a kind of international campground membership card, is required at some sites, handy at others. It is available for $10 through the National Campers and Hikers Association, Inc. (7172 Transit Road, Buffalo, N.Y. 14221), AAA or at many European campgrounds. The "Carnet" will get you an occasional discount or preferential treatment in a very crowded situation. Sometimes you are required to leave either your passport or your camping Carnet at the office. In this case, the Carnet is handy.

European sites called "week-end campings" are rented out on a yearly basis to local urbanites. Too often "week-end" sites are full or don't allow what they call "stop and go" campers (you). Your camping guidebook will indicate which places are the "week-end" type.

Even if you don't have a car or trailer, but are a camper at heart, camping may still be the way to go. Europe's campgrounds mix well with just about any mode of transportation.

Tent and train is a winning combination for many. Nearly every train station has a tourist office across the street. Upon arrival, stop here and pick up a map with campgrounds marked, local camping leaflets and bus directions. Busses shuttle campers from station to campground with ease. Every station has lockers where those with limited energy can leave unneeded bulk. Very light modern campgear makes this approach to camping better than ever. "How to Camp Europe by Train" by Bakken is a popular guide on this subject.

Hitch-hikers find camping just right for their tender budget. Many campgrounds are located near the major road out of town where long rides are best snared. Any hitching camper with average social skills can find a friend driving his way with an empty seat. A note on the camp bulletin board can be very effective.

Tents and bikes also mix well. Bikers enjoy the same we-can-squeeze-one-more-in status as hikers and will rarely be turned away.

Camping by car is my favorite combination. A car carries all your camp gear and gets you to any campground fast and easy. Road maps always pinpoint "campings" and when you're within a few blocks, the road signs take over. I almost always take the bus downtown, leaving the car next to my tent.

Remember, many campgrounds offer "bungalows" with four to six beds. These are very comfortable and much cheaper than hotels. Scandinavian bungalows are especially popular.

Camping with kids has many advantages. A family in a tent is a lot cheaper than one in a hotel. There's plenty to occupy your children, and many campings have playgrounds that come fully equipped with European kids. As your kids make European friends, your campground social circle will naturally widen.

Commit yourself to a camping trip or to a no camping trip and pack accordingly. Don't carry a sleeping bag and a tent as a security blanket.

Your camping trip deserves first class equipment. Spend some time and money outfitting yourself before your trip. There are plenty of stores with exciting new gear and expert salespeople to get you up-to-date in a hurry. European campers prefer a very lightweight "three season" sleeping bag (consult a climate chart for your probable bedroom temperature) and an ensolite closed-cell pad to insulate and soften your bed. A campstove is right for American-style camping, but probably not your cup of tea in Europe. Start without a stove. If you figure you need one, buy one there. In Europe it's much easier to find fuel for a European camp stove than for its Yankee counterpart. I kept it simple, picnicking and enjoying food and fun in the campground restaurant.

Informal camping, or "camping wild" is legal in most of Europe. Low profile, pitch-the-tent-after-dark-and-move-on-first-thing-in-the-morning informal camping is usually allowed even in countries where it is technically illegal. Use good judgement and don't pitch your tent informally in cities, resorts or Eastern European states.

It's always a good idea to ask permission when possible. In the countryside, a landowner will rarely refuse a polite request to borrow a patch of land for the night.

Many cities, especially in France, allow camping in local stadiums. Formal camping is safer than camping wild. Never leave your gear and tent unattended without the gates of a formal campground to discourage thieves.

There are several good camping guidebooks out. The comprehensive "Europe Camping and Caravanning" catalog is available in many bookstores. Each country's national tourist office in the U.S.A. will send you plenty of helpful information on camping in that country.

Camping allows you to explore Europe cheaply. You'll have no trouble finding a spot and you'll meet plenty of Europeans. Camping in Europe has its discomforts just like it does here. If you can put up with those, a camping adventure in Europe is just a plane ticket away.

Sleeping Free

There are still people traveling in Europe on $5 a day — and less. The one thing they have in common is that they sleep free. If even cheap pensions and youth hostels are too expensive for your budget, you too can sleep free. I once went twenty-nine out of thirty nights without paying for a bed. It's neither difficult nor dangerous, but it's not always comfortable and convenient. This is not a vagabonding guide but any traveler may have an occasional free night. Faking it until the sun returns can be, at least in the long run, a good memory.

Sleeping Out   Europe has plenty of places to throw out your sleeping bag. This sort of vagabonding is a bad idea, however, in police states like those in Eastern Europe. Some large cities like Amsterdam and Athens are flooded with tourists during peak season, and many of them spend their nights in a city park. Some cities enforce their "no sleeping in the parks" laws only selectively. Away from the cities, in forests or on beaches, you can pretty well sleep where you like. It's best to keep a low profile when camping unofficially. I have found that summer nights in the Mediterranean part of Europe are mild enough that I am comfortable with just my sweater and hostel sheet. I no longer encumber myself with a sleeping bag in Europe, but if you'll be vagabonding a lot, bring a light bag.

Friends and Relatives The nicest way to sleep free is as a guest of friends or relatives. I've had nothing but good experiences (and good sleep) at my "addresses" in Europe. There are two kinds of addresses: European addresses from home and those you pick up in Europe.

Before you leave, do some research. Find out where your relatives are in Europe. No matter how distant they are, unless you are a real slob, they're tickled to have an American visitor. I always send mine a card announcing my visit to their town and telling them when I will arrive. They answer, writing either "please come visit us" or "have a good trip." It is obvious from their letter (or lack of letter) if I am invited to stop by. Follow the same procedure with indirect contacts. I have dear "parents away from home" in Austria and London. My Austrian "parents" are really the parents of my sister's ski teacher. In London, they are the parents of a friend of my uncle. Neither relationship was terribly close . . . until I visited. Now we are friends for life. There is no better way to really enjoy a strange country than as the guest of a local family.

The other kind of address is the kind you pick up during your travels. Exchanging addresses is almost as common as a handshake in Europe. When people meet, they invite each other to visit sometime. I warn my friend that I may very well show up someday at his house, whether it's in Osaka, New Zealand, New Mexico, or Dublin. When I do, it's a good experience.

I'm not a freeloader when I stay with a friend or relative in

Europe. I am freely invited. I honestly would welcome them into my home in Seattle (although a Seattle-ite is pretty safe, living in such an untouristy corner of the world). Both parties benefit from such a visit. Never forget that a Greek family is just as curious and interested in you as you are in them. Equipped with home town postcards and pictures of my family, I make a point to give as much from my culture as I am taking from the culture of my host. In this sort of cultural intercourse there are only winners. I insist on no special treatment, telling my host that I am most comfortable when no fuss is made over me. I don't wear out my welcome, and follow up each visit with postcards to share the rest of my trip with my friends.

House Swapping   Many families enjoy a great budget option year after year. They trade houses (sometimes cars and pets too — but you've got to draw the line somewhere) with someone in the destination of their choice. Ask your travel agent for information or write to Vacation Exchange Club, 12006 111th Ave., Youngtown, AZ 85363 or The Travelers Directory, Box 1547, Church St., Lancaster, PA 17604.

Sleep free as you travel on Europe's trains.

Trains and Stations can be great for sleeping free. On the trains, success hinges on getting enough room to stretch out, and that can be quite a trick. See "How to Sleep on the Train" in the train transportation chapter.

When you have no place to go for the night in a city, you can always retreat to the station for a warm and safe place to spend the night for free (assuming the station stays open all night). Most popular tourist cities in Europe have stations that are painted nightly with a long rainbow of sleeping bags. This is allowed, but everyone is cleared out at dawn before the normal rush of travelers converges on the station. In some cases you'll be asked to show a ticket. Any ticket or your Eurailpass entitles you to a free night in a station's first class waiting room — you are simply waiting for your early train. First class is nice because hobos and degenerates are found "lodging" in second class waiting rooms.

It's tempting, but quite risky to sleep in a train car that's just sitting there going nowhere. No awakening is more rude than having your bedroom jolt into motion and roll towards God-knows-where. Don't sleep in these cars.

An airport is a large, posh version of a train station, offering a great opportunity to sleep free. After a late landing, I crash on a comfortable sofa, rather than wasting sleeping time looking for a place that will sell me a bed for the remainder of the night. I usually spend the night before a very early flight in the airport as well. Many cut-rate inter-European flights leave or arrive at ungodly hours. The Frankfurt airport is served very conveniently by the train and is great for sleeping free — even if you aren't flying anywhere.

With a little imagination Europe is one big free hotel (barns, churches, buildings under construction, ruins, college dorms, etc.). Just carry your passport with you, attach your belongings to you so they don't get stolen and use good judgment in your choice of a free bed.

... Eating Cheap

Many vacations revolve around great restaurant meals, and for good reason: Europe serves some of the world's top cuisine at some of the world's top prices. I'm no gourmet, so most of my experience lies in eating well cheaply. Galloping gluttons thrive on five dollars a day — by picnicking. Those with a more refined palate and a little more money can mix picnics with satisfying, atmospheric and enjoyable restaurant meals and manage just fine on ten dollars a day.

This $10 a day budget includes a $1-2 continental breakfast (usually figured into your hotel bill), a $2-3 picnic mid-day feast, and a $6 restaurant dinner.

Equate restaurant prices anywhere in the world with those in your hometown. The cost of eating is determined not by the local standard — but by your personal standard. Many Americans can't find an edible meal for less than $12 in their hometown. Their neighbors enjoy eating out for half that. If you can enjoy a five dollar meal in Boston, Detroit, or Seattle, you'll eat well in London, Tokyo, or Helsinki for the same price.

Forget the scare stories. Anyone who spends $50 for a steak in Tokyo has no right to beef. People who spend $40 for a dinner in Dublin and complain either enjoy complaining or are fools.

Let me fill you in on filling up in Europe.

Restaurants

Restaurants are the most expensive way to eat. They can rape, pillage and plunder a tight budget — but it would be criminal to pass through Europe without sampling the local specialties served in good restaurants. You should relish a country's high cuisine — it's just as important culturally as its museums.

When I go for a restaurant meal (about one a day — less in

the expensive north and more in the cheaper Mediterranean countries), I require a good value.

Average tourists are attracted, like flies to cowpies, to the biggest neon sign that boasts "we speak English and accept Visa cards." Wrong! The key to finding a good meal is to find a restaurant packed out with loyal, local customers enjoying themselves. After a few days in Europe, you'll have no trouble telling a local hangout from a tourist trap. Take advantage of local favorites.

Restaurants listed in your guidebook are usually fine, but too often when a place becomes famous by making Fodor's or Frommer's book it goes downhill.

You can find your own good restaurant. Leave the tourist center, stroll around until you find a happy crowd of locals eating. Ask your hotel receptionist, or even someone on the street, for a good place.

European restaurants post their menus outside. Check the price and selection before entering. If the menu's not posted, feel free to go inside and ask to see one.

Finding the right restaurant is half the battle. Then you need to order a good meal. Ordering in a foreign language can be fun or it can be an ordeal. Any restaurant may have an English menu laying around. Ask for one — if nothing else, you may get the waiter who speaks the goodest English. Most waiters can give at least a very basic translation — pork, chicken, zuppa, green salat, etc. A pocket phrase book or menu reader is very helpful.

If you don't know what to order go with the waiter's recommendation, or look for your dream meal on another table and order by pointing. You can't go wrong. People are usually helpful and understanding to the poor monoglot tourist. If they aren't, you probably picked a place that sees too many of them. Europeans with the most patience with tourists are the ones who rarely deal with them.

People who agonize over each word on the menu season the whole experience with stress. Get a basic idea of what's cooking, have some fun with the waiter, be loose and adventurous and just order something.

To max out culturally, I never order the same meal as my partner. We share, sampling twice as many dishes. My groups cut every dish into bits and our table becomes a lazy susan. If anything, the waiters are impressed by our interest in their food and very often they'll run over with a special treat for all of us to sample — like squid eggs.

I like to order a high risk and a low risk meal with my partner. At worst we learn what we don't like and split the veal and fries.

The "menu turistico" (tourist menu) or "prix fixe" menu is very popular. For a set price you get a multi-course meal complete with bread, wine and service. When I'm lazy and the price is right, I go for it, and it usually turns out OK. Many times, however, the meal they served was only enough to satisfy what was promised — and that just barely. Local people don't order "prix fixe." The people eating best order á la carte. Too often, I order the cheapest "prix fixe" meal and leave unsatisfied, wishing I had invested only half that "budget" price in a hearty feast of a picnic.

The best values in European entrees are fish, veal and chicken. The drink and desserts are the worst value. Skipping those, I can enjoy some very classy meals for six or seven dollars.

Before the bill comes, make a mental tally of roughly how much your meal should cost. When the bill comes (get it by catching the waiter's eye and, with raised hands, scribble with an imaginary pencil on your palm), it should vaguely resemble the figure you expected. It should have the same number of digits. If the total is a surprise, ask to have it itemized and explained. All too often waiters make the same "innocent" mistakes repeatedly, knowing most tourists are so befuddled by the money and menu that they'll pay whatever number lies at the bottom of the bill.

Fast food places are everywhere. You'll find Big Mac's in

every language — not exciting (and double the American price), but at least at McDonald's you know exactly what you're getting — and it's fast. A hamburger, fries and shake are fun half way through your trip (I hope I haven't disillusioned too many people just now). Each country has its equivalent of the hamburger or hot dog stand. Whatever their origin, they're a hit with the young locals and a handy place for a quick cheap bite. A sure value for your dollar, franc, or shilling is a department store cafeteria. These places are designed for the shopping housewife who has a sharp eye for a good value and that's what you'll get — housewives with sharp eyes and good values.

Tipping

I'm not known for flashy tipping (in fact I think it's a pretty archaic way of paying people) and tipping is a miniscule concern of mine during a European trip. Traveling through the Back Door, the only tipping I do is in restaurants when service isn't included, rounding the taxi bill up, and when someone assists me in seeing some sight and is paid no other way (like the man who shows people an Etruscan tomb that just happens to be in his backyard).

In restaurants, service is usually included. (It should say so on the menu or bill.) Tip more only if the service was way above and beyond the call of duty. Over-tipping is an ugly-American act that does a disservice to the local people. Waiters who are over-tipped begin to expect the same treatment from other tourists and locals who follow. Americans in the days of the big buck shaped an image that Yankees in the days of the smaller dollar are having a hard time living down.

Countries like Egypt have been especially corrupted by conspicuously affluent tourists, and now Cairo taxis refuse to use their meters for tourists so they can arbitrarily charge (and usually get) triple the normal fare. Egyptian children never say "hello," they say "hello, bakshish," ("hello, give me money!"). And, in Cairo markets, perfect price discrimination runs rampant. If bucks talk for you at home, muzzle them in Europe. As a matter of principle, if not economy, the local price should prevail. Don't over tip.

Morsels — One Country at a Time

Greece

The menus are very difficult to read. (It's all Greek to me.) Go into the kitchen and physically point to the dish you want. This is a good way to make some friends, sample from each kettle, get things straight and have a very memorable meal. (The same is true in Turkey.) This is a common and accepted practice among tourists. Be brave, try the far-out local food. My favorite snack is souflaki. Souflaki stands are all over Athens (like an American hot dog stand). A souflaki is a tasty shish kebab in a muffin. That and a cold Coke make a great snack. On the islands, eat fresh seafood. If possible, go to a wine festival. The Daphni Wine Festival (nightly July-September) just outside of Athens is best. Eat when the locals do — late, and for American-style coffee order Nescafe.

Italy

Italy is no longer so cheap. In fact, it's caught up with and passed most of Europe pricewise. Florence, Venice and Rome are most expensive, elsewhere it's easy to find a decent meal for five dollars.

Italians eat huge meals. The pasta course alone is enough to fill to the gill most tourists. While some restaurants won't serve just pasta, I usually find one that will, and enjoy lasagna and a salad reasonably. Any time you sit down you'll be charged a cover ("coperto") charge of a dollar or so. That, plus service makes a cheap restaurant meal rare. The most inexpensive Italian eateries are called "tavola calda," "rosticceria," "trattoria," "pizzeria," or, recently, "self-service." A big pizza and a cold beer is my idea of a good, fast, cheap Italian meal. Look for a "Pizza Rustica" for a stand-up super bargain meal.

Gelati! Delizioso!

Just point to the best looking pizza, tell them how much you want, they heat it up and it's yours.

One of the most important words in your Italian vocabulary is "gelati," probably the best ice cream you'll ever taste. A big cone with a variety of flavors costs less than a dollar. Cappuccino, rich coffee and milk with a marshmallow-like head, is everywhere, and it should be. Tiny coffee shops are tucked away in just about every street. All have a price list and most have a system where you pay the cashier and take the receipt to the man with the drinks. Experiment, try coffee or tea "freddo" (cold) or a "frappe." Discover a new specialty each day. Bar hopping is fun. A bottle of wine serves six or eight people for three dollars and most bars have delicious "chequitas" (munchies).

Spain

The greatest pleasure in Spanish eating is the price tag. However, cheapness and healthiness can be inversely correlated. Take advantage of the house wine. It is very important to fit the local schedule — lunch late and dinner later. Restaurants are generally closed except at meal times. At other times, "Bocadillos" (sandwiches) and "omelets" (omelets) are served along with "tapas" (hors d'oeuvres) as snacks in bars and coffee spots.

Portugal

Portugal has perhaps the best and cheapest food I've found in Europe. Find a local sailors' hangout and fill up on fresh seafood. It's delicious. Clams and cockles should not be missed. While Portuguese restaurants are not expensive, food stands in the fairs and amusement parks are even cheaper.

Switzerland

A fondue should be a must on your checklist. I order one steak-and-potatoes dish and a cheese fondue for two people. Swiss chocolates are famous and rightfully so. The Migros and Co-op grocery stores sell groceries for about the same price as you'd find in American stores — cheap by European standards. Youth hostels usually serve large family-style dinners at a low, low price. Expensive Swiss restaurant prices make these budget food alternatives especially attractive. Eat at remote mountain huts. Many have provisions helicoptered in, are reasonably priced, and bubble with Alpine atmosphere.

The Netherlands

My favorite "Dutch" food is Indonesian. Indonesia, a former colony of the Netherlands, fled the nest, leaving plenty of great Indonesian restaurants. The cheapest meals, as well as some of the best splurges, are found in Indonesian restaurants. The famous "rijstafel" (rice table) is the ultimate Indonesian meal, with as many as thirty-six delightfully exotic courses, all eaten with rice. One meal will stuff two large men, so order carefully. The Bali Restaurant in Scheveningen is, according to many Hollanders, the best Indonesian restaurant in Holland. I've eaten there on four different trips and have no reason to disagree.

In a budget restaurant "rijstafel" can be a great bargain —
12 exotic courses with rice for less than five dollars. Indonesian
restaurants are found all over Holland. In Amsterdam, the best
budget ones are on Bantammerstraat, just beyond the sailors'
quarters (Red Light District).

Scandinavia

Some of the most expensive restaurants in Europe are
found in Scandinavia. The key to budget eating in this part of
Europe is to take advantage of the smorgasbord. For incredible prices (cheap), the breakfast smorgasbords of Denmark,
Norway, and Sweden will fill you with plenty of hearty food.
Smorgasbords do not provide "doggie bags," but I have
noticed many empty rucksacks being brought in and not many
empty ones carried out. Since my stomach is the same size all
day long and both meals are, by definition, all-you-can-eat, I
opt for the budget breakfast meal over the fancier and more
expensive "mid-dag" (mid-day) smorgasbord. Many train stations and boats serve smorgasbords. The boat from Stockholm
to Helsinki, the boat from Puttgarden to Rodbyhavn, and, best
of all, the lovely Centralens restaurant right in the Stockholm
train station all serve especially good smorgasbords. No seasoned traveler leaves the Stockholm station after his overnight
train ride from Oslo or Copenhagen without enjoying a smorgasbord breakfast. If you don't smorgasbord, Stockholm
could very well break your budget.

"Kro" restaurants in Denmark and "Bundeheimen" (literally, "farmer's house"), found all over Norway serve, like their
name suggests, good hearty "meat-and-potatoes" meals that a
peasant would like and could afford.

Fresh produce, colorful markets and efficient super-
markets abound in Europe's most expensive corner. Picnic.

Germany

Germany is ideal for the "meat-and-potatoes" person.
With straightforward, no nonsense food at budget prices, I eat
very well in Deutschland. Small town restaurants serve up

wonderful plates of hearty local specialties for $4-5. The wurst is the best anywhere and kraut is entirely different from the stuff you hate at home. Eat ugly things whenever possible. So many tasty European specialties come in gross packages. Drink beer in Bavaria and wine on the Rhine, choosing the most atmospheric brauhaus or winestubes possible. Browse through supermarkets and see what Germany eats when there's no more beer and pretzels. Try Gummi Bears, a bear-shaped jelly bean with a cult following, and Nutella, a choco-nut spread that will turn a cookie into a first class dessert.

France

France is famous for its cuisine — and rightly so. Surprisingly, dining in France is easy on a budget, especially in the countryside. Small restaurants throughout the country love their local specialities, and take great pride in what they serve up. Wine is the cheapest drink (more expensive labels run upward of four dollars) and every region has its own wine and cheese.

"Degustation gratuite" is not a laxative, but an invitation to sample the wine. You'll find it throughout France's wine-growing regions. When buying cheese, be sure to ask for samples of the local specialities. Croissants are served warm with breakfast and baguettes (long, skinny loaves of French bread) are great for munching on.

Picnicking is, appropriately, a French word and, as you spread out your tablecloth every passerby will wish you a cheery "bon appetit!"

French cuisine deserves the coverage normally reserved for Europe's more tangible attractions so I've included a Back Door on French Eating on page 295.

Mensas

When you're in a European university town, with a wallet as empty as your stomach, find a "mensa." Mensa is the universal word for a government-subsidized university cafeteria. Here you can fill yourself with a plate of dull but nourishing food in the company of local students for an unbeatable price. Student identity isn't required and Mensas usually close during school holidays.

This is a sure-fire way to meet educated English-speaking young locals with open and stimulating minds. They're often anxious to practice their politics and economics as well as their English on a foreign friend. This idea is especially valuable in Third World Countries.

The Continental Breakfast

On the Continent, (except for Holland and Scandinavia) breakfast is a roll with marmalade or jam, occasionally a slice of ham or cheese, and coffee and tea. The finest hotels serve the same thing — on better plates. It's the European way to start the day. It's nice to supplement your CB's with a piece of fruit and a separately wrapped chunk of cheese. If you're a coffee drinker, remember, this is the only cheap time to caffinate yourself. Most hotels will serve you a bottomless cup of a rich brew only with breakfast. After that, it'll cost you a fortune to support your habit — one costly little cup at a time.

I'm a big breakfast person at home. When I feel the urge for a typical American breakfast in Europe, I beat it to death with a hard roll. You can find bacon, eggs, and orange juice in the morning but it's nearly always over-priced and a disappointment.

One alternative to the Continental breakfast, if your hotel doesn't require it, is to brunch in a park. Get an early start, stop by a public market by mid-morning when it's a hopping sight in itself. Put together a feast and enjoy it in a choice picnic spot.

Drinks

As I will discuss in the health chapter, European water has a different bacterial content than what our systems are accustomed to. Many (but not all) people will have some problem adjusting — not because their water is dirty, but because our systems are weak.

The trouble involved in avoiding European water out-weighs the benefits. As long as my sources are obviously for drinking, I drink the water — even in Italy, Sicily, Greece, Spain and Portugal. Generally, avoid water in North Africa and east of Bulgaria.

Restaurants play on the tourists' fears of getting sick. Even in places as safe as Switzerland, they caution the tourist about the water. This is done to scare you into a $2 Coke or beer at their restaurant. Don't believe them. Order water "nat-ural." If you are not careful, you may get mineral water. Insist on tap water if you want a free drink.

Tap water in five languages
Italian — *l'agua du robinetto*
French — *l'eau du robinet*
German — *heitungs wasser*
Spanish — *la agua del grifo*
Portuguese — *a agua a torneira*
In all other languages just do the international charade: hold imaginary glass in left hand; turn on tap with right, make sound of faucet. Stop it with a click and drink it with a smile.

If your budget is tight and you want to save $3 to $4 a day, never buy a restaurant drink. Scoff if you have the money, but remember — the drink is, along with the dessert, the worst value on any menu. Water is jokingly called "the American champagne" by the waiters of Europe.

Drink like a European. Cold milk, orange juice and ice cubes are American habits, either over-priced or nonexistent in European restaurants. Insisting on cold milk or ice cubes will get you nothing but strange looks and a reputation as the ugly — if not downright crazy — American (see article on "The Ugly American"). Order local drinks, not just to save money, but to experience that part of the culture and to get the best quality and service. If you must have them, the "American waters" (Coke, Fanta and Seven-Up) are sold everywhere these days.

Buying local alcohol is much cheaper than insisting on your favorite import. A shot of the local hard drink in Portugal should cost 25 cents while an American drink would cost several dollars. Drink the local stuff with the local people in the local bars; a better experience altogether than a gin and tonic in your hotel with a guy from L.A. Drink wine in wine countries and beer in beer countries. Sample the local specialties. Let a local person order you her favorite. You may hate it, but you'll never forget it.

Picnic — Spend Like a Pauper, Eat Like a Prince

There is only one way left to feast for two or three dollars anywhere in the world — picnic. I am a fanatical picnicker. I think I eat better while spending $8 to $10 a day less than those who eat exclusively in restaurants.

While I am the first to admit that restaurant meals are an important aspect of any culture, I picnic for the majority of my meals. This is not solely for budgetary reasons. I love to dive into a marketplace and actually get a chance to do business. I can't get enough of Europe's varied cheeses, meats, fresh fruits, vegetables and bread that is still warm out of the bakery oven. Many countries in Africa, Asia and South America have fruits and vegetables that I didn't even know existed. They had their debut in a picnic. I pride myself in my ability to create unbeatable atmosphere for a meal by choosing just the right picnic spot.

I don't like to spend a lot of time looking for a decent restaurant, then waiting around to get served. And, nothing frustrates me more than to tangle with a budget-threatening menu, finally ordering a meal, then walking away feeling unsatisfied, like my money could have done much more for my stomach if I had invested it in a marketplace. So, let me talk a bit about picnicking.

Every town, large or small has at least one outdoor marketplace. This is the most colorful and natural place to go to

Youngsters picnicking on a Swiss Mountain top.

assemble a picnic. The unit of measure throughout the Continent is a kilo, which is 2.2 pounds. A kilo has 1,000 grams. 100 grams, which is a little less than a quarter of a pound, is a common unit of measurement. 100 grams of meat or cheese will make several good sandwiches. Make an effort to communicate with the merchants in the markets. Know what you are buying and what you are spending.

You may want only one or two pieces of fruit. Sometimes merchants refuse to deal in such small quantities. The way to get what you want and no more is to estimate about what it would cost if he were to weigh it, and then just hold out a coin worth about that much in one hand and the apple, or whatever, in the other. Rarely will he refuse the deal. Timidity will get you nowhere.

If no prices are posted, be wary. I've seen terrible cases of tourists getting ripped-off by market merchants in tourist centers. I find places that print the prices. I suspect that any market with no printed prices has a double price standard — one for locals and a more expensive one for tourists. If all else fails, I watch carefully while a local woman buys her groceries. Even if I don't totally understand what went on, the merchant thinks I do and he's less likely to take advantage of me. If I don't like the price, I just say "No thanks."

I'll never forget a friend of mine who bought two bananas for our London picnic. He grabbed the fruit, held out a handful of change and said "How much?" The merchant took two 50 pence coins. My friend turned to me and said, "Wow, London really is expensive." People like this go home and spread these wild misleading rumors ("Bananas sell for a buck a piece in London!"). Anytime you hold out a handful of money to a banana salesman you've had it.

Picnic Drinks

There are plenty of cheap ways to wash down a picnic. Milk is always cheap, available in quarter, half or whole liters. Be sure it's normal drinking milk. More than once I've been stuck with buttermilk or something I didn't want. Nutritionally, milk can't be beat. Half a liter provides about twenty-five percent of your daily protein needs. Cold milk is rare in most countries. You will often find a "long-life" kind of milk that needs no refrigeration. (This milk will never do two things — go bad or taste good.)

Liter bottles of Coke are cheap, as is wine in most countries. The local wine gives your picnic a very nice touch. Fruit juice comes in handy boxes costing about fifty cents per quart. I have often brought a baggie full of Tang from home to provide orange juice instead of water for picnics. The cheapest way to get a good hot drink, for those who have more nerve than pride, is to get your plastic water bottle filled with free boiling water at a cafe, then add your own instant coffee or tea bag later. (A sturdy plastic bottle will not melt.)

Atmosphere

There is nothing second class about a picnic. A few special touches will even make your budget meal a first class affair.

Proper site selection can make the difference between just another meal and a banquet you'll always remember. Since you've decided to skip the restaurant, it's up to you to create the atmosphere. I try to incorporate a picnic brunch, lunch or dinner into the day's sightseeing plans. For example, I'll start the day by scouring the thriving market with my senses and my camera. Then I'll fill up my shopping bag and have brunch on a river bank. I combine lunch and a siesta in a cool park to fill my stomach, rest my body and escape the early afternoon heat. It's fun to eat dinner on a castle wall enjoying a commanding view and the setting sun.

It's very efficient to plan a picnic meal to coincide with a train or boat ride. This is a pleasant way to pass time normally wasted in transit. When you arrive, you are nourished, fat, happy, rested and ready to go, rather than weak and in search of food. Mountain hikes are punctuated nicely by picnics. Food tastes so good on top of a mountain. Europeans are great picnickers, and I've had many a picnic become a potluck. By the time the meal is over, I have a new friend as well as a full stomach.

Nutritionally, a picnic is unbeatable. Consider this example: 100 grams of cheese, 100 grams of thin-sliced salami, fresh bread, peaches, carrots, a cucumber, a half liter of milk and yoghurt for dessert. When sandwiches get old, there are plenty of variations. A pizza to go is fun. Cold, canned ravioli is not as bad as it sounds. In fact, I have acquired a taste for it. Cold cereal is not outside the realm of possibility. Cornflakes can be found in any small grocery store.

"Table Scraps"

Bring zip-lock baggies (large and small), a little can opener and a good knife; a dish towel serves as a small tablecloth and comes in very handy. Bread has always been cheap in Europe. (Leaders have learned from history that the masses are much more pacific when their stomachs are full.) Cheese is a specialty nearly everywhere and is, along with milk, one of the cheapest sources of protein.

In some countries eating can be hazardous to your health. When recommended, eat only peelable fruit and vegetables A travelers' guidebook to health or your doctor can tell you where you'll have to be careful. Don't worry in Europe. Tourists who have been in a country for awhile usually know how to stay healthy and are excellent information sources.

Know which foods in each country are reasonably priced and which are expensive by doing quick market surveys. For instance, tomatoes, cucumbers and watermelons are good deals in Italy. Citrus fruits are terribly expensive (and not very good) in Eastern Europe, while the Eastern countries have some of the best and cheapest ice cream anywhere. Ice cream is costly in Scandinavia (what isn't?) and wine is a buy in France. Anything American is usually expensive and rarely satisfying. Europeans have not yet mastered the fine art of the American hamburger.

My big meal of the day is a picnic lunch. Only a glutton can spend more than three dollars for this mid-day feast. In a park in Paris, on a Norwegian ferry, or high in the Alps, picnicking is the budget traveler's key to cheap eating.

Eating and Sleeping on a Budget — The Five Commandments

You could get eight good hours of sleep and three square meals in Europe for $10 a day if your budget required it. If you have any budget limitations at all — keep these rules of thumb in mind:

1. Budget for Price Variances Prices as much as triple from south to north. Budget more for the north and get by on less than your daily allowance in Spain, Portugal, and Greece. Exercise those budget alternatives where they will save you the most money (a hostel saves a buck in Crete and ten in Finland.

I walk, sleep on trains, and picnic in Sweden and live like a king where my splurge dollars go the farthest.) And, if your trip will last as long as your money does, travel fast in the north and hang out in the south.

2. Adapt to European Tastes   Most unhappy people I meet in Europe could find the source of their problems if they examined their own stubborn desire to find the USA in Europe. If you accept and at least try doing things the European way, besides saving money, you'll be happier and learn more on your trip. You cannot expect the local people to be warm and accepting of you if you don't accept them. Things are different in Europe — that's why you go. European travel is a package deal, and you have no choice but to accept the good with the "bad." If you require the comforts of home . . . you'd better stay there.

3. Avoid the Tourist Centers   The best values are not in the places that boast, in neon signs, "We Speak English." Find local restaurants and hotels. You will get more for your money.

4. Swallow Pride and Save Money   This is a personal matter, dependent largely upon how important pride is to you and how much money you have. Many people cringe every time I use the word "cheap" — others appreciate the directness. I'm not talking about begging and groveling around Europe. I'm talking about being able to ask a hotel for the most inexpensive room; order water even if the waiter wants you to order wine; ask how much something costs before ordering it, and saying "no thanks" if the price isn't right. Demand equal and fair treatment as a tourist (unless it's not available), when appropriate fight the price, set a limit and search on. Remember, even if the same thing would cost much more at home, the local rate should prevail.

5. Minimize the Use of Hotels and Restaurants   Enjoying the sights and culture of Europe has nothing to do with how much you're spending to eat and sleep. Learn about and take advantage of the many alternatives to hotels and restaurants.

If your budget dictated, you could feel the fjords and caress the castles without hotels and restaurants — and probably learn, experience and enjoy more than the tourist who spends in a day what you spend in a week.

Savor Europe's small-town flavor.

4
Finances and Money

Travelers Checks

Smart travelers use travelers checks. They are replaceable if lost or stolen. Before you buy your checks, choose the best company, currency and mix of denominations.

What Company? Choose a big well-known company — American Express, Cooks, Barclays or First National City. Travelers checks only cost about 1% and it's not worth getting obscure checks to save. Any legitimate check is good at banks, but it's nice to have a check that private parties and small shops will recognize and honor. (In some countries travelers checks get a 2-3% better rate than cash so they even save you money.)

Check into refund policies and services provided. I like AmExCo for its centrally located "land mark" offices, travel service, clients' mail service, refund policy — and they're free through AAA. (Ask around, there are plenty of ways to avoid that 1% charge.)

You'll hear many stories about slow or fast refunds. None of them matter. Extenuating circumstances dictate the refund speed. If you wear a money belt and aren't too scatter-brained you won't lose your checks anyway. Choose the cheapest famous company.

If you're only traveling in England go with Barclays — a British bank with a branch in every town. They waive the service charge if you have their checks, saving you a dollar per transaction.

What Kind of Currency? Travelers checks come in US dollars, Swiss francs, British pounds, Deutsch Marks and even Japanese yen. There was a time when the dollar was shakey and unpredictable and some banks wouldn't even accept them. Those days are long gone and the American dollar is once again the world's super-currency. Get your travelers checks in US dollars, they're strong, stable, and merchants around the world generally know what their currency is worth in dollars, and it's simpler — we think in dollars.

If your trip, on the other hand, is mostly in one country it's best to buy your checks in that currency.

What Denomination Should You Choose? Large bills and small bills each have advantages and disadvantages. Large checks save on signing and bulk. Small checks are more exact and, in some cases, easier to cash. If you're only passing through a country, you may just want ten dollars. If you have only $100 checks, you'll have to change back $90. You'll be changing a total of $190 at a uniform percent loss for the privilege of spending ten expensive dollars. If you're out of cash and the banks are closed it's easy to find a merchant or even another traveler who will change a $10 or $20 travelers check. Changing a large check in that circumstance would be tough.

For $1000 in checks, I would choose three $100, ten $50 and ten $20 checks.

Remember, travelers checks are replaceable if lost or stolen — but you must keep track of the serial numbers. Leave a copy of all your check numbers (along with your passport number, flight number, and any other vital statistics) with someone at home, and carry a copy in your luggage and in your wallet. Update your list once a week so, if you lose them, you'll know exactly which checks to claim a refund on.

Changing Money in Europe

Remember, it's expensive to change money. You lose money and time every time you change so estimate carefully what you'll need and get it. In touristy places bank charges can be high — several dollars — and it's not uncommon to spend an hour in a bank line.

You need your passport to change a check. There are many "lost" checks floating around Europe and only a fool would change a check without a passport to match. (All the fools went bankrupt so bring your passport with you.) Whenever possible, don't change in hotels, shops, nightclubs, etc. These places change money, but only for a profit.

Many Americans exclaim with glee, "Gee, they accept bank cards and dollars! There's no need ever to change money." Without knowing it, they're changing money everytime they buy something — at a loss. Use the local money and get it at banks.

Paper money of any western country is good anywhere. The dollar is just one of many currencies all floating in the international exchange market. If you leave Italy with paper money, that 10,000 lire note is just as good as dollars throughout Europe. Many people change excess local money back to dollars, then change those dollars into the next country's money. That makes no sense and is expensive.

Coins, on the other hand, are generally worthless outside their country. Since many countries have coins worth over $2 each, a pocket full of change can be an expensive mistake. Spend them or change them into paper, before you cross the border. Otherwise you've just bought a bunch of little souvenirs. (Most border regions use both currencies interchangeably.)

Credit cards are widely accepted throughout Europe. This is exciting news to all the people who have put an extra middleman into our financial lives. Credit cards work in Europe — but not in the market or at Pedro's Pension. They kick you right out of "The Back Door." Be careful when you use your plastic money. Many people have been terribly ripped off. Take one if you must for cash advances and major purchases (car rentals, plane tickets, etc.). But it's best to go with cash. (Editorial note: only a naive person believes he's getting "free" use of the money. We're all absorbing the 4% the banks are making in higher purchase prices.)

While paper money from any western country is good at banks in every other country, the money of Eastern Europe is "soft" — falsely valued at several times its true worth. You can't avoid buying this money when you're in Bulgaria, Romania, Hungary, Czechoslovakia, East Germany or Poland. It's a government-sponsored rip-off designed to get "hard" western currency — desperately needed to purchase western goods on the international market. This money is worthless in western Europe so exchange it, spend it — or give it away if you have to — but don't take it out of its country.

Carry Cash

Carry plenty of cash. In some places it's getting expensive and difficult to change a travelers check — but hard cash is cash. You don't need a bank — people always know roughly what a dollar, mark or pound is worth and, for a price, you can sell it. Several hundred dollars cash in your money belt (completely safe) comes in handy for emergencies, like when banks go on strike. I've been in Greece and Ireland when every bank went on strike — shutting down without warning.

Bring one day's budget in each country's currency with you from home. Your bank can sell you one bill worth about $30 from each country for the same price you'll pay in Europe. For no extra cost, risk or bulk (six bills — for six countries — hide safely in the money belt) you'll have enough money to get settled in each new country without worrying about banking. This is a wonderful convenience — especially if you arrive at night or when the banks are closed. Most stations have a bank open when others are closed but lines there after normal hours can be horrendous.

"Tip Packs," sold by many banks, are an ingenious way to lose 20 to 40% on your dollar. They are unnecessary. I'd be embarrassed to spend $10 for the privilege of carrying around $7 worth of coins and paper so I could practice in advance and tip upon arrival. Get a good sampling of coins after you arrive and in two minutes you'll be comfortable with the nickels, dimes and quarters of each new currency.

Many Americans refuse to understand the "strange" money of Europe. You won't find George Washington or Abe Lincoln but it's all logical. Each system is decimalized just like ours. There's a hundred "little ones" (cents) in every "big one" (dollar). Only the names have been changed — to confuse the tourist. Upon arrival, make a point to figure out the money. Equate the unit of currency (franc, mark, krona, etc.) into American cents. (For example, there are two and a half Deutsch Marks in a dollar. Each DM is a 40-cent piece.) If a hot dog costs 5 marks, then it cost five 40-cent pieces, or $2.00. Fifty little ones (pfennig) is half a mark (20 cents). If mustard costs 25 pfennig (a quarter of a 40-cent piece), it costs the equivalent of 10 cents. Ten marks is $4, 150 DM = $60. Quiz yourself. Soon it will be second nature. You can't survive on a budget until you are comfortable with the local currency.

Keys to Successful Bargaining

In much of the world the price tag is only an excuse to argue. Bargaining is the accepted and expected method of finding a compromise between the wishful thinking of the merchant and the tourist.

Prices are "soft" in much of Asia, Africa and Latin America. In Europe bargaining is common only in the south. You should fight the price in "flea markets" and with people selling handicrafts and tourist items on the streets in all but the most developed countries.

While bargaining (if you're traveling beyond Europe) is important from a budgetary standpoint, it can also become an enjoyable game. Many travelers are addicted hagglers who would gladly skip a tour of an Egyptian temple to fight it out with the crazy local merchants. Here are the ten commandments of the successful haggler:

1. Determine whether or not bargaining is appropriate It's bad shopping etiquette to "make an offer" for a sweater in a London department store. It's foolish not to at a Moroccan souvenir stand. To learn if the price is fixed, fall in love with that item right in front of the merchant. Look longingly into the eyes of that porcelain Buddah, then decide that "it's just too much money." You've put him in a position to make the first offer. If he comes down even two percent there's nothing sacred about the price tag. Now you're free to haggle away.

2. Determine the merchant's cost   Many merchants will settle for a nickel profit rather than lose the sale entirely. Promise yourself that, no matter how exciting the price becomes, you won't buy. Then work the cost down to rock bottom. When it seems to have fallen to a record low rip yourself away. That last price he hollers out as you turn the corner is usually about a nickel above cost. Armed with this knowledge you can confidently demand a fair price at the next souvenir stand — and probably get it.

3. Find out what the locals pay   If the price is not posted, you should assume that there is a double price standard — one for locals and one for tourists. If only tourists buy the item you're pricing, see what an Arab, Spanish or Italian tourist would be charged. I remember thinking I did very well in Istanbul's Grand Bazaar until I learned my Spanish friend bought the same shirt for thirty percent less. Many merchants just assume American tourists have more money to spend.

In a taxi, demand the meter. They seem to conveniently break when a tourist gets in, allowing the cabbie to "estimate" the price of the ride. Know what the locals pay.

4. Pre-price each item   Remember that the price tags are totally meaningless and can serve only to distort your idea of an item's true worth. The merchant is playing a psychological game. People often feel that if they can cut the price fifty percent, they are doing great. Well, the merchant responds by quadrupling his prices. Then the tourist haggles the price in half and happily pays twice what that souvenir should sell for. The best way to deal with crazy price tags is to ignore them. Before you even see the price tag, pre-price the item that you are interested in. Determine what it's worth to you, considering the hassles involved in packing it or shipping it home. This value, not the price tag, should be your guide in determining a souvenir's worth.

5. Don't hurry Get to know the shopkeeper. Accept his offer for tea, talk with him. Leave him to shop around and get a feel for the market. Then return. He'll know you are serious.

6. Be indifferent — never look impressed As soon as the merchant perceives the "I gotta have that!" in you, you will never get the best price. He knows you have plenty of money to buy something you really want. He knows about USA prices. Never be openly crazy about an item. (Commandments 1 and 6 are contradictory, but then, as Emerson said, "Consistency is the hobgoblin of little minds." Which one you obey depends on the situation.)

7. Impress him with your knowledge — real or otherwise This way he respects you, and you are more likely to get good quality. Istanbul has very good leather coats for a fraction of the USA cost. I wanted one. Before my trip, I talked to some leather coat salesmen and was much better prepared to confidently pick out a good coat in Istanbul for $50.

8. Employ a third person Use your friend who is worried about the ever-dwindling budget, or who doesn't like the price or who is bored and wants to return to the hotel. This trick may work to bring the price down faster.

9. Show the merchant your money Physically offer him "all you have" to pay for whatever you are bickering over. The temptation will be greater for him just to grab your money and say, "Oh, all right."

10. If the price is too much — leave Never worry about having taken too much of the merchant's time and tea. They are experts at making the tourist feel guilty for not buying. It's all part of the game. Most merchants, by local standards, are financially well off.

A final point for the no-nonsense budget shopper: you can generally find the same souvenirs in large department stores at true values and often with government-regulated prices. Department store shopping is quicker, easier, often cheaper — but not nearly as much fun.

Theft and the Tourist

Thieves plague tourists throughout the world. As the economy gets tighter, pick-pockets and purse-snatchers get hungrier, and the tourist becomes a very tempting target.

Many countries depend on the USA economically. When we are in a recession they feel it, too. In much of the world, your camera is worth one year of hard labor to the man on the street. Gross inequities like this enable many thieves to rationalize their crimes.

If you are not constantly on guard, you'll have something stolen. One summer, four out of five friends I traveled with lost cameras in one way or another. (Don't look at me.) I have heard countless stories of tourists getting ripped-off: pickpocketed in a bad neighborhood in London; shoulder bag snatched by a motorcycle bandit in Rome; suitcase taken from the train during a long, dark French tunnel; camera slipped right off the neck of a fellow napping in Bangkok. And so on.

You can't be too careful. A tourist is an easy target. Loaded down with all her valuables in a strange new environment, she is a favorite victim of thieves — many of whom specialize solely in "the tourist trade." I read of people whose trips are ruined by thieves who snatch their purse or wallet. There is no excuse for this kind of vulnerability. Nearly all crimes suffered by tourists are non-violent and are avoidable simply by thinking. If you exercise the proper caution and are not overly trusting, you should have no problem.

Here are some hints on how not to be ripped-off during your trip:

First of all, don't bring things that will ruin your trip if they are lost, broken or stolen. Everything that is crucial should fit into your money belt. Purses and wallets are fine for odds and ends and one day's spending money but not for irreplaceables. Luxurious luggage lures thieves like a well-polished flasher lures fish. Why brag to the thief that your luggage is the most expensive? The thief chooses the most impressive suitcase in the pile.

My key to peace of mind is my money belt. (Buckle up for safety.) I'll never again travel without one. The money belt is a small, nylon, zipper bag that ties around the waist under your clothes. It costs only a few dollars. In it, I keep my passport, cash, travelers checks, train pass and any very important documents, vouchers or identity cards. Bulky or replaceable documents are kept in a small zipper bag (a three-ring notebook pencil bag) that I sew to the inside of my rucksack or suitcase. It's important to keep the money belt slim so it's comfortable and hidden. I wear it all summer, even sleeping with it when necessary, and it is never uncomfortable (see catalog p. 366).

With my money belt, if I ever did get all my luggage stolen, the trip would not be threatened. I could re-outfit myself for $200 and carry on. The photographic equipment and film would be the only real loss, and I considered that risk when I decided to pack it in the first place.

My camera is, to a potential thief, the most tempting item in my luggage. I never leave it lying around where hotel workers and others can see it and be tempted. It is either around by neck or safely out of sight.

If I ever sleep in public (on a train or at an airport or wherever), I clip or fasten my pack (or suitcase) to the chair or the luggage rack or to me. Even the slight hang-up of undoing a clip foils most thieves. I also sew a small button flap to my back pocket and automatically button my wallet in each time after I use it.

Be on guard for the imaginative "artful dodgers" of the 1980's. Thief teams often create a fight or commotion to distract their curious victims. Groups of Gypsy girls with big eyes and colorful dresses play a game where they politely mob the unsuspecting tourist, beggar-style. As their pleading eyes grab yours and they hold up their sad message scrawled on cardboard, your purse or rucksack is being delicately rifled. (This is particularly common in Paris and Rome.) Keep things zipped, buttoned and secure. Be alert and aware! Somewhere, sometime, when you least expect it most — you'll meet the Gypsies.

Cars are a favorite target of thieves. Be very careful never to leave anything even hinting of value in view in your parked car. Put anything worth stealing in the trunk. Leave your glove compartment open so the thief can look in without breaking in. Choose your parking place carefully. Cars get ripped-off *anywhere* at night. In Paris I was warned to take absolutely everything inside my hotel. I did. They stole my mirror! In Rome my pension was next to a large police station — a safe place to park (if you're legal).

Invest in an extra key. Most rental cars come with only one, and that is needlessly risky. (Besides, it's convenient for two people to have access to the locked car.)

Get a photocopy of your valuable documents and tickets. It is a lot easier to replace a lost or stolen plane ticket, passport, Eurailpass, or rental voucher if you have a picture proving that you really owned what you are claiming is lost. This is especially true in the case of your Eurailpass, which is not always, as the rules say, non-replaceable.

Now that you have taken these precautions, there's one more thing — relax and have fun. There's no sense in letting fear limit your vacation. Most people in every country are on your side. If you exercise adequate discretion and don't put yourself into risky situations your travels will be about as dangerous as home-town grocery shopping. Please don't travel afraid — travel carefully.

Soft Currency and the Black Market

Sooner or later in your travels you'll be approached by a local person wanting to buy money or goods from you. You have encountered the "Black Market."

Most of the world's currencies have their true value determined by the international exchange market. Some countries, however, artificially overvalue their money. At a bank you'll be charged the "official" rate of exchange — more than that money is really worth. When this happens, the currency becomes "soft" — difficult or impossible to change outside of that country. "Hard," realistically valued currency, like dollars and all Western European currencies, are in high demand in that country for purchasing imported goods. A black market is created, and people everywhere seem to be in search of "real money" and the special items only it can buy. Tourists are known to have plenty of hard money and will commonly be approached by people who are trying to gather enough hard cash to buy a car or stereo or camera that cannot be purchased with that country's soft money.

Most Eastern European countries tie their currencies to the Russian ruble. The ruble is soft as a banana, and as a result, these countries have a thriving black market. Many factory workers make well under $200 a month and have a difficult time spending their money. What they want can only be purchased with hard foreign currency, so they will pay up to triple the official rate to acquire hard dollars. That means a Polish or Bulgarian worker will trade one month's pay for $70 US to save for his imported dream. As governments continue to artificially control the value and flow of money and goods they stimulate their own black markets.

Dealing in the black market is illegal and obviously risky. Nevertheless, in many countries, the underground economy is the one that keeps things going. You will be tempted by the black market. When traveling in the USSR, Eastern Europe or elsewhere, the black market is the forbidden fruit — don't mess with it thoughtlessly. You should, however, know something about it.

Many people finance their travels by playing the black market. They know what to buy, what to sell — and where. I'm not talking about drugs and sub-machine guns. I'm talking pettiness: a bottle of gin, a Beatles record, a pair of Levis, $20 bills. Here are some examples of black market activity. Names won't be used, to protect the guilty.

In a Warsaw nightclub, a man wearing a large money pouch — complete with "change maker" — sits down with a couple of Americans and loudly announces that he will pay them triple the official exchange rate for their dollars. Poland is Eastern Europe's bargain basement — even at the government's inflated exchange rate.

In Moscow, a traveler sells a Playboy magazine for $50 (that's $50 worth of Russian currency at the official rate), a Beatles "White Album" for $70, and a Bible (in Ruski) for $100. The total paid was well over one month's local wages.

In East Berlin's most popular disco, a young American pays the five mark ($2) cover charge in West German marks rather than East German soft marks. For his hard currency he is given hard drinks — free, all night long.

On a Bulgarian train, the conductor checks the tickets. Then, with the excitement of a little boy, he asks eagerly, "Black market? Change dollars?" The tourist follows him to the train's WC where the conductor gives him triple the going rate. He is undoubtedly a middle-man who makes more money buying and selling hard currency than he does punching tickets. He'll have no trouble selling those dollars at a profit to Bulgarians in need of hard cash.

The governments of these countries often require tourists to spend a minimum amount of hard currency per day. In Romania, as you enter by train you are issued a seven-day visa only after changing seven times their minimum daily expenditure requirement. To extend your visa you must show a bank slip proving that you changed enough money — legally. In the USSR and several other countries there are special shops, gas stations, tours and hotels that are especially for foreign visitors and accept only hard currency. In some cases, these are the only hotels, tours or gas stations the guests are allowed to use. Countries with soft currencies generally require proof that you changed your money through official channels before you're allowed to make a major purchase. This includes hotel bills, plane tickets and car rentals. Because of this tight control, many tourists who "make a killing" on the black market have a very difficult time spending all their local wealth. That money can't be exchanged again for hard currency, and it becomes "funny money" once it crosses the border. It's a strange feeling, not knowing how to blow your money. You can only eat so many ice cream cones.

Certain items that are very popular but can't be purchased with local currency make wonderful gifts — if you can get them across the border. If the customs official sees your gifts and determines that they aren't for your personal use he will probably confiscate them — and take them home. I know of a tourist who brought a Romanian friend well-chosen gifts costing $40: a Sony recording tape, a pair of jeans, a rock and roll album (the "harder" the better), and a T-I pocket calculator. That Romanian glowed with pride as he wore his "real American

jeans." Within two days his record was taped a dozen times —
all over the village. He figures the value of those gifts at two
month's wages.

Black market dealings are illegal, and a tourist is expected
to understand and obey the laws of the country he is visiting. I
just thought you might be interested.

*Buy and sell exchange rates displayed in a bank window. You
always lose. Notice U.S. dollars — 4% loss; Yugoslavian money
— 24% loss!*

5
Hurdling the Language Barrier

Communicating in a Language You Don't Speak

That notorious language barrier is about two feet tall. It can keep you out of Europe, or, with a few tricks, you can step right over it. I speak only English. My linguistic limitations have never hindered my travels. Of course, if I spoke more languages, I could enjoy a much deeper understanding of the people and cultures I see. But, logistically speaking — getting transportation, rooms, eating, and seeing the sights — you can manage fine speaking only English.

We English-speakers are the one linguistic group that can afford to be lazy. English is the world's linguistic common-denominator. When a Greek meets a Norwegian, neither speaks the other's language. They'll communicate in English.

While Americans are terrible monoglots, Europeans are very good with languages. Most young North Europeans speak several languages. Scandinavian students of our language actually decide between English and "American." My Norwegian cousin speaks with a touch of Texas, and knows more slang than I do! Most Swiss grow up tri-lingual like their country. People speaking minor languages (Dutch, Belgians, Scandinavians) have more reason to learn German, French or English since very few people outside their small states speak their tongue.

Imagine if each of our states spoke its own language.

That's the European situation. They have done a great job of minimizing the communication problems you'd expect to find in a small continent with such a babel of tongues. Not only are most educated people multi-lingual, but most signs that the traveler must understand (e.g., road signs, menus, telephone instructions, museum info, etc.) are printed either in several languages or in universal "imbe-symbols." Europe has a uniform road sign system, so the driver rarely faces any language problems.

While English may be Europe's "linguafranca," and we don't need to be afraid of the language barrier, communicating does require some skill. How well you communicate with the Europeans you meet depends on how well you can get a basic idea across — not how many words you know in that language. Here are some keys to communicating with people who don't speak your language.

Speak slowly, clearly and with well chosen words. The "Voice of America" is in business to communicate and they use what they call "simple English." You're dealing with someone who learned English out of a book — reading British words, not hearing American ones. Choose easy words and pronounce each letter (Cris-py po-ta-to-chips. Borrow a singer's enunciation exercises and exaggerate each letter). Most Americans speak louder when they aren't understood and if they still can't communicate, they toss in a few extra words. Listen to other tourists and you'll hear your own shortcomings.

Use no contractions. Cut out all slang. Our American dialect has become a super-deluxe slang pizza not found on any European menu. The sentence "Cut out all slang," for example, would baffle the average European. "Speak no idioms" would be better understood. If you learned English in school for two years how would you respond to the American who explains "What a day!" Listen to yourself. If you want to be understood, talk like a Dick and Jane book.

Keep your messages and sentences very simple. When asking for something, a one word question (Photo?) is much more effective than an attempt at something more grammatically correct ("May I take your picture, sir?").

Be a caveman. Keep it grunt simple. Your first priority when communicating in Europe is to strip your message naked and transmit only the basic ideas. Even with no common language, rudimentary communication is easy. Don't be afraid to look like a fool. Butcher the language if you must — but communicate. I'll never forget the lady in the French post office who flapped her arms and asked, "Tweet, tweet, tweet?" I understood immediately, answered with a nod, and she gave me the air mail stamps I needed. If you're hungry, clutch your stomach and growl. If you want milk, "moo" and pull two imaginary udders. If the liquor was too strong, simulate an atomic explosion starting in your stomach and mushrooming to your head. If you're attracted to someone, pant.

Pick up gestures. Every culture has peculiar — and fun — hand and face gestures. In Turkey you signal "no" by jerking your eyebrows and head upward. In Bulgaria, "yes" is indicated by happily bouncing your head back and forth as if you were one of those oriental dolls with a spring neck and someone slapped you. "Expensive" is often shaking your head and sucking in like you just burned yourself.

Figure things out. Most major European languages are related, coming from Latin. With that awareness and an effort to make some sense of the puzzle, lots of words become meaningful. *Lundi* (lunar), means *Monday* (moonday). *Sonn* is sun so *Sonntag* is Sunday. If *"bongiorno"* means good day, *"suppa del giorno"* must mean soup of the day. Think of *kindergarten* (children's garden), *bon marche* (good bargain), *vater, mutter, trink, gross, gut, nacht, rapide, grand, economico, delicioso,* and you can *muy comprendo.*

Many letters travel predictable courses as one language melts into the next over the centuries. For intance, "p" often becomes "v" in the next language. Italian menus always have a charge for *"coperto"* — a "cover" charge.

Practice understanding. Read time schedules, concert posters, multi-lingual signs in bathrooms, and newspaper

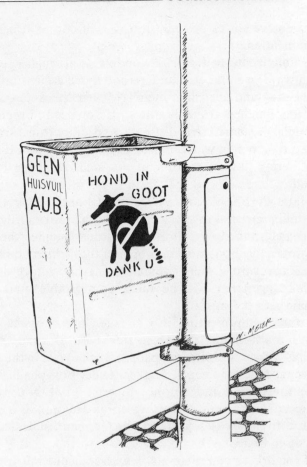

What language barrier?

headlines. It's a puzzle and the more you play it, the better you get.

Be melodramatic, exaggerate the accent of the language you're working with. In France, if you sound like Maurice Chevalier you're much more likely to be understood. The locals won't be insulted — they'll be impressed. Even English, spoken with a sexy French accent, will make more sense to the French ear. In Italy, be melodic, exuberant, and wave those hands. You've got to be uninhibited. Self-consciousness kills communication.

A small note-pad works wonders in a tough spot. The written word or number is understood much easier than when it's spoken — and mispronounced. (My backpocket notepad is one of my handiest travel buddies.) If you need to repeatedly communicate something difficult and important (medical instructions, "boiled water," "well-done meat," "your finest ice cream," etc.), have it written in the local language in your notepad.

Many Europeans are self-conscious about their English and would prefer not to speak than to speak broken English. If you are determined to communicate, and butcher their language doggedly enough, sooner or later they'll break down and surprise you with some English. After what you've done to their language, they will be more comfortable working in less-than-perfect English.

Your communicating job is made much easier if you choose a multi-lingual person to start with. Business people, urbanites, young well-dressed people, and anyone in the tourist trade is most likely to speak English. Older Europeans, Turks, Eastern Europeans, and anyone who was school age during the Nazi occupation is more likely to speak German as a second language. In these cases, your broken German "ist besser" than your native English.

If you draw a complete blank with someone but you want to communicate, just start hurling bits and pieces at each other. Consider this profound conversation I had with a cobbler in Sicily:

"Spaghetti," I said with a very saucy Italian accent.

"Ronald Reagan," was the old man's reply.

"Mama mia!" I said tossing my hands and head into the air.

"Yes, no, one, two, tree," he returned slowly and proudly.

Then I whispered secretly, "Molto buono, ravioli."

He spit, "Be sexy, drink Pepsi!"

And I waved goodby saying, "Arrividerci."

"Ciao," he smiled.

You are surrounded by expert, native-speaking tutors in every country. Let them teach you. Spend bus and train rides learning. Start learning the language when you arrive. Psychologically, it's hard to start later because you'll be leaving so soon. I like to learn five new words a day. You'd be surprised how handy a working vocabulary of 20-50 words is. The practical phrase lists following this chapter are a good place to start.

The Berlitz "14 European Languages Phrasebook" is ideal for the average traveler. Their individual language books provide more information than most people will ever need. While phrasebooks can be helpful in your efforts to communicate, I find them more fun than practical. I can't imagine anyone ever hauling out their phrasebook to say, "I've broken my leg. Can you please show me to the nearest hospital?" In that case, a point and a scream works in any language. A phrasebook is more helpful in a situation like when you are sitting, bored, in a restaurant waiting for your meal. Call the waitress over and, with a pained look, ask for shampoo.

Assume you understand. My master key to communication is that I make an educated guess at the meaning of a message — verbal or written — and act with confidence as if I understood it correctly. This applies to rudimentary things like instructions on custom forms, museum hours, menus, questions the hotel maid asks you, etc. 80% of the time I'm correct. 20% I misunderstand the message. Half of the time I am wrong I never know it, so it doesn't really matter. So, 10% of the time I really blow it. That makes my trip easier — or more interesting.

Let's take a border crossing as an example. I speak no Bulgarian. At the border, a uniformed guard struts up to my car and asks a question. Not understanding a word he said, but guessing what the average border guard would ask the average tourist, I look at him and answer with a solid "Nyet." He steps back, swings his arm open like a gate and says, "OK." I'm on my way, quick and easy. I could have got out of the car, struggled with the phrasebook and made a big deal out of it, but I'd rather fake it, assuming he was asking if I'm smuggling anything in, and keep things simple. It works.

International Words

As our world shrinks, more and more words leap their linguistic boundaries and become international. Sensitive travelers develop a knack for choosing words most likely to be universally understood ("auto" instead of "car," "kaput" rather than "broken," "photo" not "picture"). They also internationalize their pronounciation. "University," if you play around with its sound (Oo nee vehr see tay) will be understood anywhere. The average American is a real flunky in this area. Be creative. Analogy communication is very effective. In every language on earth, "Attila" means "the crude bully." When a big Italian crowds in front of you say, "Scuzi, Ah tee la." and retake your place. If you like your haircut and want to compliment your Venetian barber, put your hand sensually on your hair and say "Casanova." Nickname the hairstylist "Michelangelo."

Here are a few internationally understood words. Remember, cut out the Yankee accent and give each word a Pan-European sound.

Stop	Kaput	Vino
Restaurant	Ciao	Bank
Hotel	Bye-Bye	Rock-n-Roll
Post, Par Avion	Camping	OK
Auto	Picnic	Amigo
Autobus(boos)	Nuclear	English (Engleesh)
Yankee, Americano	Tourist	Mama mia
Michelangelo (artistic)	Beer	Oo la la
Casanova (romantic)	Coffee	America's favorite
Disneyland (wonderland)	Tea, Chai	four-letter words
Hercules (strong)	Coke, Coka	Elephante (a big clod)
Attila (mean, crude)	Sexy	Europa
Self-serve	Toilet	Police

Super	Taxi	Telephone
Photo	Central	Information
Manana	University	Passport
Chocolate	Pardon	Fascist

A Yankee-English Phrase Book

Oscar Wilde said, "The English have really everything in common with the Americans — except, of course, language." On your first trip to England you'll find plenty of linguistic surprises. I'll never forget checking into a small town Bed and Breakfast — a teenager on my first solo European adventure. The landlady cheerily asked me, "And what time would you like to be knocked up in the morning?" I looked over at her husband, who winked, "Would a fry at eight be suitable?" The next morning I got a rap on the door at 7:30 and a huge British breakfast a half hour later.

Traveling through England is an adventure in accents and idioms. Every day you'll see babies in "prams," sucking "dummies," as mothers change wet "nappies." Soon the kids can trade in their "nappies" for "smalls" and "spend a penny" on their own. "Spend a penny" is British for a visit to the "loo" (bathroom). Older British kids enjoy "candy floss" (cotton candy), "naughts and crosses" (tic-tac-toe), "big dippers" (roller coasters), "sultanas" (raisins), "iced lollies" (popsicles), and are constantly in need of an "elastoplast" (band-aid).

If you're just "muckin' about," it's fun to browse through an "iron mongers" (hardware store), "chemists shop" (pharmacy) or Woolworths and notice the many familiar items with unfamiliar names. The school supplies section includes "sticking plaster" (adhesive tape), "rubbers" (erasers), and "scribbling blocks" (scratch pads). Those with "green fingers" (a green thumb) might pick up some "courgette" (zucchini), "broad bean" (lima bean), "swede" (turnip) or "aubergine" (eggplant) seeds.

In England, "chips" are fries and "crisps" are potato chips. A hamburger is best on a toasted "bap" and if you ask for a napkin, you'll get a funny look but no more (that's what the British call a tampon). You wipe your fingers with a serviet — never a napkin! (No, Russians don't call them "soviets.") The English have a great way with names. You'll find towns with names like Upper and Lower Piddle, Once Brewed and Itching Field. I saw a hair salon called "Curl Up and Dye." This cute coziness comes through in their language as well. Your car is built with a "bonnet" and a "boot" rather than a hood and trunk. You drive it on "motorways," and when the freeway divides, it becomes a "dual carriageway." Gas is "petrol," a truck is a "lorry," and when you hit a traffic jam, don't "get your knickers in a twist" (make a fuss), just "queue up" (line up) and study your American-English phrase book.

A two-week vacation in England is unheard of, but many locals "holiday for a fortnight" in a "homely" (pleasant) rural cottage. They'll pack a "face flannel" (wash cloth), "torch" (flashlite), "hoover" (vacuum cleaner), and "hair grips" (bobbie pins) before leaving their "flat" (apartment). The cottage can be lovely. Every day I'd "post" a letter in the "pillar box" and give my "bird" (girl friend) a "trunk" (long distance call), "reversing the charges" (collect), of course. On a cold evening it's best to find a "pimp" (bundle of kindling) and make a fire or take a walk wearing the warmest "mackintosh" (raincoat) you can find or an "anorak" (parka) with "press studs" (snaps).

Many times after "washing up" (doing the dishes) I'd go up to the first floor (second floor) with a "neat" (straight) Scotch and a plate of "biscuits" (sweet cookies) with "dessicated" (shredded) coconut and just enjoy the view. It's a "smashing" view, guaranteed to give you "goose pimples" (goose bumps) every time.

All across the British Isles, you'll find new words, crazy local humor and countless accents. Pubs are coloquial treasure chests. Church services, sporting events, The House of Parliament, live plays featuring local comedy, the streets of Liverpool, the docks of London and children in parks are playgrounds for the American ear. One of the beauties of touring the British Isles is the illusion of hearing a foreign language and actually understanding it — most of the time.

European Travel Glossary

"ATS" Airplane type seats, advertised for buses and boats, they recline just enough so you can't sleep solidly, like those on airplanes.

"The American Waters" Coke, Pepsi, Fanta, Sprite and Seven-Up. Found (and bottled) all over Europe. Five-year olds in Turkey greet foreigners with "Be sexy, drink Pepsi!"

Auto-stop The most common European term for hitchhiking; Also called "tramp" in some countries.

Balkans The name for the Greece, Bulgaria, Yugoslavia region.

Celtic The Irish, Welsh, and Scottish people and those who live in Brittany.

"The Continent" Continental Europe. England is an island and not really part of what she thinks of as "The Continent."

Etruscans The highly civilized people who inhabited Italy from Rome to Florence in the thousand years before Christ. Rome was originally an Etruscan town.

Germanic Countries Those countries that speak German — Germany, Switzerland, and Austria.

Hard and Soft Currency Hard currency is sold at its true value at home and is accepted at banks in other countries. Soft currency is falsely valued at home and is impossible or very difficult to change outside its borders. All of Western Europe has hard currency.

Homesick A problem suffered by people who don't mentally travel with their home with them. Be "at home" on the road — it works wonderfully.

Iberia The peninsula of Spain and Portugal.

The Industry Organized tourism, all the facets of the business side of travel working together.

"Lerks and Perks"   A popular topic of conversation among tour guides and bus drivers in parking lots — kick backs and special incentives they enjoy for encouraging a group of stark raving shoppers to consume in a certain direction.

Low Countries   Belgium, Netherlands, and Luxembourg (Benelux). They're called low because they are. Half of Holland is below sea level, reclaimed from the sea.

Mensa   The European word for university cafeteria, usually government subsidized, always cheap.

Moors   The Arabs that flourished in Spain and Portugal from 711 til 1492.

Open-jaws   Flying into one European city and home from another. A very efficient itinerary strategy.

"Option"   The half-day or evening tours or activities that are not included in a bus tour's price. In many cases, they are barely "optional".

Peak season   The busiest tourist season. In Europe, about June 20 through August 20. It's so crowded you can only "peek" at the most popular sights.

Shoulder season   Still crowded, but not quite "peak". Shoulder season is between "peak" and "off" season. In Europe, roughly May 20 to June 20 and August 20 to September 30. You've got elbow room in shoulder season.

Sound and Light Shows   Very popular with sedentary tourists, these are evening shows in a romantic and historic setting where bus tours gather, sit on folding chairs and listen to a recorded narration with a musical and dramatic touch while colored lights play on the surrounding buildings. Generally not worth the time or money.

WC   Water closet, international symbol for toilet. Also "loo."

Practical Foreign Phrases
FRENCH

1.	hello	bonjour	bohn-ZHOOR
2.	goodbye	au revoir	oh-VWAH
3.	see you later	a bientot	ah byuhn-TOH
4.	goodnight	bonne nuit	bohn NWEE
5.	please	s'il vous plait	see voo PLAY
6.	thank you	merci	mehr-SEE
7.	yes/no	oui/non	wee/noh
8.	one/two/three	un/deux/trois	uh/DOO/twah
9.	cheap/expensive *good bargain*	bon marche/cher	bohn mar-shay/shehr
10.	good/bad	bon/mauvais	bohn/mo-VAY
11.	beautiful/ugly	joli/laid	zho-LEE/lay
12.	big/small	grand/petit	grahn/pehTEE
13.	fast/slow	rapide/lent	rah-PEED/lehn
14.	very	tres	tray
15.	where is . . . ?	ou est . . . ?	oo ay
16.	how much . . . ?	combien	kohm-bee-UHN
17.	I don't understand	je ne comprends pas	zhuh neh KOHM-prahn PAH
18.	What do you call this?	qu'est-ce que c'est?	KESS koo SAY
19.	I'm lost	je me suis perdu	zhuh meh swee pehr-DOO
20.	complete price (everything included)	tout est compris	too-tay kohm-PREE
21.	Im tired	je suis fatigue	zhuh swee fah-tee-GAY
22.	I'm hungry	j'ai faim	zhay fam
23.	cheers!	sante!	sahn-TAY
24.	food	nourriture	new-ree-TOOR
25.	grocery store	epicerie	eh-PEES-eh-REE
26.	picnic	pique-nique	peek-neek
27.	delicious	delicieux	de-lee-syoh
28.	market	marche	mar-SHAY
29.	drunk	soul	SOO
30.	money	argent	ar-ZHA
31.	station	gare	gar
32.	private accommodations	chambre	shambr
33.	toilet	w.c.	VAY say
34.	I	je	zhuh
35.	you	vous	voo
36.	love	amour	ah-MOOR
37.	sleep	sommeil	so-MAY
38.	train	train	tran
39.	The bill, please	L'addition, s'il vous plait	lah-dee-see-OHN, see voo play
40.	friend	ami	ah-MEE
41.	water/tap water	eau/eau douce	OH/OL dooss
42.	castle	chateau	shat-TOH
43.	How are you?/I'm fine	ca va?/ca va	sah VAH
44.	Tourist Information	syndicat d'initiative	san-dee-KAH dan-EE-see-ah-TEEV

GERMAN

1. hello	guten tag	goo-ten tock
2. goodbye	auf wiedersehn	awf VEE-der-sayn
3. see you later	bis spater	beess SHPAY-tuh
4. goodnight	gute nacht	GOO-tuh nahkt
5. please	bitte	BIT-teh
6. thank you	danke schon	DONG-kuh shayn
7. yes/no	ja/nein	yah/nine
8. one/two/three	eins/zwei/drei	aintz/tzvy/dry
9. cheap/expensive	billig/teuer	BIL-ikh/TOY-err
10. good/bad	gut/schlecht	goot/shlehkht
11. beautiful/ugly	schon/hasslich	shurn/HESS-leek
12. big/small	gross/klein	groass/kline
13. fast/slow	schnell/langsam	shnel/LONG-zahm
14. very	sehr	zair
15. where is . . . ?	wo ist . . . ?	voh ist
16. how much . . . ?	wieviel	vee-FEEL
17. I don't understand	ich verstehe nicht	ikh vehr-SHTAY-er nicht
18. what do you call this?	wie heisst das?	vee HEIST dahss
19. I'm lost	ich habe mich verirrt	ikh hah-beh mikh fehr-IRT
20. complete price (everything included)	alles ist inbegriffen	AHlerss ist IN-ber-grif-ern
21. I'm tired	ich bin mude	ikh bin MEW-duh
22. I'm hungry	ich habe hunger	ikh hah-beh HOONG-guh
23. cheers!	prosit!	proast
24. food	speise	SHPY-zuh
25. grocery store	laden	LODD-en
26. picnic	picknick	pik-nik
27. delicious	lecker	LECK-uh
28. market	markt	markt
29. drunk	betrunken	beh-TROHN-ken
30. money	geld	gelt
31. station	bahnhof	BAHN-hof
32. private accommodations	zimmer	TSIMM-er
33. toilet	klo	kloh
34. I	ich	eekh
35. you	du	doo
36. love	liebe	LEE-beh
37. sleep	schlaf	shloff
38. train	zug	tsoog
39. The bill, please	die Rechnung, bitte	dee RECK-nung, BIT-teh
40. friend	freund	froint
41. water	wasser	VOSS-ehr
42. castle	schloss	shlohss
43. How are you/ I'm fine, thanks	wie geht es?/ Es geht mir gut, dahnke	vee GATES/ ess GATE mehr GOOT, DONG-kuh
44. Tourist Information	Reiseburo	RIE-suh-BYOO-ro

GREEK

1.	hello	YAHSS-ahss
2.	goodbye	YAHSS-ahss
3.	see you later	EESS to ehpahneeDHEEN
4.	goodnight	kahleeNEEKtah
5.	please	pahrahkahLO
6.	thank you	ehvkhahreeSTO
7.	yes/no	neh/O-khee
8.	one/two/three	EHnah/DHEEo/TREEah
9.	cheap/expensive	ftee-NOHSS/ah-kree-VOHSS
10.	good/bad	kah-LOHSS/kah-KOHSS
11.	beautiful/ugly	or-AY-ohss/AHSS-kee-mahss
12.	big/small	meh-GAH-lohss/mee-KROHSS
13.	fast/slow	GREE-gor-ohss/ahr-GOHSS
14.	very	poLEE
15.	where is . . . ?	poo IN-neh
16.	how much . . . ?	POH-so
17.	I don't understand	DEN kah-tah-lah-VENN-o
18.	What do you call this?	poss LEHyehteh ahvto
19.	I'm lost	KAHtheekah
20.	complete price	Olah pehreelahmVAH-nondheh
	(everything included)	
21.	I'm tired	EEmeh koorahSMEHnoss
22.	I'm hungry	peeNO
23.	cheers!	YAH-sahss
24.	food	tro-FEE
25.	grocery store	mah-gah-ZEE
26.	delicious	thaumasios
27.	market	aGORa
28.	money	lep-TAH
29.	station	stathmos
30.	private accommodations	doeMAHtooo
31.	toilet	meros
32.	I	AY-go
33.	you	eh-SAYSS
34.	love	ah-GAH-pay
35.	sleep	kim-MOM-may
36.	train	TREN-no
37.	The bill, please	Toh log-a-ree-ahz MO, pah-rah-kah-LOH
38.	friend	FEE-lohss
39.	water	neh-RO
40.	Tourist Information	toor-is-MOHSS

ITALIAN

1. hello	bongiorno	bohn-ZHOOR-no
2. goodbye	ciao	chow
3. see you later	civediamo	chee vey-dee-OMM-o
4. goodnight	buona notte	BWONN-ah NOT-tay
5. please	per favore	pair fah-VOR-ay
6. thank you	grazie	GRAH-tsee-ay
7. yes/no	si/no	see/no
8. one/two/three	uno/due/tray	oo-noh/doo-ay/tray
9. cheap/expensive	economico/caro	ay-koh-NO-mee-koh/CARR-o
10. good/bad	buone/cattivo	BWON-o/kaht-TEE-vo
11. beautiful/ugly	bello/brutto	BEHL-lo/BROOT-to
12. big/small	grande/piccolo	GRAHN-day/PEEKkoh-lo
13. fast/slow	rapido/lento	RAHH-pee-do/LEHN-to
14. very	molto	MOHL-to
15. where is . . .?	dov'e . . .?	do-VAY
16. how much . . .?	quanto?	KWAHN-to'
17. I don't understand	Non capisco	nohn kay-PEESS-ko
18. what do you call this?	che cosi questo?	kay KO-see KWAY-sto
19. I'm lost	mi sono perso	mee SOH-no PEHR-so
20. I'm tired	sono stanco	SOH-no STAHNG-ko
21. I'm hungry	ho fame	oh FAH-may
22. food	cibo	CHEE-bo
23. grocery store	drogheria	dro-GAY-ree-ah
24. picnic	picnic	picnic
25. delicious	delizioso	day-leet-see-OH-so
26. market	mercato	mayr-COT-to
27. drunk	ubriaco	oo-bree-AH-co
28. money	denaro	day-NAHR-ro
29. station	stazione	STAHT-see-OH-nay
30. private accommodations	camera	CAH-may-rah
31. toilet	toilet	toy-LET
32. I	io	ee-OH
33. you	lei	lay
34. love	amore	ah-MOH-ray
35. sleep	dormire	dor-MEER-ay
36. train	treno	TREN-no
37. The bill, please	Il conto, prego	ell KON-to, pray-go
38. friend	amico	ah-mee-ko
39. water/tap water	acqua/acqua naturale	AH-kwa nah-toor-ALL—ay
40. castle	castello	kah-STELL-o
41. church	chiesa	kee-AY=za
42. How are you?	come va?	KO-may VAH
43. Tourist Information	ufficio informazioni	oo-FEE-see-o EEN-for-MOTZ-ee-OH-nee
44. You're welcome	prego	PRAY-go
45. Doing sweet nothing	dolce far niente	DOL-chay far nee-YEN-tay

PORTUGUESE

1. hello	bom dia	bohm DEE-ah
2. goodbye	adeus	eh-DAY-oosh
3. see you later	ate logo	eh-TAY LO-go
4. goodnight	boa noite	BOH-eh NOY-teh
5. please	por favor	poor feh-VOR
6. thank you	obrigado	obree GAHdhoo
7. yes/no	sim/nao	see/NAH-oh
8. one/two/three	um/dois/tres	uh/doysh/traysh
9. cheap/expensive	barato/caro	beh-RAW-to/CARR-o
10. good/bad	bom/mau	BOHM/MAH-oh
11. beautiful/ugly	belo/feio	BEHloo/FAYoo
12. big/small	grande/pequeno	GRAHN-day/peh-KAYN-yo
13. fast/slow	rapido/lento	RAHpeedo/LENN-to
14. very	muito	MOO-to
15. where is . . . ?	donde esta . . . ?	OHN-deh eesh-TAH
16. how much . . . ?	quanto?	KWAHN-to
17. I don't understand	nao compreendo	NAH-oh kohm-pree-AYN-do
18. what do you call this?	como se chama isto?	KO-moo sehr SHAR-ma EESH-to
19. I'm lost	estou perdido	esh-TOH-ah perr-DEE-do
20. complete price (everything included)	tudo incluido	TOO-do ANN-kloo-EE-do
21. I'm tired	estou cansado	esh-TOH-ah cahn-SAH-do
22. I'm hungry	tenho fome	TEN-no FO-meh
23. cheers!	saude!	sah-OO-duh
24. food	alimento	ah-lee-MEN-tu
25. grocery store	mercearia	mehr-say-ah-REE-ah
26. picnic	piquenique	PEEK-ah-NEEK
27. delicious	delicioso	deh-LEE-see-OH-zuh
28. market	mercado	mehr-KA-du
29. drunk	bebado	be-BA-du
30. money	dinheiro	dee-NEER-u
31. station	estacao	eh-stah-SAH-oh
32. private accommodations	case particular	casa parr-teek-u-LARR
33. toilet	retrete	ray-TRAY-tay
34. I	eu	yo
35. you	tu	tu
36. love	amor	a-MOHR
37. sleep	dormir	dor-MEE
38. train	trem	trehm
39. The bill, please	A conta, por favor	ah KOHN-tah, poor feh-VOR
40. friend	amigo	eh-MEE-go
41. water	agua	AH-guah
42. castle	castelo	coss-TELL-o
43. Tourist Information	informacao turistico	ann-for-mah-SAH-o too-REE-stee-ko
44. How are you?	Como vi?	CO-MO VIE

SERBO-CROATION

1. hello	dobar	DO-bar DUN
2. goodbye	dan	DUN
3. see you later	dovidjenja	do-vee-TEN-ya
4. goodnight	laku noc	LAH-koo NOACH
5. please	molim	MO-leem
6. thank you	hvala	HVAH-lah
7. yes/no	da/ne	dah/neh
8. one/two/three	jedan/dva/tri	YEH-dahn/dvah/tree
9. cheap/expensive	jeftino/skupo	YEHF-tee-no/SKOO/po
10. good/bad	dobro/lose	DObro/LOsheh
11. beautiful/ugly	lepo/ruzno	LEHpo/ROOzhno
12. big/small	veliko/malo	VEHleeko/MAHlo
13. fast/slow	brzo/sporo	BERzo/SPOro
14. very	vrlo	VERlo
15. where is...?	gde je...?	g'DAY-yeh
16. how much...?	koliko?	koLEEko
17. I don't understand	ne rezumem	neh rah-ZOO-mem
18. What is that?	Sto je to?	SHTAH yeh-toh
19. I'm lost	zalutao sam	zah-LOOT-ow sahm
20. complete price (everything included)	sve je uracunato	sveh yeh OOrachoonahto
21. I'm tired	umoran sam	OOmorahn sahm
22. I'm hungry	gladan sam	GLAHdahn sahm
23. cheers!	ziveli	ZHEEvehlee
24. food	hrana	HRA-na
25. grocery store	bakalnica	bah-KAHL-nee-kah
26. picnic	izlet	EEZH-let
27. delicious	ukusan	OO-koo-shawn
28. market	trg	turg
29. drunk	pijan	PEE-yahn
30. money	novac	NOH-vak
31. station	stanica	STAHN-eetz-ah
32. private accommodations	podesavanje	poh-deh-sah-VAHN-yeh
33. toilet	toaleta	toh-LET-tah
34. I	ja	yah
35. you	vi	vee
36. love	ljubav	LYOO-bahv
37. sleep	spavati	SPAH-va-tee
38. train	voz	voze
39. The bill, please	Racun, molim	RAW-choon, MO-leem
40. friend	prijatelj	PREE-yah-tell
41. water	vode	VO-day
42. Tourist Information	turisticki ured	TOO-rist-eech-kee-OO-red
43. How are you?	kako ste?	KOCK-O stay

SPANISH

1. hello	hola	OH-lah
2. goodbye	adios	AH-dee-OHSS
3. see you later	hasta luego	AHSS-tah LWAY-go
4. goodnight	buenas noches	BWAY-nahss NOH-chayss
5. please	por favor	por fav-VOHR
6. thank you	gracias	GRAH-see-ahss
7. yes/no	si/no	see/no
8. one/two/three	uno/dos/tres	OO-no/dohs/trayss
9. cheap/expensive	barato/caro	bah-RAH-to/KAH-ro
10. good/bad	bueno/malo	BWAY-no/MAH-lo
11. beautiful/ugly	bonito/feo	bo-NEE-to/FAY-o
12. big/small	grande/pequeno	GRAHN-day/pay-KAYN-yo
13. fast/slow	rapido/lento	RAH-pee-do/LAYN-to
14. very	muy	mwee
15. where is...?	donde esta...?	DOHN-day ayss-TAH
16. how much...?	cuanto?	KWAHN-to
17. I don't understand	no comprendo	no kom-PRAYN-do
18. what do you call this?	como se llama esto?	KO-mo say YAH-ma AYSS-to
19. I'm lost	me he perdido	may ay pehr-DEE-do
20. complete price	todo esta incluido	TOH-doh ayssTAH eenklooEEdo
(everything included)		
22. I'm hungry	tengo hambre	TAYNG-go AHM-bray
23. cheers!	a su salud!	ah soo sah-LOOD
24. food	alimento	ah-lee-MAYN-to
25. grocery store	abaceria	ah-bah-say-REE-ah
26. picnic	comida a escote	ko-ME-da AH eskoy-tay
27. delicious	delicioso	day-lee-see-OH-so
28. market	mercado	mayr-KAH-do
29. drunk	borracho	boh-RAH-choh
30. money	dinero	dee-NAY-ro
31. station	estacion	ay-STAH-see-OHN
32. private accommodations	casa particular	KAH-ssah pahr-tee-koo-LAHR
33. toilet	retrete	ray-TRAY-tay
34. I	yo	yo
35. you	usted	usted
36. love	amor	ah-MOHR
37. sleep	sueno	SWAYN-yo
38. train	tren	train
39. The bill, please	La cuenta, por favor	lah KWAYN-tah, por fah-VOHR
40. friend	amigo	ah-MEE-go
41. water	agua	AH-gwah
42. castle	castillo	coss-TEE-yoh
43. How are you?/I'm fine, thanks	Como esta?/Estoy bien, gracias	co-mo STAH/stoy bee-AYN, EEN-for-MAH-see-OHN
44. Tourist Information	Informacion turistica	too-REES-tee-kah

SWEDISH

1. hello	god dag	goo dah
2. goodbye	adjo	ah YUR
3. see you later	vi ses	vee SAYSS
4. goodnight	god natt	goo NUT
5. please	varsagod	VAHR-sah-gude
6. thank you	tack	tock
7. yes/no	ja/nej	yah/nay
8. one/two/three	ett/tva/tre	eht/tvaw/tray
9. cheap/expensive	billig/dyr	BIL-lig/deer
10. good/bad	god/dalig	gude/DAW-lig
11. beautiful/ugly	vacker/ful	VAHkeer/fewl
12. big/small	stor/liten	stoor/LEE-tern
13. fast/slow	snabb/langsam	snob/LONG-sahm
14. very	mycket	MEWkert
15. where is . . . ?	var ar . . . ?	VARR ai
16. how much . . . ?	hur mycket?	hewr MEWkert
17. I don't understand	jag forstar inte	yar furr-SHTOAR IN-ter
18. what do you call this?	vad heter det har?	vod HET-ter det HARE
19. I'm lost	jag har gatt vilse	yar harr got VIL-ser
20. complete price (everything included)	allt ingar	ahlt in-GOAR
21. I'm tired	jar ar trott	yog ayr TRUTT
22. I'm hungry	jag ar hungrig	jog ayr HEWN-grig
23. cheers!	skal!	skoal
24. food	naring	NAYR-ing
25. grocery store	specerihandel	SPEES-er-ee-HAN-del
26. picnic	utflykt	OOT-flekt
27. delicious	harlig	HAR-lig
28. market	torg	torg
29. drunk	drucken	DROO-ken
30. money	pengar	PENG-gar
31. station	station	stah-SHONE
32. private accommodations	husrom	HOOSS-rum
33. toilet	toalett	to-ah-LET
34. I	jag	yog
35. you	du	doo
36. love	karlek	KAYR-lik
37. sleep	sova	SO-vah
38. train	tag	tawg
39. The bill, please	var vanlig ge mignotan	var VAYN-lig yay mee NO-tahn
40. friend	vann	vayn
41. water	vatten	vott-en
42. castle	borg	borg
43. How are you?	Hur stat det till?	hoor STOAR det till

The insults that follow are taken from **The Insult Dictionary — How to Snarl Back in Five Languages,** *which can be ordered through James H. Heineman, Inc., 475 Park Ave., New York, NY 10022.*

English	German	French	Italian	Spanish
Hairy creep	Oller Leisetreter (Oller lysetrayter)	Troglodyte (Troglodeet)	Stupido scimmione (Stoo-peedoh scheemee-ohneh)	Espantapajaros (Spantahpahharos)
Moron	Nackter Wilder (Naackter veelder)	Cretin (Craytan)	Deficiente (Deh-fee-chenteh)	Carcamal (Carcamahll)
Ass	Narr (Naarr)	Ane bate (Ann battay)	Somaro (Soh-mah-roh)	Asno (Assnoh)
Donkey	Esel (Ayzel)	Bourricot (Booreeko)	Asino (Ah-zeenoh)	Burro (Boorroh)
Crazy in the head	Schwach im Kopf (Shvaach im kopf)	Dingue (Dang)	Pazzoide (Pah-tzo-ee-deh)	Majareta (Mahharetah)
Ugly	Hasslich (Haesslich)	Laideron (Laidron)	Brutto (Broot-toh)	Asqueroso (Askehrosoh)
Useless vampire	Blutsaugendes Gespenst (Blootsaagendes geshpenst)	Vampire a la gomme (Vampeer a la gom)	Vampiro inutile (Vam-peeroh in-ootee-leh)	Vampiro caduco (Bahm-peeroh cadookoh)
Blood-sucking leech	Schmarotzer (Shmaarotser)	Sangsue (Sansi)	Sanguisuga (Sangoo-ee-sooga)	Tacano (Tahkanyoh)
Repulsive, evil-smelling dog	Widerlicher Lump (Veederlicher loomp)	Repugnant voyou (Raipinian vwahyoo)	Ributtante vagabondo puzzolente (Ree-boot-tanteh vagabond-oh poot-zolenteh)	Ronoso (Ronyoso)
Dribbling, senile fool	Bloder Sabberer (Bloeder zaabberer)	Vieux baveux (Vyer bavehr)	Stupido vecchio vincitrullito (Stoopeedah veh-keeoh reen-chee-trool-leeto)	Viejo baboso (Beeyehho babbosoh)

English	German	French	Italian	Spanish
This isn't just second class, it's degradation	Das ist nicht nur zweite Klasse sondern auch jammerlich (*Daas ist neecht noor tsvvyte Klaasse zondern aoch yaemmerlish*)	C'est pas seulement une deuxieme classe, c'est de la pourriture! (*Say par sehrlman in derzyaim klarss, say d'lar pooreetir!*)	Questa non e una seconda classe, e una degradazione (*Kwestah non eh oonah seh-con-dah clahs-seh, eh oonah deh-grah-dah-tzee-oh-neh*)	Esto no es Segunda Clase, es una degradacion. (*Estoh no ess segoondah classe, ess oona degradathion*)
Put that dirty cigarette out — this is a non-smoker	Drucken Sie Ihre lausige Zigarette aus, das ist ein Nichtraucher (*Drueken Zee eere laozege Tsee-garette aos, daas eest eyn Neecht-raocher*)	Eh eh, la, la cigarette — c'est un non-fumeur ici! (*Eh eh, lar, lar seegaret — stan non-fimehr eessee!*)	Spenga quella sigaretta puzzolente, qui e vietato fumare. (*Spehngah kwella see-gah-reht-tah pootz-oh-lenteh, kwee eh vee-eh-ta-to foomareh*)	Tire esta colilla de una vez. Aqui es para no fumadores (*Teereh estah koleelya deh oona beith. Akee ess parah no foomahdores*)
Just wait your turn, you ill-mannered jerk	Drangen Sie sich nicht vor, Sie ungeschliffener Banause (*Drayngen zee zich neecht for, zee oongeshliffener baanaose*)	Eh! Attends done ton tour, paysan! (*Eh! Attan donk ton toor, paysan!*)	Aspetti il suo turno, zoti-cone maleducato (*Ahs-peh-tee eel soo-oh tor-no, tzo-tee-ko-neh mah-leh-doo-cah-to*)	Pongase en la cola, mal educado! (*Pongaseh en lah kawla, mal eddokadoh!*)
Stand on your own feet	Konnen Sie nicht auf Ihren eigenen Fussen stehen? (*Coennen zee nisht aof eeren ygenen fussen shtayn?*)	Vous avez fini de me marcher dessus? (*Voo zavay feenee derm marshay dersi?*)	Ci sta bene sul mio pierde? (*Chee stah beh-neh sool mee-o pee-eh-deh?*)	Aguantese usted solo, quiere? (*Agooanteseh oosteh soloh, kyereh?*)

Gossiping, malicious old bag	Bosartige alte Klatsche (Boesaartige aalte Klaatsche)	Pipelette venimeuse (Peeplet verneemerz)	Pettegola maligna (Peht-teh-gola mah-leeneeah)	Chismoso (Cheesmosoh)
Boo!	Boo! (Boo!)	Hou! Hou! (Oo! Oo!)	(In Italy to show disapproval at the theatre one whistles)	Bu! (Boo!)
Rotten!	Schrecklich (Shrayklish)	Quel four! (Kel foor!)	Fa schifo (Fa skeefoh)	Putrefacto (Pootrefactoh)
Road hog!	Strassen-Schnecke (Shtraassen-shnayke)	Chauffard! (Shaufahr!)	Criminale! (Cree-mee-nah-leh)	Mamarracho! (Mamarrachoh!)
So what?	Na und? (Naa oond?)	Et alors? (eh alohr?)	E chi se ne frega? (Eh kee seh neh freh-gah?)	Que pasa? (Ke passah?)
Get lost	Hau'ab (Hao aap)	Allez vous faire voir! (Allay voo fair vvar!)	Va all'inferno (Vah ahll'in-ferno)	A ver si te pierdes de vista! (A ber see te peeyerdes de beestah!)
Go jump in the lake	Hang' Dich auf (Hayng deesh aof)	Allez vous faire pendre ailleus! (Allay voo fair pandr ayehr!)	Vada a farsi friggere (Vahdah ah far-see free-dje-reh)	Tirate de cabeza al lago! (Teerahte de cabetha al lagoh!)
Your lips are like wet liver	Deine Lippen sind so zarte wie nasse Leber (Dyne lippn zind zo tsart vee nasse layber)	Vous avez les levres comme du foie meurtri! (Voo zavay lay laivr kom di fwar mehrtree!)	Le tue labbra sono come fegato crudo (Leh too-eh lah-brah sono comeh feh-gah-to croo-do)	Tus labios son como la hiel (Toos labbyos son comoh la yel)
Get your cotton-picking hands off me	Horen Sie 'mal mit der Fummelei auf (Hoern zee maal meet dair foommely aaf)	Vous avez fini de me peloter! (Voo zavay feenee d'mer perlotay?)	Tenga la mani a posto (Teh-ngah leh mah-ny ah posto)	Guarde sus pezunas para otra ocasion (Guardeh soos pehthoonyas parah otrah ocassion)

English	German	French	Italian	Spanish
This place is a flea-pit	Dieses Theater ist eine Flohkiste (*Deezes teater ist yne flo-keeste*)	Quel trou a puces! (*Kel troo ar pis!*)	Questa sala e infima (*Kweh-sta sahla eh eenfeema*)	Este asiento es un nido de pulgas (*Esteh aseeyentoh ess oon needoh de poolgas*)
B.O.!	Schweissgeruch! (*Shvyssgerooch!*)	Hold your nose between forefinger and thumb in a disdainful manner.	Che puzza di sudore! (*Keh poo-tzah dee soo-do-reh!*)	Huele! (*Ooele!*)
I asked for a porter, not a pygmy	Ich brauche einen Gepacktrager, keinen Zwerg (*Eekh braoch eynen Gepaektraeger keynen tsverg*)	Je veux un porteur, pas un gringalet! (*Sher ver an portehr, pazan grangallay!*)	Ho bisogno di un facchino non di un pigmeo. (*Oh besonio dee oon fak-keeno non dee oon pigmeh-oh*)	He pedido un mozo, no un mequetrefe. (*Eh pedidoh oon mohaw, noh oon meketrefeh*)
It's fragile, you clumsy idiot	Das ist zerbrechlich. Sie Trampeltier (*Daas eest tsairbraychlich, Zee Traampltier*)	Eh, brute! C'est fragile! (*Eh, britt! Say frasheel!*)	E fragile, pezzo d'idiota. (*Eh frah-jee-leh, peh-tzo deedeeotah*)	No ve que es fragil, idiota? (*Noh ve ke ess frahheel, eediotah?*)
Do any of your customers ever come back?	Ist schon einer Ihrer Kunden wiedergekommen? (*Eest shon yner eerer koonden veedergekommen?*)	Vous avez des clients qui reviennent manger ici? (*Voo zavay day cleeyan keer vyen manshay eecee?*)	Capita mai che un cliente torni una seconda volta? (*Cah-pee-ta mah-ee keh oon clee-ehn-teh tornee oona seh-conda volta?*)	Hay algun cliente que vuelva por segunda vez? (*Ay algoon cleeyenteh ke bwelbah por segoondah beth?*)
May I have another plate for the maggots?	Bringen Sie mir doch noch bitte einen Teller fur die Maden (*Breengn zee meer doch noch bitte y-nen tayller fuer dee maaden*)	Donnez-moi donc une cuvette pour y mettre les vers! (*Donnay muvar donk in kivett poor ee mettr'er lay vair!*)	Mi darebbe un piatto a parte per i vermi? (*Mee darehb-beh oon pee-aht-to ah parteh per ee vehr-mee?*)	Tiene otro plato para dejar los gusanos? (*Teeyene otroh platoh para dehhar los goosanos?*)

6
Health

Before Your Trip

See your doctor Just as you would give your car a good check-up before a long journey, it's a good idea to meet with your doctor before your trip. Get a general check-up. Tell the doctor everywhere you plan to go and anywhere you may go. Then you can have the flexibility to take that impulsive swing through Turkey or Morocco knowing that you are prepared medically and have the required shots. At the time of this printing, no shots are required for European travel, but it's always wise to check. Get advice on maintaining your health and about drinking the water. Obtain recommended immunizations and discuss proper care of any medical conditions. In the case of such conditions it is wise to take with you to Europe a letter from the doctor describing the problem. If you plan to travel beyond Europe, ask your doctor about gamma globulin and the anti-diarrhea "miracle pill," doxycycline.

Investigate the weather conditions you expect to encounter and pack proper clothing. Will you need an umbrella, or a sunscreeen ointment?

Have a dental check-up Emergency dental care during your trip is time- and money-consuming, and it can be hazardous and painful.

```
┌──────────Assemble a Traveler's First Aid Kit──────────┐
│    Your kit should contain:                            │
│                                                        │
│  soap                      aspirin                     │
│  supplemental vitamins     bandages                    │
│  thermometer               medications — anti-diarrheal│
│                            antibiotic   motion sickness │
└────────────────────────────────────────────────────────┘
```

Soap prevents and controls infections. Young travelers concerned about acne (which can be especially troublesome when traveling) should wash with soap twice a day. Those with corrected vision should bring extra glasses in a solid protective case, as well as the lens prescription. Contact lenses are used all over Europe and the required solutions for their care are easy to find. Soft lenses can be boiled like eggs. (Be sure to remind your helpful landlady to leave them in their case.) Do not assume that you can wear your contacts as comfortably in Europe as you can at home. I find that the hot, dusty cities and my style of travel make contacts impossible, and every summer I end up wearing my glasses and carrying my contacts.

Supplemental vitamins (with iron, for women) are most effective when taken with the day's largest meal. Aspirin is a great general pain reliever for headaches, sore feet, sprains, bruises, hangovers and many other minor problems. A thermometer in a protective case is important because, if you have a fever, you should seek medical help. (To convert from Celsius to Fahrenheit, use the formula $F = [(C \times 9/5) + 32]$. $98.6° F = 37° C$.) Medication for motion sickness ("Dramamine") should be taken several hours before the upsetting motion is expected to begin. This medication can also serve as a mild sleeping pill. Ask your doctor to recommend an anti-diarrheal medication. Certain medications prescribed in other countries (like chloramphenicol and enterovioform) are very dangerous and should be avoided. Bandages help keep wounds clean, but are not a substitute for thorough cleaning. A piece of clean cloth can be sterilized by scorching it with a match. Bandages or tape can prevent or retard problems with the feet. Simply cover any irritated area when you first notice it.

Health in Europe

Europe is generally safe All the talk of gamma globulin, doxycycline and treating water with purification tablets is applicable only south and east of Europe.

Many people might disagree with me, but I would say that, with discretion and common sense, you can eat and drink whatever you like in Europe. If any area deserves a little extra caution it is the southern countries of Spain, Portugal, Italy and Greece.

I was able to stay healthy while traveling from Europe to India. By following these basic guidelines, I never once suffered from "Tehran Tummy" or "Delhi Belly."

Outside of Europe Use good judgment when eating. Avoid unhealthy-looking restaurants. Wash and peel all fruit. When in serious doubt, eat only thick-skinned fruit (uh, peeled). Even in the worst places, anything cooked and still hot is safe. Meat should be well-cooked. (Have "well-done" written on a piece of paper in the local language and use it when ordering.) Avoid possibly-spoiled foods, and remember, pre-prepared foods gather germs. The train station restaurants are India's safest because they have the fastest turnover. Germs just don't have time to congregate.

Honor your diet An adequate diet is very important for a traveler. The longer your trip, the more you will be affected by an inadequate diet. Budget travelers often eat more carbohydrates and less protein to stretch their travel dollar. This is the root of many nutritional problems encountered by travelers. Protein is necessary for resistance to infection and to rebuild muscles. Protein should be consumed with the day's largest meal because that is when the "essential" amino acids are most

likely to be present to allow complete protein utilization. I
bring supplemental vitamins and take them religiously.

Drink the Water

You can drink the water anywhere in Europe. Please, no
matter what you hear, drink the water. You can drink the water
in Europe. Read signs carefully, however, because some taps,
like those on the trains, are not for drinking. A decal showing a
glass with a red "X" over it or a skull and crossbones should be
taken as a subtle hint that it is not *trinkwasser*. Water served in
a restaurant is obviously drinking water. A new game is being
played all over Europe. Many waiters are telling tourists that
the water is no good. "It's only for brushing your teeth." This is
a lie to scare you into ordering a two dollar drink.

East of Bulgaria and south of the Mediterranean, do not
drink the water without treating it. Water can be treated by
boiling it for twenty minutes. I prefer the two percent tincture
of iodine treatment. I carry it in an eye-dropper bottle. Eight
drops per quart or liter or one drop per glass is all that is
required to purify the questionable water. This is very handy in
a restaurant, because my glass of water is purified in time to
drink it still cold with my meal. Iodine is fast, easy, kills just
about everything, and doubles as a good disinfectant.

Beer, wine, boiled coffee and tea, and bottled soft drinks
are safe. Coca-Cola products are safe to drink anywhere in the
world.

You Will Get Sick

Get used to the fact that travel is a package deal. You will
get sick in Europe. You'll have diarrhea for a day. When you
get the runs, take it in stride, and if you stay healthy, you'll feel
lucky.

The water may, sooner or later, make you sick. It is not
necessarily dirty. The bacteria in European water is different
from that in American water. Our systems are the most pam-
pered on earth. We grew up on bread that rips in a straight line.
We are capable of handling American bacteria with no prob-

lem at all, but some people can go to London and get sick. Some French people visit Boston and get sick. Some Americans travel around the world, eating and drinking everything in sight, and don't get sick — others spend weeks on the toilet. It all depends on the person.

If you do get diarrhea, it will run its course (so to speak) and the only thing for you to do is keep "plugging" along, revise your diet and don't panic. When I get diarrhea, I make my diet as bland and as boring as possible for a day or so (bread, rice, potatoes, soup, tea, 7-Up). Keep telling yourself that tomorrow you will feel much better. You will. Most conditions are self-limiting. Like most tourists, I bring Lomotil pills, but I have found that the bland diet is the best remedy. If your loose stools persist, be sure to replenish all lost liquids and minerals. (Bananas are very effective in replacing potassium which is lost during a bout with diarrhea.) If you have a prolonged case of diarrhea (which is especially dangerous for an infant), a temperature greater than 101° F (38.3° C), or if you notice blood in your stools, contact a doctor for help. As I mentioned before, Europeans use a pill called Enterovioform which is unsafe. American doctors advise that you avoid that treatment.

I visited the Red Cross in Athens after a miserable three-week tour of the toilets of Syria and Jordan, and the remedy that finally stopped all of my troubles was simply boiled rice and plain tea. After five days on that dull diet, I was as good as new — and constipated.

Constipation, the other side of the coin, seems to be nearly as prevalent as diarrhea. Know what roughage is and everything will come out all right in the end.

A basic hygiene hint is to wash your hands often, keep your nails clean and never touch your fingers to your mouth.

If You Do Get Sick

Medical treatment in Europe is generally of high quality. To facilitate smooth communication, it is best to find an English-speaking doctor. Information leading you to these

"I want to see a doctor."   English
"Deseo ver al medico."   Spanish
"Je voudrais voir le docteur."   French
"Desidero verde il dottore."   Italian
"Jag vill traffa doktorn."   Swedish
"Ich mochte den Arzt sehen."   German
"Gormek istiyorum doktorn."   Turkish

"Traveling makes a man wiser, but less happy."

— *Thomas Jefferson*

doctors can be obtained through agencies that deal with Americans, such as embassies, consulates, American Express Companies and large hotels.

American Embassies and consulates have lists of American or British trained doctors. This is most important outside of Europe. Primitive medicine men are fun — unless your bed is the one they're dancing over.

A physical injury is often accompanied by swelling which is painful and retards healing. For twenty-four to thirty-six hours after a sprain or bruise occurs, you should apply ice to and elevate the injured area. An "ace" bandage is useful to immobilize, to stop swelling and, later, to provide support. It is not helpful to "work out" a sprain.

Venereal disease has reached pandemic proportions (an epidemic not limited to a specific area). Obviously, the best way to prevent V.D. is to avoid exposure. A rubber prophylactic is fairly effective in preventing tranmission for those who are unable to avoid exposure. Cleaning with soap and water before and after exposure is also helpful if not downright pleasurable.

Traveler's Toilet Trauma

Foreign toilets can be traumatic to some and nearly impossible to find for others. An experienced traveler learns to overcome toilet-shock and can find a WC quickly and easily.

First, about toilet-trauma. Be prepared for toilets that are dirtier and different than those at home. Only Americans need disposable bibs to sit on and a paper strip draped over their toilet, assuring them that no one has sat there yet. In fact, those of us who need a throne to sit on, are in the minority. Most humans sit on their haunches and nothing more. When many refugees are oriented (or de-oriented) here, they have to be told not to stand on our rims.

So, if you plan to venture away from the international-style hotels in your travels and become a temporary local person, there's a good chance you'll really be "going" local. Experienced travelers enjoy recalling the shock they got the first time they opened the door and found only porcelain foot-prints (often called the "Turkish bombshell") or just a hole in the ground — complete with flies in a holding pattern.

Toilet paper (like spoons and forks) is another "essential" that most people on our planet don't use. What they use varies, and I don't care to get too graphic in this area. Just remember that a billion people in South Asia never eat with their left hand.

A week's supply of toilet paper — don't leave home without it. When you run out, tour a first-class hotel or restaurant and borrow ten or twelve yards of good soft stuff. Local grade TP is often closer to wax or crepe paper — good for a laugh but not much more.

Finding a decent public toilet can be frustrating. I once dropped a tour group off for a potty stop. When I picked them up 20 minutes later, none had found relief.

Public conveniences are inconveniently rare. I can sniff out a good john in a jiffy but it's rarely "public." Any place that serves food or drinks has a bathroom. No restaurateur would label his WC so those on the street can see, but you can walk into any cafe or restaurant, politely and confidently, and find a bathroom somewhere in the back. It's easiest in places that have outdoor seating, because waiters will think you're a customer just making a quick trip inside. Some call it rude, I call it survival. If you feel like it, ask permission. Just smile, "Toilet?" I'm rarely turned down. Timid people buy a drink they don't want in order to leave one. That's unnecessary. Just be polite and say thank you and good-bye. When nature beckons and there's no restaurant or bar handy, look in parks, train stations, on trains, in museums, hotel lobbies, government buildings and on upper floors of department stores.

In many countries you'll need to be selective to avoid the gag-a-maggot variety of toilets. Public toilets and those in parks are often repulsive. I never leave a museum without taking advantage of its restrooms — free, clean, and full of artistic graffiti. Use the toilets on the train rather than in the station to save time and money. Toilets on first-class cars are a cut above those on second-class. I go first-class even with a 2nd class ticket. Train toilets are located on the ends of cars, where they shake the most. A trip to the train's john always reminds me of the rodeo.

Large, classy, old hotels are as impressive as many places you'll pay to see. You can always find a royal retreat here and plenty of very soft TP. This is really an oasis in Third World countries where western sit-down toilets are rare.

And finally, there are countries where the people don't use restrooms at all. I've been on buses that have just stopped, and fifty people scatter. Three minutes later they reload, relieved. It takes a little adjusting, but that's travel. When in Rome, do as the Romans do . . . and before you know it . . . Euro-peein'.

7
The Woman Traveling Alone

Every year more and more single women are traveling alone around Europe. Women outnumber the men in the travel classes I teach. And (while many of them, no doubt, flock in just to see me) most are asking: "Is it safe for me to travel alone in Europe?" This is a topic that is best understood and discussed by a woman. Pam Kasardi, who has traveled more than any woman I know, has agreed to share her thoughts on the subject in this chapter.

* * * * *

A woman traveling alone faces two special problems: first off, the usual danger associated with solo travel (crime) may be greater because a woman is seen as more vulnerable than a man; and secondly, a woman traveler may have to endure more sexual harassment while on the road than she would find acceptable at home. Aside from these problems, however, there are some great advantages to traveling alone as a woman.

If you have the desire to travel alone in Europe, do it. While I don't recommend traveling alone in North Africa or the Middle East, I have never regretted traveling alone in Europe. My feeling (as well as the general consensus of the solo women travelers I've met) is that you will be safe as long as you are careful and exercise the same common sense you would in any big American city. Be very wary of the people you meet. Withhold your trust much longer than you would at home. To put it bluntly, Europe has more than its share of horny men roaming about with no other purpose in mind than to hustle women tourists.

As far as crime and your safety are concerned, I would say Europe is on par with the U.S. If you don't feel safe traveling alone in America, think twice before embarking upon a solo European adventure. You are most likely to run into problems in Italy, Greece, Spain, Portugal and in the countries bordering Europe to the south and southeast, where men are most enthralled by the woman traveler. The Moslem countries, while not necessarily a criminal threat, are generally considered the leaders of the pack in hassling women travelers. In these countries you are safest in the more touristed areas, where the Western traveler is a relatively common sight.

Fit in. Women's Liberation has yet to reach Southern Europe. When you enter a new country, observe. See how the women are treated and how they are expected to act. Don't forget that you are in a different culture with different morals and mores. Just as you must learn to fit in as a guest, you must learn to adapt to the local expectations of proper relations between the sexes. Learn to see your actions as the local people see them. Don't flaunt your relative liberation. If you wear skimpy cut-offs and a tight tee-shirt amidst women shrouded from head to toe in black, you will certainly be calling attention to yourself, offending people and asking for trouble. In a situation such as this, a skirt or long pants would be more appropriate — even if less comfortable.

Don't be a temptation. The flashy female tourist is often equated with the dreamy women the Southern European man sees in American movies. You may be considered "loose" just because you are American. Work hard to fit in so you don't encourage that sort of appraisal of your character. Be especially careful with your clothing and physical movements (stares, smiles, winks, and so on). I'll never forget the day I left my Naples hotel wearing a cool halter top. Within a few minutes I realized that, heat or no heat, I would have to wear something much less interesting.

Many foreign men will look at you for anything they can interpret as a sexual invitation. I have found that the most harmless gesture, like a warm smile or eye contact, can be misinterpreted. Sadly, you will sometimes have to act colder than you really are to remain unharassed.

No matter how you dress or act, you will probably be the object of much admiration, some advances and plenty of less-than-discreet stares. Try not to let gestures of appreciation (whistles and so forth) bother you. I have found them to be generally harmless compliments as well as invitations. The best policy is to ignore them and keep on walking. If things get out of hand, a harsh scolding, in any language, especially in the presence of onlookers, will usually work wonders. "Basta!" means "enough" in Italian.

Stares are a fact of traveling. The farther off the beaten path you get, the more you'll be stared at. In the countryside of Spain, foreigners of any sex are stared at constantly. Admittedly, stares, wolf whistles, pinches and macho come-ons are not to your or my liking, but they are as much a part of Italian and Spanish culture as spaghetti and bullfights. Even if you don't like it, accept it as inevitable.

Southern European women have a habit of strolling arm in arm to let men they pass know that they are in no need of "companionship." When traveling in the South with another woman, I do the same thing. It works very well in reducing harassment.

If you find yourself in a conversation that is leading in the wrong direction, you may want to tell the man or men involved about your husband or children — even if they are imaginary. One summer I wore a fake wedding band whenever I wanted to be considered unavailable and uninterested. When I want to sit unpestered in a cafe, I write in my journal. If you are doing something, you don't look like you're just waiting to be picked up.

In Europe it's macho to try. Train conductors may lay down next to you on the train, hotel managers may try to escort you farther than your room, shoe shine boys may polish your thighs. These are not rape attempts. These are frustrated men asking for a date with a very impressive woman from a sky-scraper land that speaks and thinks a strange language. Don't get shook up — just firmly refuse.

Be very careful who you trust. Believe me, European men, especially the ones who get a lot of practice, can be incredibly smooth and impressive. I've heard several stories about women travelers who joined up with some "classy" European only to wake up abandoned and left without any of their belongings. This unfortunate condition can be avoided by withholding your trust.

Women traveling in pairs are less likely to find themselves in difficult situations than those traveling alone. Many people start their trips alone, intending to pick up partners as they go along. This is easy since there are many solo travelers of both sexes all over Europe traveling with the same intention — befriending and teaming up with a compatible travel partner. I find this particularly easy in youth hostels. European hotels don't care if the couples they rent to are married or not.

You will enjoy rewarding experiences and wonderful hos-pitality because you are a woman — dinner invitations, escorted tours, rides, cups of tea, and so on. American women are often looked upon with awe by foreign men. While there may be hassles, I think these hassles are more than compen-sated by the generous offers of hospitality. You will have many advantages over your male counterpart. Most men would have to travel months to receive the same amount of tangible hospi-tality that a woman receives in a few days. Needless to say, this sort of friendliness can make a visit to any country special. As you travel beyond Europe you will notice even greater hospi-tality and attention. I'll never forget the Egyptian man who let me ride his donkey. As I rode sleepily up the bank of the Nile he begged me to stay with him in Egypt. He promised to build me "a castle on the hilltop."

The problem of course is that all too often those kind of acts come with strings attached. (My Egyptian friend fondled my leg while he promised me the world.) I find that these amount to little more than minor irritations. Before you curse the attention you are getting, remember that you may actually miss it a little after you get home.

A woman who finds herself in any sort of serious trouble should know that a few well-placed tears will often do wonders to clear things up. While a man could conceivably starve on the street corner, a woman in distress is never far from help.

I think the most common negative result from this kind of harassment is that the woman escapes to more comfortable terrain, like England or Germany, and takes with her a disdain for "those rude men in the south."

Now that you've read this chapter, keep in mind that, if anything, I have made the situation sound worse than it really is. Proceed with a cautious but positive attitude and you'll have a great trip.

Pam Kasardi

8
Travel Photography

My most prized souvenirs are the pictures I've taken. Every year I ask myself whether it's worth the worry and expense of mixing photography with my travels. After my film is developed and I relive my trip through those pictures, the answer is always, "Yes!"

If you are going to take pictures during your travels, some hints on the subject can be very helpful. I'm not a professional photographer. I have taken thousands of pictures in the last decade, however, and I'd like to share with you some of the lessons I've learned from that experience.

The Camera

Good shots are made by the photographer — not the camera. For most people, a very expensive camera is a bad idea. Your camera is more likely to be lost, stolen or broken than anything else you'll travel with. A very expensive model may not be worth the risks and headaches that accompany it.

A good, basic 35 mm single lens reflex camera provides everything I need. (I'm talking about something like my Pentax K-1000, which costs about $150.) I have used a more expensive automatic camera. It had its advantages, but I found myself longing for the dependable simplicity of my old K-1000. When buying a camera, think about size, weight and durability.

Before you buy a camera do your research. Camera owners love to talk photography. Learn from them. Visit some camera shops and ask questions. Most people are limited not by the shortcomings of their camera but by their lack of knowledge. You may put a lot of expense and energy into your travel photography. If you don't understand ASA numbers, "f-stops" or "depth of field" find a photography class or workshop and learn. Camera stores offer many good books on photography and even on travel photography. I shutter to think how many people are underexposed or at least lacking depth in this field.

Lenses

Most cameras come with a "normal" 50-55 mm lens. To start with, this is all you need. The "f-stop" numbers indicate how wide you can open the aperture. A more expensive lens can be opened wider (set at a lower "f-stop"), enabling you to take a picture when less light is available. Your lens should go as low as f-2.

The length of the lens (e.g., 55 mm) determines the size of the image it takes. A wide-angle lens (28 or 35 mm) lets you fit more into your picture. This is especially useful when photographing interiors where it's impossible to back up enough to get much in. Wide-angle lenses can distort the picture. A 28 mm lens is considered as wide as you can go without too much distortion.

A longer telephoto lens (e.g., 150 mm) allows you to get a closer shot of your subject. A telephoto lens is especially handy for taking portraits inconspicuously. The longer or more powerful the lens, the more it magnifies any vibrations, thus requiring a faster shutter speed for a good, crisp shot.

A zoom lens has an adjustable length. A common size zoom lens has a range from 70 to 205 mm. You could fit your subject's entire body in the picture (at 70 mm), then "zoom" right in to get just the face (at 205 mm). This is a lot of fun, but, like the telephoto, it is substantially bulkier and heavier than either the regular or the wide-angle lenses. I would say that for travel photography, unless you are particularly interested in portraiture, the wide-angle is a more valuable second lens than the telephoto or zoom.

There is a mid-range zoom lens that gives the photographer a range from about 35 to 70 mm. Many travelers are very happy with this three-lens-in-one concept. There is also a device called a doubler (or tripler) which is attached between the body of the camera and the lens. This doubles (or triples) the power of that lens' magnification. The cost of the doubling is a loss of light.

Filters

There is a wide variety of filters available for the photographer to play with. Every lens should have either an ultraviolet or a haze filter to protect the lens. The only other filter I use is a polarizer to intensify colors. A polarizer will sharpen the contrast between the white and blue of a cloudy sky, giving you a more powerful picture.

Film

Travel photographers around the world debate the merits of different kinds of film. There's no real right or wrong choice — just a personal preference.

Each brand is a little different. For instance, Kodak yields pictures that are bluer, while Agfa is a little stronger in its treatment of reds. Rather than trying to evaluate all films, I will simply explain what I buy and why.

I shoot slides rather than prints. Prints are much more expensive so I take slides, and get prints made only of the shots I really like. I buy rolls of 36 rather than 20 exposures. It's cheaper, less bulky and you don't have to change film as often.

Films come with different ASA numbers or "speeds." The average traveler carries film with ASA numbers ranging from 25 to 400. The ASA number indicates how sensitive to light the film is. Greater light sensitivity allows you to take pictures in darker settings. There is a trade-off, however, since greater light sensitivity produces pictures with a "grainy" quality. In choosing your film, you must decide how "fast" you need it and how important it is for you to minimize graininess. I have never found graininess to be a problem. In a small print or on a slide projected on a screen, I see no difference in graininess between ASA 400 and ASA 64. Graininess does become a factor in large prints. Colors seem to vary a little from one ASA numbered film to another. It's a confusing field. You will make the best choice if you understand the trade-offs between speed, color and graininess. Kodachrome 64 is the best selling slide film and is the best general purpose film on the market. I get Kodak film in ASA 64, 200 or 400.

Film prices vary, and if you find a good price you can stock up. (Keep what film you don't use fresh by freezing it.) Before buying film or any photographic equipment it's wise to pick up a photography magazine and read the advertisements. Wholesale warehouses all over the country sell cameras, accessories and film at prices no retail outlet can match.

Gadgets

Like many hobbies, photography is one that allows you to spend endless amounts of money on a galaxy of gadgets. I have some favorites that are particularly useful to the traveling photographer.

First of all you need a gadget bag. The most functional and economical one is simply a small nylon stuff bag made for hikers. When I'm in a market or somewhere taking a lot of pictures, I like to wear a nylon belt pouch (designed to carry a canteen). This is a handy way to have your different lenses and filters accessible, allowing you to make necessary changes quickly and easily.

A mini C-clamp/tripod is a fantastic gadget. About 5″ tall, this tool screws into any camera, sprouts three legs and holds the camera perfectly still for slow shutter speeds and time exposure shots. (It looks like a small "lunar landing module.") The C-clamp works where the tripod won't, such as on a fence or a hand rail. A conventional tripod is much too large to lug around Europe. A cable release is a gadget that allows you to snap a shot or hold the shutter open without moving the camera. Proper use of this and a C-clamp/tripod will let you take some exciting time exposures and night shots.

A lot of time exposure photography is guesswork. The best way to get good shots of difficult lighting situations is to "bracket" your shots by trying several different exposures of the same scene. You will have to throw out a few slides that way, but one good shot is worth several in the garbage can. Automatic cameras usually meter properly up to eight or ten seconds, making bracketing unnecessary.

A "no-frills" camera like the Pentax K-1000 will not have a timed shutter release. An accessory self-timer is fun and reasonably priced. If you are traveling alone, you can attach that device to your camera and get into your own picture. (If you're not quick you may get a little behind in your photography.) If you are traveling with a friend and want to share lenses, it's possible to buy an adapter ring that will make lenses of different mounts compatible. A dust blower, lens cleaning tissue and a small bottle of cleaning solution are wise additions to any gadget bag.

Tricks For a Good Shot

A sharp eye with a wild imagination is more valuable than a third lens. Develop an eye for what will look good and be interesting after the trip. Weed out dull shots before you take them, not after you get them home. It's cheaper. Postcard-type shots are boring. Everyone knows what the Eiffel Tower looks like. Find a unique or different approach to sights that everyone has seen.

Buildings, in general, are not interesting. It doesn't matter if Karl Marx or Beethoven was born there, a house or building is as dead as they are. As photographers gain experience, they take more "people shots" and fewer buildings or general landscapes. Show the personal and intimate details of your trip: how you lived, who you met, what made each day an adventure (e.g., a close-up of the remains of a picnic, your leech bite or a shot of how you washed your clothes).

Vary the perspective of your camera — close, far, low, high, day, night, etc. Break rules and be gamey. For instance, we are told never to shoot into the sun. Some into-the-sun shots bring surprising results. Try to use bad weather to your advantage. Experiment with strange or difficult light situations. Buy a handbook on existing light photography.

People are interesting subjects. It takes nerve to walk up to someone and take their picture. It can be difficult, but if you want some great shots, be "nervy." Ask for permission. The way to do this in any language is to point at your camera and ask, "Photo?" Your subject will probably be delighted. You most likely just made his day, as well as a good picture. Try to show action. A candid is better than a posed shot. Even a posed "candid" is better than a posed shot. Many photographers take a second shot immediately after the first portrait to capture a looser, warmer subject. If the portrait isn't good, you probably weren't close enough. My best shots are so close that the entire head can't fit into the frame. I traveled through Morocco and Spain with a professional photographer. One of the lessons I learned from him was to not intimidate your subject. If you walk right up, shake his hand and act like a bloody fool, he will consider you just that and ignore you while you feast on some great material.

It's very important to be able to take a quick shot. Know your camera, practice setting it, understand depth of field and metering. In a marketplace situation, where speed is crucial, I preset my camera. I set the meter on the sunlit ground and focus at, let's say, 12 feet. Now I know that, with my depth of field, anything from about 10 to 15 feet will be in focus and, if it's in the sunshine, properly exposed. I can take a perfect picture in an instant, provided my subject meets these preset requirements. If I must shoot secretly or with a low profile (which is a good idea for the most interesting candids), I take off the case. A camera hanging around my neck is bad enough, but with the case open and hanging from my camera, I'm announcing my intentions loud and clear. My gun is cocked. It's possible to get some good shots by presetting the camera and shooting from the waist. Ideally, I get eye contact while I shoot from the hip.

You will hear that the focal length of your lens will dictate the slowest safe hand-held shutter speed you can use. For instance, a 50 mm lens should shoot no slower than a 50th of a second. That rule is a bit conservative. I have been able to get fine shots out of my 50 mm lens at a 30th of a second, even a 15th. Don't be afraid to hand-hold a slow shot, but do what you can to make it steady. If you can lean against a wall, for instance, you become a tripod instead of a bipod. If you have a self-timer, hold the camera still and let that mechanism click the shutter rather than your finger. Using these tricks, I can get good-looking pictures inside a museum at an 8th of a second.

Contrary to what you may think, you won't be able to remember the name of every monastery and mountain that you take a picture of. I record the name of anything I want to be sure to remember on a small piece of paper that I store in between the back of my camera and its case.

When you put your slide show together, remember to limit the length of your show. Nothing is worse than to sit through an endless parade of lackluster shots. Set a limit (e.g., two carousels of 140 slides each, about an hour's worth) and prune your show down to where you've had to leave out some shots that you really like. It should be tight. Keep it moving. Leave the audience crying for more.

A good eye is more important than an extra lens.

9
Museums

Culture for the Uncultured

Europe is a treasure chest of great art. Many of the world's greatest museums will be a part of your trip. Here are a few hints on how to get the most out of these museums.

I have found that some studying before the trip makes the art I see in Europe much more exciting. It's criminal to visit Rome or Greece or Egypt with no background in those civilizations' art. I remember touring the National Museum of Archeology in Athens as an obligation, and it was really quite boring. I was convinced that those who were enjoying it were actually just faking it. Two years later, after a class in ancient art history, that same museum was a fascinating trip into the world of Pericles and Socrates — all because of some background knowledge.

A common misconception is that a great museum has only great art. A museum like the Louvre in Paris is so big (that building was, at one time, the largest in Europe), you can't possibly cover everything properly in one visit — so don't try. Be selective. Only a fraction of a museum's pieces are really "greats," and generally, it is best to enlist the services of a guide or guidebook to show you the best two hours of a museum. Brief guide pamphlets recommending the best basic visit are available in most of Europe's great museums. With this selective strategy, you'll appreciate the highlights when you are fresh. If you still have any energy left, you can explore other areas that you are specifically interested in. For me, museum

A victim of the Louvre.

going is the hardest work I do in Europe, and I'm rarely good for more than two or three hours.

If you are determined to cover a large museum thoroughly, the best strategy is to tackle one section a day for several days.

As I mentioned earlier, if you are especially interested in one piece of art, spend half an hour studying it and listening to each passing tour guide tell his or her story about "David" or the "Móna Lisa" or whatever. They each do their own research and come up with different information to share. There's really nothing wrong with this sort of tour freeloading. Just don't stand in the front and ask a lot of questions.

Before leaving, I always thumb through a museum guidebook index or look through the postcards to make sure I have not missed anything of importance to me. For instance, I love Dali. I thought I was finished with a museum, but in the postcards I found a painting by Dali. A museum guide was happy to show me where this Dali painting was hiding. I saved myself the agony of discovering after my trip was over that I was there but didn't see it.

Remember, most museums are closed one day during the week. Your local guidebook or tourist information should have that information. Free admission days are usually the most crowded. In some cases, it's worth the entrance fee to avoid the crowds.

Open Air Folk Museums

Many travel in search of the old life and traditional culture in action. While we book a round-trip ticket into the archaic past, those we photograph with the old world balanced on their heads are struggling to dump that load and climb into our world. Many are succeeding.

More than ever, the easiest way to see the "real culture" is by exploring that country's Open Air Folk Museum. True, it's culture on a "lazy susan," about as real as Santa's Village in a one-stop climate-controlled shopping mall, but the future is becoming the past faster than ever and, in many places, it is the only "Old World" you're going to find.

An Open Air Folk Museum is a collection of traditional buildings from every corner of the country or region carefully reassembled in a park, usually near the capital or major city. These sprawling museums are the best bet for the hurried (or tired) tourist craving a walk through that country's past. Log cabins, thatched cottages, mills, old school houses, shops and farms come complete with original furnishings and usually a local person dressed in the traditional costume who's happy to answer any of your questions about life then and there.

Folk museums buzz with colorful folk dances, live music performances and young craftsmen specializing in old crafts. Many traditional arts and crafts are dying and these artisans do what they can to keep the cuckoo clock from going the way of the dodo bird. Some of my favorite souvenirs are those I watched being dyed, woven, or carved by folk museum craftsmen.

To get the most out of your visit, pick up a list of special exhibits, events and activities at the Information Center and take advantage of any walking tours. These sightseeing centers of the future were popularized in Scandinavia, and they're now found all over the world.

The best folk museums I've seen are in the Nordic capitals. Oslo's, with 150 historic buildings and a 12th century stave church, is just a quick boat ride across the harbor from the city hall. Skansen in Stockholm gets my first place ribbon for its guided tours, feisty folk entertainment and its Lapp camp complete with reindeer.

Switzerland's Ballenberg Open Air Museum near Interlaken is a good alternative when the Alps hide behind clouds.

The British Isles have no shortage of folk museums. For an unrivaled look at the Industrial Revolution, be sure to spend a day at the new Blists Hill Open Air Museum at the Iron Bridge Gorge, north of Stratford. You can cross the world's first iron bridge to see the factories that lit the fuse of our modern age.

The "Knotts Berry Farm" of Bulgaria is in Gabrovo and

offers a refreshing splash of free enterprise-type crafts in a rather cold, communal world.

Barcelona's Pueblo Espanol is a disappointment.

Every year new folk museums open. Travel with a current guide and use tourist information centers abroad. Before your trip send a card to each country's National Tourist Office in San Francisco or New York (see page 20). Request the general packet of trip-planning information and specifics like schedules of festivals and cultural events and lists of Open Air Folk Museums.

Folk museums teach traditional life-styles better than any other kind of museum. As the world plunges towards 50 billion MacDonald's hamburgers, these museums will become even more important. Of course, they're as realistic as Santa's Village — but how else will you see the elves?

Here is a list of some of Europe's best open air Folk Museums:

Norway

Norwegian Folk Museum, at Bygdoy near Oslo. 150 old buildings from all over Norway and a 12th-century stave church.

Maihaugen Folk Museum, at Lillehammer. Folk culture of the Gudbrandsdalen.

Trondheim and Trondelag Folk Museum, at Sverresborg fortress near Trondheim. 60 buildings showing old Trondheim, Lapp village and farm life.

Sweden

Skansen, in Stockholm. One of the best museums, with over 100 buildings from all over Sweden, craftspeople at work, live entertainment and a Lapp camp complete with reindeer.

Kulturen, Lund. Features Southern Sweden and Viking exhibits.

Finland

Seurasaari Island, near Helsinki. Buildings reconstructed from all over Finland.

Handicrafts Museum, Turku. The life and work of 19th-century craftsmen.

Denmark

Funen Village (Den Fynske Landsby), just south of Odense.

Old Town, Arhus. 60 houses and shops show Danish life from 1580-1850.

Lyngby Park, north of Copenhagen.

Hjerl Hede Iron Age Village, 10 miles south of Skive in northern Jutland. Lifestyles in prehistoric times.

Oldtidsbyen Iron Age Village, near Roskilde.

Germany

Cloppenburg Open-Air Museum, southwest of Bremen. Traditional life in Lower Saxony, 17th and 18th centuries.

Unterhuldingen Prehistoric Village, on the Boden Sea (Lake Constance).

Switzerland

Ballenberg Swiss Open-Air Museum, just northeast of Lake Brienz. A fine collection of old Swiss buildings with furnished interiors.

Netherlands

Netherlands Open-Air Museum, north of Arnhem. 70 old Dutch buildings.

De Zeven Marken Open-Air Museum, in Schoonoord.

Bokrijk Open-Air Museum, between Hasselt and Genk, in Belgium. Old Flemish buildings and culture in a native reserve. Outstanding.

Great Britain

Blists Hill Open-Air Museum, near Coalport. Shows life from the early days of the Industrial Revolution.

Beamish Open-Air Museum, northwest of Durham. Life in Northeast England in 1900.

Welsh Folk Museum, at St. Fagans near Cardiff. Old buildings and craftsmen illustrate traditional Welsh ways.

Ireland

Bunratty Folk Park, near Limerick. Buildings from the Shannon area and artisans at work.

Glencolumbkille Folk Museum, Donegal. Thatched cottages show life from 1700 to 1900. A Gaelic-speaking cooperative runs the folk village and a traditional crafts industry.

Irish Open-Air Folk Museum, at Cultra near Belfast. Traditional Irish lifestyles. Buildings from all over Ireland.

Bulgaria

Gabrovo Folk Museum, Gabrovo. Old buildings and skilled craftsmen.

Spain

Pueblo Espanol, Barcelona. Buildings from all over Spain depict regional architecture, costumes and folk craft.

This is not a complete listing and new open-air folk museums are being built every year. Ask for more information at European tourist offices.

The Louvre — A Talk With a Guide

The Louvre in Paris is considered by most art historians to be our civilization's finest art museum. Many people visit France soley to see this granddaddy of museums. Sadly, many of them leave disappointed. Overwhelmed by its enormous size and the thunder of its crowds, they take a quick look at the Mona Lisa — and flee. You can avoid this if you tackle the Louvre thoughtfully.

Catherine Bounout, a veteran Louvre guide and art historian, shared with me her intimate knowledge, respect and love of this building. There is no doubt, she stressed, that the more you know about the Louvre, the more you will enjoy it.

Avoid the crowds, especially during the peak months of

July and August. The Louvre, like most tourist attractions in Paris, is closed on Tuesdays. (Open other days from 9:45 to 5:00.) This makes it particularly crowded on Mondays and Wednesdays. Thursday or Friday is best. Try to arrive just before the 9:45 opening time.

For the average visitor, a guided tour is the best way to approach the Louvre's enormous collection. Museum-going is very hard work. Big museum-going is slave labor. Many people set out on their own to cover the museum thoroughly, but run out of steam long before the Louvre runs out of art. I like an expert to show me the best two hours while I'm fresh. If you were to lay the Louvre's 208,500 works of art end to end, they would stretch from Paris to New York and back — at least that's what a drunk in a Dublin pub told me. Take advantage of the English tours which leave daily from 10:00 to 4:00 and cost less than $2. If you miss the tour (or are with a group) it's easy to hire a private Louvre guide for about $20 an hour. The guides enjoy private tours most because they can tailor the tour specifically to the group's interests. "If you want only paintings, you get only paintings."

Catherine, like most guides I met, maintains a fresh and enthusiastic delivery. She explains, "I like art and people. This job is a perfect mix. But if I don't see enthusiasm, I get bored. If people sleep in front of me, I sleep along with them. An enthusiastic group makes my job much easier. I love them to ask questions. Then I can stop at a new painting and I will be soooo happy. I don't mind people who 'freeload' on my tours because they are generally more interested than those who pay."

When asked about her pet peeve she didn't hesitate to answer: "Tourists are too noisy. Please respect the art. Don't go just to see the Mona Lisa. If someone wants to see the Mona Lisa we show them a poster."

Paris has dozens of museums, covering the entire spectrum of Western art. The artistic traveler with limited time and energy should plan selectively and efficiently. You can follow the evolution of Western art chronologically from start to finish by visiting the Louvre, Jeu de Paume, Palais de Tokyo and the Centre Georges Pompidou, in that order.

The Louvre covers Western art very nicely through the 18th century. Impressionism was the style that followed. Artistic rebels like Monet and Van Gogh pioneered this striking break from the traditional art of Europe. Their paintings weren't considered "real art" worthy of the Louvre, so were housed near the Louvre in the Galerie du Jeu de Paume. (Open M, W, Th, F 9:45-5:15, weekends 11:00-5:15, closed Tuesdays.) Now the water lilies, pastel-dotted landscapes and moody umbrellas of this period are accepted, but they remain in the same small museum, just off the Place de la Concorde. It is an excellent collection. You may find a new favorite artist!

The next stop on your Parisian walk through the history of art is the Palais de Tokyo. Catherine calls this fine Post-Impressionist collection the most underrated and overlooked museum in Paris. I discovered it only through her recommendation. Exciting art with no crowds, just off the Place d'Iena near the Eiffel Tower — don't miss it. In the near future, Paris will be building one grand museum to house all of the art of the 19th century.

The "Musee National d'Art Moderne" (Who says you can't read French?) in the new Georges Pompidou Center will bring you right up to the artistic present — and then some. This crazy, colorful, "exo-skeletal" building will refresh you with Europe's greatest collection of 20th-century art. After so much "old art" this place is a lot of fun. Where else can you see a piano smashed to bits and glued to a wall?

10
Coping Abroad

City Survival

Many Americans are overwhelmed by European big city shock. Struggling with the LA's, Chicagos and New Yorks of Europe is easier, if you follow three rules: 1) get and use information; 2) orient yourself; 3) take advantage of the public transportation systems.

Information

Without information and planning, you'll be Mr. McGoo in a large city. Spend the last hour as you approach by train or bus reading and planning. Know what you want to see and put it in an efficient order. Your sightseeing strategy should cover the city systematically, one neighborhood at a time, keeping closed days and free days in mind.

All big cities have English bookstores. Large bookstores and university bookstores have English sections. European editions of American news magazines and newspapers are sold in most places. The European edition of "Time" comes out every Tuesday.

Find a good map. The best and cheapest map is often the public transit map. Try to get a map that shows bus lines, subway stops and major sights. Many hotels can give you a free city map.

If you find yourself in a town with no information and the

tourist office is closed, a glance through the postcard rack will quickly show you the most interesting and scenic town sights. Big European cities bubble with entertainment, festivities and night life. But it won't come to you. Without the right information and not speaking the local language, it's easy to be completely oblivious to a once-in-a-lifetime event erupting just across the bridge. In this case, a periodical entertainment guide is the ticket. Every big city has one, either in English like London's "What's On," or "This Week" in Oslo, or in the local language, but easy to decipher, like the "Pariscope."

Ask at your hotel and at the tourist office about entertainment. Read posters. Events are posted on city walls everywhere. They are in a foreign language but that really doesn't matter when it comes to: Winefest, Musica Folklorico, Juni 9, 21:00, Piazza Major, Entre Libre, and so on. Read the signs — or miss the party.

Orientation

Get the feel of the city. Once you get oriented, you're more at home in a city — it warms up and sightseeing is more enjoyable. Study the map to understand the city's layout. Relate the location of landmarks — your hotel, major sights, the river, main streets and station — to each other. Use any viewpoint like a church spire, tower or hilltop to look over the city. Retrace where you've been, see where you're going. Back on the ground you won't be in such constant need of your map.

Many cities have fast orientation bus tours like London's famous "Round London" tour. If you're feeling overwhelmed, these make a city less whelming.

Public Transportation

When you master a city's subway or bus system, you've got it by the tail. Europe's public transit systems are so good that many Europeans never own a car. Trains, buses and subways are their wheels.

The buses and subways all work logically and are run by people who are happy to help the lost tourist locate himself.

Anyone can decipher the code to cheap and easy urban transportation. Too many timid tourists never venture into the subways or on to the buses and end up spending needless money on taxis or needless time walking.

Paris and London have the most extensive, and the most needed, subway systems. Both cities are covered with subway maps and expert subway tutors. Paris even has maps that show you which way to go. Just push a button and the proper route lights up! Subways are speedy and comfortable, never slowed by traffic jams. Buses are more scenic. Some cities have one tourist-oriented bus route — cruising you by the major sights for the cost of a ticket.

Make a point to get adequate transit information. Pick up a map. Find out about any specials — like packets of tickets sold at a discount (Paris) or tourist tickets allowing unlimited travel for a day or several days (London). These may seem expensive, but if you do any amount of running around, they can be a convenient money-saver.

Have a local person explain your ticket to you. A dollar may seem expensive for the bus ride until you learn that your ticket is good for round-trip, two hours, or several transfers. Bus drivers and local people sitting around you will generally mother the foreigner through the ride. Just make sure those around you know where you want to go.

Taxis are often a reasonable option. In southern countries they are cheap and, while expensive for the lone budget traveler in the north, a group of three or four people can often travel cheaper by taxi than by buying three or four bus tickets. Don't be bullied by cabbie con-men. Insist on the meter, agree on a rate, or know the going rate. Taxis intimidate too many tourists. If I'm charged a ridiculous price for a ride, I put a reasonable sum on the seat and say goodbye.

Guided Tours
Tourist: (toor'ist)n. 1. a person who makes a tour

Throughout your trip you'll encounter sightseeing tours. There are several kinds of tours. Orientation tours are fast,

Shrink cities with preparation, orientation and transportation.

inexpensive and superficial. Rarely do you even get out of the bus. Their only redeeming factor is that they serve to orient the traveler. I suppose if you only had three hours in London, for example, the "Round London Tour" would be the best you could do to "see" the place.

Walking tours are my favorite. They are thorough, cover only a small part of a city. They are usually conducted by a well-trained local person who is sharing his town for the noble purpose of giving you an appreciation of the city's history, people and culture — not to make a lot of money. The walking tour is personal, inexpensive and a valuable education. I can't recall a bad walking tour. Many local tourist offices organize the tours or provide a walking tour leaflet. For the avid walking tourist there are some great walking tour guidebooks. Pick up one that covers the cities you'll be visiting.

Fancy coach tours, the kind that leave from the big international hotels, are expensive and often boring. They are so depersonalized, sometimes to the point of multi-lingual taped messages, that you may decide to tune in to the Chinese soundtrack. These tours can, however, be of value to the budget-minded do-it-yourselfer. Pick up the brochure, and you have a well-thought-out tour itinerary. Now do it on your own, taking local buses at your leisure, touring every sight for a fraction of the cost.

The best guides are often those that you pick up at the specific sight. These guides usually really know their museum or castle or whatever.

Bus Tour Self-Defense

Guided tours can be a great way to travel — if the tourist knows how to get the most out of it and doesn't allow himself to be taken advantage of. Here are some hints for the traveler who books a typical budget bus tour. Keep in mind that many people take escorted coach tours year after year only for the hotels, meals and transportation provided. Every day they do their own sightseeing, simply applying the skills of independent

How you travel determines who you meet; big bus tourists can be a disappointment.

travel to their coach tour. This can be a very economical and easy way to go "on your own."

Having escorted several European coach tours and organized some of my own, I've learned that you must understand the guide and his position. Leading a tour is a demanding job with lots of responsibility, paperwork and miserable hours. Most guides treasure their time alone and, socially, keep their distance from the group. Each tourist has personal demands, and when you multiply that by a bus of fifty, you get one big headache.

To the guide, the best group is one that lets him do the thinking, is happy to be led around like sheep, and depends on him to spoonfeed Europe to them. The guide's base salary is often low, but an experienced guide can do very well when that is supplemented by his percentage of the optional excursions, kickbacks from merchants that he patronizes and the trip-end tips from his busload. The best guide is a happy one. It's very important to keep him on your side. If the guide wants to, he can give you a lot of unrequired extras that will add greatly to your tour — but only if he wants to. Your objective, which requires some artistry, is to keep the guide on your side without letting him take advantage of you.

Most tours do not include the daily sightseeing programs. These are optional. Budget tours are highly competitive and profit margins on the base cost are thin. For this reason, it's very important for the guide to sell the "options."

Discriminate among options. Some are great, others are not worth the time or money. I have found that, in general, the half-day sightseeing tours of cities are a good value. A local guide will usually show you his or her city in a much more thorough fashion than you would be able to do on your own given your time limitations. Illuminated night tours of Rome and Paris can be marvelous. Other "illuminated" tours and "nights on the town" I prefer to miss. Usually, several bus tours combine for the "evening of local color." Two hundred tourists having a glass of local wine in a huge room with buses lined up outside isn't really local. I would prefer to save $10 by taking a cab or a bus downtown to just poke around. One summer night in Regensburg, the great-great-great grandson of Johannes Kepler bought me a beer, and we drank it under the stars, overlooking the Danube, while most of the tour waited to get off the bus.

The guide may pressure you into taking the "options." Stand firm. In spite of what you may be told, you are capable of doing plenty on your own. Maintain your independence. Get maps and tourist information from your hotel desk (or another hotel desk) or a tourist information office. Hotels are often located outside the city where they cost the tour company less and where they figure you are more likely to book the options just to get into town. Some tours promise to take you downtown if the hotel is outside the city limits. Ask the man or woman behind the desk how to get downtown on the public transportation. Taxis are always a possibility, and with a group, they're not expensive.

Team up with others on your tour to explore on your own. No city is dead after the shops are closed. Go downtown and stroll.

Do your own research. Know what you want to see. Don't just sit back and count on your guide to give you the Europe you're looking for. The guide will be happy to feed you Europe — but it will be from his menu. This often distorts the importance of sights in order to fit the tour. For instance, many tours seem to make a big deal out of a statue in Lucerne called "the Dying Lion." Most tourists are impressed upon command. The guide declares that this mediocre-at-best sight is great and that is how it is perceived. What makes it "great" for the guide is that, one, Lucerne (which doesn't have a lot of interesting sights) was given too much time in the itinerary, and two, it's easy for the bus to park and wait. "The Last Supper" by Leonardo da Vinci, on the other hand, is often passed over by bus tours in Milan. It is an inconvenient sight.

Many people make their European holiday one long shopping spree. The guide is happy to promote this. According to the merchants I talked to in Venice and Florence, 15% is the standard commission that a store gives a tour guide who brings in a busload of tourists. Don't necessarily reject your guide's shopping tips, just keep in mind that the prices you see often include that 15% kickback. Shop around and never swallow the line, "This is a special price available only to your tour, but you must buy now." The salesmen who prey on tour buses are smooth. They zero right in on the timid and gullible group member who has no idea what a good buy is. If you buy — buy carefully.

When you're traveling with a group, it's fun as well as economical to create a kitty for communal "niceties." If each person contributes $10, the "kitty-keeper" can augment dry Continental breakfasts with fresh fruit, provide snacks and drinks at rest stops for a fraction of the exorbitant prices you'll find in the freeway restaurants, get stamps for postcards so each person doesn't have to find the post office himself, etc.

Remember that the best selling tours are the ones that promise you the most in the time you have available. No tour can give you more than twenty-four hours in a day or seven days in a week. What the "blitz" tour *can* do is give you more hours on the bus. Choose carefully among the itineraries available and don't assume more is better. In Europe, pace yourself. Be satisfied with what you can see comfortably.

The groups I have escorted on European bus tours have been almost universally happy and satisfied with their vacations. They got the most out of their tour — and their tour didn't get the most out of them — because they exercised a measure of independence.

Telephoning in Europe

The more I travel, the more I use the telephone. I call hotels and hostels to make or confirm reservations, tourist information offices to check my sightseeing plans, restaurants, train stations, and local friends. In every country the phone can save you lots of time and money. Each country's phone system is different — but each one works — logically.

The key to figuring out a foreign phone is to approach it without comparing it to yours back home. It works for the locals and it can work for you. Many people flee in terror when a British phone starts its famous "rapid pipps." They go home telling tales of the impossibility of using England's phones.

Each country has phone booths with multi-lingual instructions. Study these before dialing. Operators generally speak English and are helpful. International codes, instructions and international assistance numbers are usually in the front of the phone book. If I can't manage in a strange phone booth, I let a nearby local person help me out. They are happy not only to dial for you, but, if neccesary, to do your talking as well.

Area codes are a common source of phone booth frustration. They are usually listed by city on the wall or in the book. When calling long distance in Europe you must dial the area code first. Area codes start with a zero which is replaced with the country code if you're calling international. Local numbers vary in length from three to seven digits.

Once you've made the connection, the real challenge begins — communication. With no visual aids, getting the message across in a language you don't speak requires some artistry. Some key rules are: Speak slowly and clearly, pronouncing every consonant. Keep it very simple — don't clutter your message with anything less than essential. Don't over-communicate — many things are already understood and don't need to be said. Use international or carefully chosen English words. When all else fails, let a local person on your end do the talking after you explain to him, with visual help, the message.

Let me illustrate with a hypothetical conversation with a hotel receptionist in Barcelona. I'm at the station, just came into town, read my guidebook's list of budget hotels, and I like "Pedro's Hotel." I call from a phone booth and here's what happens . . .

Pedro answers, "Hotel Pedro."

I ask, "Hotel Pedro?" (Question marks are created melodically.)

He affirms, already a bit impatient, "Si, Hotel Pedro."

I ask, "Speak Eng-leesh?"

He says, "No, dees ees Spain." (Actually, he probably would speak a little English or would say, "moment," and get someone who did. But we'll make this particularly challenging, not only does he not speak English — he doesn't want to.)

Remembering not to over-communicate, you don't need to tell him you're a tourist looking for a bed. Who else calls a hotel in a foreign language? Also, you can assume he's got a room available. If he's full he won't still be talking to you. He'd say "complete" or "No hotel" and hang-up. If he's still talking to you he's interested in your business. Now you must communicate just a few things, like how many beds you need and who you are.

I say "OK, hotel." (OK is a good "Roger" word.) "Two people" — he doesn't understand. I get fancy, "Dos people" — he still doesn't get it. Internationalize, "Dos pehr-son" — no comprende. "Dos hombre" — nope. Digging deep into my bag of international linguistic tricks. I say "Dos Yankees." "OK!" he understands, you want beds for two Americans. He says, "Si" and I say, "Very goood" or "Muy bueno." Now I need to tell him who I am. If I say, "My name is Mr. Steves and I'll be checking in in a few minutes," I'll lose him. I say, "My name Ricardo (Ree KAR do)." (In Italy, I say, "My name Luigi." Your name really doesn't matter, you're communicating a password so you can identify yourself when you walk through the door. Say anything to be understood.)

He says "OK."

You repeat slowly, "Hotel, dos Yankees, Ricardo, coming pronto, OK?"

He says "OK."

You say, "Gracias, ciao!"

Twenty minutes later you walk up to the reception desk and Pedro greets you with a robust, "Eh, Ricardo!"

E.T. (European Traveler) Phone Home

Most European countries have direct connections to the USA now and you can get through for as little as a dime. Rather than write postcards, I just call in my "scenery's here, wish you were beautiful" messages.

You can call home in several ways. Calling collect or using your telephone credit card can be complicated and more expensive. Telephoning through your hotel's phone system is easy but usually very expensive. Post offices have international phone booths that are metered. You are billed fairly after you hang up. My favorite method is to get a few coins, dial direct and keep it short and sweet.

While rare in the South, nearly all Northern European countries have "dial direct to anywhere" phone booths. US calls cost about two dollars per minute but there is no minimum. First get a pile of coins. Then find a phone booth. International booths usually have instructions in the book or on the wall. Put in a coin and dial: 1st — international code, wait for tone; 2nd — country code; 3rd — area code; and 4th — the seven digit number. If you want to call me from France, put in a franc (12 cents) dial 19-1-206-771-8303 and talk fast. Every country has its quirks — try pausing between codes if you're having trouble or dial the international operator. Remember, it's six to nine hours earlier in the states.

I start with a small coin worth 10 to 25 cents to be sure I get the person I need or can say "I'm calling back in five minutes so wake him up." Then I plug in the larger coins. I keep one last sign-off coin ready. When my time is done I pop it in and say goodby. The ·booth tells you when you're about to be cut off.

It's cheaper and easier (coin-free) if you have your friend call you back, dialing direct from the states. Give your local area code (without the first zero) and number. They can get the international and country code from their American operator.

Avoiding Some Avoidable Problems

Europeans do many things differently than we do. Simple as these things are, they can cause needless confusion.

The numbers 7 and 1 are slightly different from ours. European "ones" have an upswing, " Λ ". To make the seven more distinctive, add a cross, " $\mathcal{7}$ ".

The day and month are reversed in numbered dates. Therefore, Christmas is 25-12-85 instead of 12-25-85 as we would write it. Commas are decimal points and decimals, commas so a dollar and a half is 1,50 and there are 5.280 feet in a mile.

Floors are numbered differently. The first floor is called the ground floor. What we would call the second floor is a European's first floor. So if your room is on the second floor (European), then you will be on the third floor (American).

When counting with your fingers, start with your thumb. Making a "peace" sign to indicate the number 2 is giving the "finger" sign in some countries.

Finally, the 24-hour clock is used in any official timetable.

This includes bus, train and tour schedules, Learn to use it quickly and easily. Everything is the same until 12:00 noon. Then, instead of starting over again at 1:00 p.m., the Europeans keep on going — 1300, 1400 . . . 2400. 1800 is 6:00 p.m. (18 minus 12 = 6). Using the 24-hour clock, midnight is 2400.

11
Attitude Adjustment — For a Better Trip

The Ugly American

Europe sees two kinds of travelers: those who view Europe through air-conditioned bus windows, socializing with their noisy American friends and collecting silver spoons; and those who are taking a vacation from America, immersing themselves in different cultures, experiencing different people and lifestyles, broadening their perspective.

Europeans will judge you as an individual, not based on your government. A Greek fisherman once told me, "I hate Kissinger — but I like you." I have never been treated like the Ugly American. I've been proud to wear our flag on my lapel. My American-ness in Europe, if anything, has been an asset.

"Ugly Americans" do exist. Europeans recognize them and treat them accordingly, often souring their vacation. "Ugly Americanism" is a disease easily cured by a change in attitude.

The Ugly American:

—Lacks respect and understanding for strange customs and cultural differences. Only a Hindu can understand the value of India's sacred cows. Only a devout Spanish Catholic can appreciate the true worth of his town's patron saint. No American has the right, as a visitor, to show disrespect for these customs.

—Demands the niceties of American life in Europe, e.g., orange juice and eggs (sunny-side up) for breakfast, long beds,

English menus, punctuality in Italy or cold beer in England. He should remember that he is visiting a land that enjoys its Continental breakfasts, that doesn't grow six-foot four-inch men, that speaks a different language (with every right to do so), that lacks the "fast-food efficiency" of the USA and drinks beer at room temperature. Live as a European for a few weeks; it's cheaper, you'll make more friends and have a better trip.

—Is ethnocentric, traveling in packs, more or less invading each country while making no effort to communicate with "the natives." He talks at Europeans in a condescending manner. He finds satisfaction in flaunting his relative affluence, and rates well-being by material consumption.

You can be a "Beautiful American" Your fate as a tourist lies in your own hands. A graduate of the Back Door School of Touristic Beauty:

—Maintains a modest sense of humility, not flashing signs of affluence, such as over-tipping or joking about the local money.

—Not only accepts, but seeks out European styles of living. Forget your discomfort if you're the only one in a group who feels it.

—Is genuinely interested in the people and cultures he visits.

—Makes an effort to bridge that flimsy language barrier. Rudimentary communication in any language is fun and simple with a few basic words. While a debate over the economics of Marx on the train to Budapest (with a common vocabulary of twenty words) can be frustrating, you'll be surprised at how well you can communicate — if you only break the ice and try. Don't worry about the language — communicate! (See the chapter on *Hurdling the Language Barrier.*)

—Is positive and optimistic in the extreme. Discipline yourself to focus on the good points of each country. Don't dwell on problems. You can't go wrong with a militantly positive attitude.

I've been accepted as an American friend throughout Europe, Russia, the Middle East and North Africa. Coming as an American visitor, I've been hugged by Bulgarian workers on a Balkan Mountain top; discussed Watergate and the Olympics over dinner in the home of a Greek family; explained to a young frustrated Irishman that California girls aren't really goddesses; and hiked through the Alps with a Swiss school teacher, learning German and teaching English.

The Ugly American sees Europe through ugly eyes. There is no excuse for being an Ugly American. Go as a guest, act like one and you'll be treated like one. Your trip will be better for it.

Be Open Minded

"Experiencing the bazaar away from home" is "travel" in six words. Yet so many leave home and are repulsed by what they see. Between the palaces, quaint folk dancers and museums you'll find a living civilization — grasping for the future while we tourists grope for its past.

Today's Europe is a complex, mixed bag of tricks. It can rudely slap you in the face if you aren't prepared to accept it with open eyes and an open mind. Many will find that Europe is getting crowded, tense, seedy and far from the homogenous fairy-tale land it once was.

If you're not mentally braced for some shocks, local trends can tinge your travels. Hans Christian Andersen's statue has internationally understood four-letter words scrawled across its base. Whites are now the minority in London, Amsterdam's sex shops and McDonald's share the same street lamp, Paris has a man from the Sudan selling Ivory bracelets and crocodile purses on every corner. You may meet an Italian hotel keeper who would consider himself a disgrace to his sex if he didn't follow a single woman to her room — he's turned away as easily as a Girl Scout selling cookies. Drunk punk rockers do their best to repulse you as you climb to St. Patrick's grave in Ireland, and Greek ferryboats dump mountains of trash into their Mediterranean. An eight-year old boy in Denmark smokes a cigarette like he was born with it in his mouth and, in a Munich beerhall, an old drunk spits "seig heil's" all over you. The Barcelona shoeshine man will charge you $8.00 and people everywhere put strange and wondrous things in their stomachs.

They eat next-to-nothing for breakfast, mud for coffee,

mussels in Brussels, and dinner's at ten in Spain. Beer is warm here, cold there, coffee isn't served with dinner and ice cubes can only be dreamed of. Roman cars stay in their lanes like rocks in an avalanche and very few Europeans voted for Reagan.

Contemporary Europe is alive and groping. Today's problems will fill tomorrow's museums. Feel privileged to walk the crazy streets of Europe as a sponge — not a judge. Absorb, accept, learn, and at all costs — be open-minded.

Don't Be a Creative Worrier

Travelers tend to be creative worriers. Many sit at home before their trip, all alone, just thinking of things to be stressed by. Travel problems are always there; you just notice them when they're yours. (Like people only notice the continual newspaper tire sales when they're shopping for tires.) Every year there are air controller strikes, train strikes, terrorist attacks, new problems, and old problems turning over new leaves.

Travel is ad-libbing, incurring and conquering surprise problems. Make an art out of taking the unexpected in stride. Relax, you're on the other side of the world, playing games in a Continental back yard. Be a good sport, enjoy the uncertainty, frolic in the pits, have fun.

Tackling problems with relish opens some exciting doors. Even the worst times rosy up into cherished memories after your journal is shelved and your trip is stored neatly in the slide carousel of your mind.

The KISS Rule — "Keep It Simple, Stupid!"

Don't complicate your trip — simplify! Travelers get stressed and cluttered over the silliest things. Here are some common complexities that in their nibbly way can suffocate a happy holiday:

Registering your camera with customs before leaving home, spending several hours trying to phone home on a sunny day in the Alps, worrying about the correct answers to meaningless bureaucratic forms, making a long distance hotel reservation in a strange language and then trying to settle on what's served for breakfast, having a picnic in pants that can't sit on grass, sending away for Swedish hotel vouchers.

People can complicate their trips with audio-recorder-movie cameras, leadlined film bags, special tickets for free entry to all the sights they won't see in England, immersion heaters, instant coffee, 65 handi-wipes and a special calculator that figures the value of the franc out to the third decimal. They ask for a toilet in 17 words or more, steal "sweet-n-low" and plastic silverware off the plane and take notes on facts that don't matter.

Travel more like Gandhi — with simple clothes, open eyes, and an uncluttered mind.

Be Militantly Humble — Attila Had a Lousy Trip

As one of the world's elite who are rich and free enough, you are leaving home to experience a different culture. If things aren't to your liking — don't change the "things," change "your liking."

Legions of tourists tramp through Europe like they are at the zoo — throwing a crust to the monkey, asking the guy in lederhosen to yodel, begging the peacock to spread his tail again, and bellowing Italian arias out Florentine hotel windows. If a culture misperforms or doesn't perform they feel gypped.

By treating Europe like a royal, but spoiled child, always right, even if undeservedly so, and demanding nothing, approaching it like Oliver Twist, humbly but firmly asking for "more soup," I leave the Attila-type tourists mired in a swamp of complaints.

All summer long I'm pushing a bargain, often for groups.

It's the hottest, toughest time of year and tourists and locals clash. Many tourists leave soured.

When I catch a Spanish merchant short-changing me, I correct the bill and smile, "Adios." A French hotel owner can blow up at me for no legitimate reason. Rather than return the fire I wait, smile, and sheepishly ask again. Asking for action, innocently assertive but never demanding "justice," I usually see the irate ranter come to his senses, forget the problem and work things out.

"Turn the other cheek" applies perfectly to those riding Europe's magic carousel. If you fight the slaps the ride is over. The militantly humble can spin forever.

Swallow Pride, Ask Questions, Be Crazy

If you are too proud to ask questions and be crazy your trip may well be dignified — and dull. Make yourself an extrovert, even if you aren't one. Be a catalyst for adventure and excitement. Make things happen, or oftentimes they won't.

Be an extrovert. Ask the cute men to scoot over.

I'm not naturally a "wild and crazy guy." But when I'm shy and quiet, things don't happen. I try to keep myself out of that rut when I'm traveling. It's not easy, but this special awareness can really pay off. Let me describe the same evening twice — first, with the mild and lazy me, and then with the wild and crazy me:

The traffic held me up, so by the time I got to that great historical building that I've always wanted to see, it was six minutes before closing. No one was allowed to enter. Disappointed, I walked over to a restaurant and couldn't make heads or tails out of the menu. I recognized "steak-frites" and settled for the typical meat patty and french fries. On the way home I looked into a very colorful local tavern, but there were no tourists in there, so I walked on. In a park, I was making some noise, and a couple came out on their balcony and told me to be quiet. I went back to the room and did some washing.

That is not a night to be proud of. A better traveler's journal entry would read like this:

I was late and got to the museum only six minutes before closing. The guard said no one could go in now, but I begged, joked and pleaded with him. I had traveled all the way to see this place and I would be leaving early in the morning. I assured him that I would be out by six o'clock, and he gave me a glorious six minutes in that building. You can do a lot in six minutes when you are excited. Across the street at a restaurant that the same guard recommended, I couldn't make heads or tails out of the menu. Inviting myself into the kitchen, I met the cooks and got a first-hand look at "what's cookin'." Now I could order an exciting local dish and know just what I was getting. It was delicious! On the way home I passed a classic local bar, and while it was dark and sort of uninviting to a foreigner, I stepped in and was met by the only guy in the place who spoke any English. He proudly befriended me and told me, in very broken English, of his salty past and his six kids, while treating me to his favorite local drink. I'll never forget that guy or that evening. Later, I was making noise in a park, and a middle-aged couple told me to shut up. I continued the

Put yourself where you become the oddity. If people stare — sing to them.

*conversation, and they eventually invited me up to their apart-
ment. We joked around — not understanding a lot of what we
were saying to each other — and they invited me to their
summer cottage the next day. What a lucky break! There is no
better way to learn about this country than to spend an afternoon with a local family. And to think that I could be back in
my room doing the laundry!*

Many tourists are actually afraid or too timid to ask a
local person a question. The meek may inherit the earth but
they make lousy tourists. Local sources are a wealth of information. People are happy to help a traveler. Hurdle the language barrier. Use a paper and pencil, charades or whatever it
takes to be understood. Don't be afraid to butcher the
language.

Ask questions — or be lost. Create adventure — or bring
home a boring journal. Preceive friendliness and you'll find it.

The Travel Industry

It's a huge business — travel. Most of what the industry
promotes is decadence: lie on the beach and be catered to;
hedonize those precious two weeks to make up for the other
fifty; see if you can eat five meals a day and still snorkle when
you get into port. That's where the money is and that's where
most of the interest is. The industry caters to the rich tourist
while you (anyone who's read ten pages of this book) are just
a fringe that fits the industry like a snowshoe in Mazatlan.

I've learned a lot about the politics of tourism as a newspaper travel columnist. Advertising makes your newspaper's
travel section go. Practical consumer information does not sell
cruises. The advertisers (travel agencies) that support the travel
section of one of my newspapers approached the editor in
concert saying that they would not advertise as long as my
column was called "The Budget Traveler." The column is now
more palatably named "The Practical Traveler." The key to
marketable travel writing is not to teach or write well — but to

write stories that further myths that inhibit independent travel. Tales of Ugly Americanism, high costs, language barriers, theft and sickness help fill the cruise ships and tour buses with would-be independent adventurers.

Few travel agents could or even would want to travel "Through the Back Door." The most typical attitude I get when I hob-nob with big-wigs from the industry in Hilton Hotel ball rooms is "If you can't go first class, it's better to stay home." I'll never forget the bewilderment I caused when I turned down a free room in Bangkok's most elegant Western-style hotel in favor of a ten dollar Thai-style hotel. That just did not compute.

Of course, these comments are generalizations and there are many great travelers in the industry that do more than sell ads. These people will understand my frustration because they've also had to deal with it. Travel in a hungry world can be rich people flaunting their affluence — taking pictures of poor kids jumping off ships for small change. Or it can promote understanding — turning our American perspective into a human perspective and making our world more comfortable in its smallness. What the industry promotes is up to each individual agent, and its consumers.

Know Thy Travel Agent — A Quiz

I will never travel without the help of a good travel agent. A traveler's most valuable friend is his or her agent — but only if that agent knows budget Europe. Your travel agent's service is free. They get their commission from the airline or tour company — not by marking up your ticket price.

It's important to cultivate a loyal relationship with an agent who knows and respects your style of travel and will give you the same respect he gives his luxury cruisers. A shocking number of agents know virtually nothing about budget European travel — by choice.

The only way to be sure your travel agent is properly

suited to helping you with your trip is to ask him or her a few
questions. Here's a little quiz — complete with answers . . .

1. **What is "open-jaws"?**
   a) Yet another shark movie sequel.
   b) A tourist in awe of the Mannekin Pis.
   c) An airline ticket that allows you to fly into one city and
   out of another.

2. **Which international boat rides are covered by the
   Eurailpass?**
   a) Poland to Switzerland.
   b) All of them.
   c) Ireland to France, Sweden to Finland and Italy to
   Greece. Germany and Sweden to Denmark.

3. **What's the Youth Hostel membership age limit?**
   a) Five.
   b) As high as 30 if you like the Rolling Stones.
   c) There is none.

4. **What is the cheapest way to get from London's Heathrow
   Airport into London?**
   a) Walk.
   b) In a Youth Hostel.
   c) Don't. Spend your whole vacation at Heathrow.
   d) By subway.

5. **What is an ISIC card?**
   a) A universal way to tell foreigners you're not feeling well.
   b) It beats three-of-a-kind.
   c) International Student Identity Card.

6. **Is there a problem getting a "bed and breakfast" in England's small towns without a reservation?**
   a) Not if you live there.
   b) Yes. Carry No-Doze in England.
   c) Only for Indians.
   d) No.

7. **How much does a Yugoslavian visa cost?**
   a) "How much you have, comrade?"
   b) You can just charge it on your "Visa" card.
   c) More than a Grecian urn.
   d) It's free and can be obtained easily at the border.

12
Miscellaneous Tips and Tricks

Terrorism and Tourism

An awareness of current social and political problems is as vital to travel as a listing of top sights. Many popular tourist destinations are entertaining tourists with "sound and light" shows on one hand while quelling terrorist and separatist movements on the other. England, France, Italy and Spain are just a few countries in Europe alone that are dealing with serious or potentially serious internal threats.

Many people skip Rome because of the "Red Brigade" and avoid Spain in fear of the "militant Basques." This is unnecessary and unfortunate. Don't let these problems dictate your itinerary — they are no threat to you. Just be up on the news and exercise adequate discretion. (Don't sing Catholic songs in Ulster pubs.) I travel safely, enjoying a first-hand look at the demographic chaos that explains much of what fills the front pages of our newspapers.

Travel should broaden your perspective, enabling you to rise above the six o'clock news and see things as a citizen of the world. While monuments from the past are worthy of your sightseeing energy, travel plugs you directly into the present. There are many peoples fighting the same thrilling battles we won 200 years ago and, while your globe may paint Turkey orange and Iran green, no political boundaries can divide racial, linguistic or religious groups that simply.

Look beyond the beaches and hotels in your tourist brochures for background on how your vacation target's cultural, racial and religious make-up is causing problems today or may bring grief tomorrow. With this foundation and awareness you can enjoy the nearly unavoidable opportunities to talk with involved locals about complex current situations.

If you're looking to "talk politics" you must be approachable — free from the American mob on the air-con coach. Like it or not, people around the world look at "capitalist Americans" as the kingpins of a global game of Monopoly. On their board "Baltic Avenue" and "Boardwalk" are separated by much more than two squares. Young, well-dressed people are most likely to speak (and want to speak) English. Universities are the perfect place to solve the world's problems in English with a liberal open-minded foreigner over a government-subsidized budget cafeteria lunch.

In Ireland "the troubles" are on everyone's mind — like an on-going "hostage crisis." Hitchhiking through the Emerald Isle, I never knew if I'd get Lincoln or Douglas but I'd always get a stimulating debate. In the USSR and throughout Eastern Europe whenever I wanted some political or economic gossip I'd sit alone in a cafe. After a few minutes and some "James Bond eye-contact" I'd have company and a juicy chat with a resident dissident.

After your smashingly successful European adventure, you'll graduate to more distant cultural nooks and geographic crannies. If you mistakenly refer to a Persian or Iranian as Arabic you'll get a stern education on the distinction, and in Eastern Turkey you'll learn there is a fiercely nationalistic group of people called Kurds who won't rest until that orange and green on the globe is divided by a hunk of land called Kurdistan. (There are large Kurds and small Kurds but they have nothing to do with cottage cheese.) In a Bangkok temple befriend a saffron-robed Buddhist monk and while you teach him some slang he'll explain to you what "guided democracy" means in Southeast Asia.

Understand a country's linguistic divisions. It's next to

impossible to keep everyone in a multilingual country happy. Switzerland has four languages — the Germans dominate. In Belgium there's tension between the Germanic and French-speaking regions. Many French Canadians will tell you their language receives equal treatment only on Corn Flakes boxes.

Italian kidnappings, Basque bombs and Turkish terror should not keep you home. Victims are generally targeted, and you're not worth the terrorists' trouble.

It's refreshing to be so out of touch while traveling that you forget what day it is but it's always wise to be up on the news. American and English newspapers are available in most of the world as are English radio broadcasts. Other tourists can be valuable links with the outside world as well. Most importantly, the nearest American or British consulate can advise you on problems that merit concern. Take their advice seriously even if it means "scrubbing your mission."

A terrible bomb tore through Zion Square in Jerusalem the day before I planned to cross into Israel from Jordan. The consulate in Amman told me it was safe to cross the Jordan River. A German tourist was shot and killed on the Mekong River on the Thailand-Laos border. I called the American consulate in Chiang Mai before my "hill-tribes trek." He said the Mekong was dangerous and the German resisted the bandits. I would be OK where I was going. Before loading onto my Lebanon-bound bus in Turkey, I called the consulate and was advised to cancel my ticket. I did. Talking to people about local problems is fine. Dodging bullets isn't. I can't remember ever hearing a gun or a bomb in my travels. Many times, however, I've had the thrill of a first hand experience merely by talking with people who are personally involved.

Your tour memories can include lunch with a group of Palestinian college students, an evening walk through Moscow with a Russian dissident, listening to the "Voice of America" with curious Bulgarians in a Black Sea coast campground, and learning why the French aren't promoting the reunification of Germany. Or your travel memories can be built upon the blare of your tour guide's blow horn in dead gothic cathedrals and polished palaces.

Geriatric Globe-Trotting

More people than ever are hocking their rocking chairs and buying plane tickets. To many senior adventurers, travel is the fountain of youth. I spent six weeks last summer in Europe with a group of people who made any parents look young. They taught me many things, including the fact that it's never too late to have a happy childhood.

Special discounts in much of the world encourage many older travelers (see "The Discount Guide for Travelers Over Fifty-Five" published by Dutton, $5.95) but the trend I see lately is for energetic elders to leave their seniority at home and just run around expecting the same respect that budget travelers a third their age get.

I spent a week meeting with retired couples who were flying off to Europe with Eurailpasses, carry-on suitcases (9 by 24 by 14 inches) that convert into rucksacks, and $20 a day. Most of them were on their second or third retirement trip and each time as they walked out my door, I thought, "Wow, I've got a good 40 or 45 years of travel ahead of me."

Gertrude and Vernon Johnson, both 68, are in Europe now. Nobody knows where. Before they left, I quizzed them on geriatric globe-trotting.

Was this your first major trip abroad?   "Last year's trip was our first trip anywhere! We spent six weeks with a train pass and $50 a day for the both of us. Out of that $50, we spent $40 on room and board (going the Bed & Breakfast way) and $10 a day covered everthing else, including miscellaneous transportation, admissions, little souvenirs and even a weekly phone call home to the kids."

Were you hesitant at first?   "Yes, indeed. I remember climbing into that airplane thinking I might be making a big mistake.

But when we got over there we tackled problem after problem successfully. Friendly people were always coming out of the woodwork to help us when we needed it."

What about theft and physical safety for a couple of retired kids like yourselves running around Europe independently? "As far as retired people go, we never felt like we were 'retired.' I never felt any different from anyone else and people accepted us as just two more travelers."

Gertrude added, "Later on, as we remembered our trip, we thought maybe people treated us 'gray-haired ruck-sackers' a little kinder because of our age. We never had a bit of a problem with theft or safety. Of course, we'd wear our money-belts everyday and choose our neighborhoods carefully. It's pretty obvious when you're getting into a bad neighborhood. We never felt that Ugly American problem. People treated us very well — if anything, there was more help in public in Europe than we find at home."

Were the Europeans impressed by a retired couple with such an independent travel style? "I'd say they were. In fact, at one place, Rick, we were sitting down and . . ."

Then Gertrude interrupted Vernon saying, "Nothin' doing! That's too good an anecdote." She plans, at 68, on becoming a travel writer some day — so we'll just have to wait for the rest of that story.

Do you speak any languages? No, but we worked on a Berlitz French record for three weeks and that was helpful. We found that the best way to get along with the locals was to try to speak their language. They'd laugh a lot but they would bend over backwards to help us. They could usually speak enough English to help us out."

Did you have trouble finding rooms? "No. We traveled from May 1 to June 15 without reservations. Arthur Frommer's Guide was handy and, of course, we got help from people in the towns. We had no problems. Decent budget hotels are close to the station, and that made setting up a snap."

"We always planned to arrive early. The overnight trains were ideal because they arrived first thing in the morning. We took our Frommer's Guide into the tourist office, which was always in or near the station, and they'd call the hotel for us. A few times they charged extra for their service, but it was always very convenient. For older people, I would insist on arriving early in the day and having local money with you when you arrive."

Then Gertrude added, "People take mercy on you when you're in trouble."

The table rocked every time Vernon started a "too good anecdote" as Gertrude grabbed his knee. Age only matters if you're a cheese.

How much did you pack? "Our luggage weighed a total of 25 pounds. Gertrude carried 11 and I packed 14. We just packed a few easy-wash and fast-dry clothes. Before our first trip you told us to bring nothing electrical. We didn't listen and we almost burnt down our hotel in Paris. (The table jolted again.) So this time we're bringing nothing electrical."

What was the most important lesson you learned on your first trip? "Pack even less. When you pack light you're younger — foot loose and fancy free. And that's the way we like to be."

Travel Laundry

I met a woman in Italy who wore her tee-shirt frontwards, backwards, inside-out frontwards and inside-out backwards to delay the laundry day. A guy in Germany showed me his take-it-into-the-tub-with-you-and-make-waves method of washing his troublesome jeans. Some travelers just ignore their laundry needs and stink.

Anybody traveling anywhere has to wash clothes. My

washer and dryer won't fit under the airplane seat so I've learned to do without. Here are some tips.

Choose your travel wardrobe with washing and drying in mind — quick-dry and no wrinkle. Your self-service laundry kit should include a "travel clothesline" with suction cups. Stick those suckers over your bath tub or across the back of your car and you're on the road to dry clothes. Many hotel room sinks come sans stopper . . . to discourage in-room washing. Bring a universal sink stopper. That flat little rubber mat out-performs a sock in the drain. Pack a concentrated liquid detergent in a sturdy small plastic squeeze bottle wrapped in a zip-lock baggie. Many good squeeze bottles become leaky ones after they leave home. A large zip-lock bag (carried in most camping stores) makes a good laundry bag. (I've ignored requests from environmental groups to use stronger lead-lined receptacles.)

Hotel rooms around the world have multilingual "no washing clothes in the room" signs. This may be the most ignored rule on earth after "eat your peas." Interpret this as an

"I-have-lots-of-good-furniture-and-a-fine-carpet-in-this-room-and-I-don't-want-your-drippy-laundry-ruining-things" order. In other words, you can wash clothes very carefully, wring them nearly dry and hang them in an undestructive way.

Your laundry should keep a low profile. Don't hang it out the window. The maid doesn't notice my laundry. It's hanging quietly in the bathroom or shuffled among my dry clothes in the closet.

Some hotels will let your laundry join theirs on the lines out back or on the roof top. Many youth hostels have coin-op washer and dryers or drying rooms to ease your laundry hassles.

Wring your wet laundry as dry as possible. Rolling it in a towel can be helpful. Always separate the back and front of clothes to speed drying. Some travelers pack an inflatable hanger (especially handy in Venice or on a cruise where it doubles as a kind of laundry life-jacket). Smooth out your wet clothes, button shirts and set collars to encourage wrinkle-free drying. If your shirt or dress dries wrinkled hang it in a steamy bathroom. A piece of tape makes a good ad lib lint brush. In hot climates I wash my shirt several times a day, wring it and put it on wet. It's clean, refreshing and in fifteen minutes it's dry.

For a thorough washing ask your hotel to direct you to the nearest laundromat. Nearly every neighborhood has one. They can be expensive and terribly slow. Use the time to catch up on postcards and your journal or chat with the local crowd that's causing the delay. Laundromats throughout the world seem to give people the "gift of gab." Full service places are quicker — "just drop it off and come back this afternoon" — but even more expensive. Still, every time I slip into a fresh pair of jeans I figure it was worth the hassle.

Souvenir Strategy

If your trip includes several countries, it's a good idea to save your souvenir shopping for the cheaper ones. Gift shopping is getting very expensive. I remember buying a cuckoo clock 10 years ago for $3. Now a hamburger, shake and fries at the Munich McDonald's will cost that much.

You can buy an eight-foot dinghy in Portugal for the price of an eight-inch pewter Viking ship in Norway. On European trips I do nearly all of my souvenir and gift shopping in Turkey, Morocco, Spain, Portugal, Greece and Italy — in that order. By gift shopping in the cheaper coutries my dollar goes two or three times as far.

In the interest of packing light, try to put off shopping until the end of the trip. Ideally, you should end your trip in a cheap country, do all of your shopping, then fly home. One summer, I had a 16-pound rucksack and nothing more until the last week of my trip when, in Spain and Morocco, I managed to accumulate two medieval chairs, two sets of bongos, a camel-hair coat, swords, a mace and a lace tablecloth.

If you do some shopping before the end of your trip, it's easy and inexpensive to lighten your burden by sending a package home by surface mail. Book rate is very cheap. Be sure to wrap the package very carefully. Many post offices sell packing boxes in various sizes.

Large department stores often have a souvenir section with prices much less than what you would pay in the cute little tourist shops nearby. Shop around and remember that, in the southern countries, most things sold on the streets or in markets have soft prices. When appropriate, bargain like mad.

A Word of Caution to the Shopper

Shopping is an important part of the average person's trip, but be careful not to lose control. All too often, slick marketing and "cutesy," romantic window displays can succeed in shifting the entire focus of your trip toward the tourist shops. (It's a lucrative business. Many souvenir merchants in Italy work through the tourist season, then retire for the rest of the year.) This sort of tourist brainwashing can turn you into one of the hundreds of people who set out to see and experience Europe but find themselves wandering in a trance-like search for signs announcing "We accept Visa cards." I've seen half the members of a British Halls of Parliament guided tour skip out to survey an exciting table of plastic "bobbie" hats and English coffee mugs. Don't let your tour degenerate into a glorified shopping trip.

I think it's wise to restrict your shopping to stipulated time during the trip. Most people have an idea of what they want to buy in each country. Set aside a time to shop in each of these areas and stick to it. This way you avoid drifting through a day thinking only of souvenirs.

When you are shopping, ask yourself if your enthusiasm is merited. More often than not, you can pick up a very similar item of better quality and for a cheaper price at home. Unless you're a real romantic, the thrill of where you bought something fades long before the item's usefulness. My life has more room for a functional souvenir than for a useless symbol of a place I visited. Even thoughtful shoppers go overboard. I have several large boxes in my attic labeled "great souvenirs."

13
Europe—
The Whirlwind Tour

Let's assume that you have ten weeks, plenty of energy and a desire to see as much of Europe as possible. It's most economical to fly to London and travel around Europe with a two-month Eurailpass. You'll spend two months on the Continent and use any remaining time in England, before or after you start your train pass. Budgeting for an $800 round trip ticket to London, a $560 two-month first-class Eurailpass and $20 a day, the entire trip will cost less than $2600. It can be done. Green, but thinking, budget travelers of all ages do it all the time.

If I could relive my first two months in Europe this is the trip I'd take. I'll have to admit — this itinerary is fantastic. Fasten your seatbelts, raise your seats to their upright position and here we go . . . .

London is Europe's great entertainer, wonderfully historic and the best starting point for a European adventure. The English speak English but their accents will give you the sensation of understanding a foreign language. Every day will be busy, and each night filled with a play and a pub. But the Continent beckons.

Paris is a quick overnight train ride away. Ascend the Eiffel Tower to survey a Paris studded with architectural gems and historical "one-of-a-kinds." You'll recognize the Notre Dame, Sacre Coeur, the Invalides and much more. A busy four days awaits you back on the ground — especially with a visit to Europe's greatest palace, Louis XIV's Versailles.

On the way to Spain, explore the dreamy chateaux of the Loire Valley. Take the train to Madrid where bullfights, shopping and the Prado museum fill your sunny days. Then sleep on the train to Lisbon, Portugal's friendly capital.

Lisbon can keep a visitor busy for days. Its highlight is the Alfama. This salty old sailor's quarter is a photographer's delight. You'll feel rich in Lisbon, where a taxi ride is cheaper than a London bus ticket.

Break the long train ride to the French Riviera, with a day or two in Madrid and Barcelona. A rest on the beach is in order before diving into intense Italy.

Italy, steeped in history and art, is a bright spot in any itinerary. An entire trip could be spent climbing through the classical monuments of Rome, absorbing the art treasures of Florence and cruising the canals of colorful Venice. These cities, Pompeii, the leaning tower of Pisa, the hill towns of Tuscany and so much more just might kidnap your heart.

Your favorite place in Italy may be the Cinqueterre. Cinqueterre?! Your friends will believe it only after they see your pictures. Unknown to tourists and the ultimate Italian coastal paradise, you'll find pure Italy in these five sleepy traffic-free villages near Genoa.

Savor the old world elegance of Hapsbourg Vienna for a few days and then enjoy Salzburg's unrivaled music festival. Classical music sounds so good in its birthplace.

Tour Mad King Ludwig's fairytale castle at Neuschwanstein before visiting the Tyrolian town of Ruette and its two forgotton — yet unforgettable — hill-crowning, ruined castles. These are the Ehrenburg Ruins. (Keep them a secret.) Running along the overgrown ramparts, you'll find yourself under attack a thousand years ago.

Europe's most scenic train ride is across southern Switzerland from Chur to Martigny. Be careful, on a sunny day the Alpine beauty is intoxicating.

For the best of the Swiss Alps establish a home base in the rugged Bernese Oberland, south of Interlaken. The traffic-free village of Gimmelwald in Lauterbrunnen Valley is everything an Alp-lover could possibly want.

Munich, the capital of Bavaria, has the world's greatest street singers. But they probably won't be good enough to keep you out of the beerhalls. Huge mugs of beer, bigger pretzels and even bigger beermaids! If you are smart, you'll skip the touristy Hofbrau House and patronize Mathauser's Beerhall for the best local crowd, a rowdy oom-pah band, and thick German atmosphere.

The Romantic Road bus tour (included on the Eurailpass) is the best way to get from Munich to Frankfurt. The bus rolls through the heart of medieval Germany, stopping at Nordlingen, Dinkelsbuhl and the always popular queen of quaint German towns, Rothenburg.

After the bus tour, take the Rhine cruise (also covered by Eurail) from Bingen to Koblenze to enjoy a parade of old castles. Sleep in Bacharach's classic castle youth hostel with a panoramic view of the Rhine for $3.

Finish your Continental experience with a visit to the capitals of Scandinavia. Smorgasbords, Viking ships and healthy, smiling blondes (of both sexes) are the memories you'll pack on the train south to Amsterdam.

After a few days in crazy Amsterdam and a bike ride through the countryside, sail for England. Any remaining time is easily spent in the English countryside.

This trip is just a sampler. There's plenty more to see but I can't imagine a better first two months in Europe.

The Whirlwind Tour Itinerary — Some Specifics

If I was planning my first European trip and wanted to see as much as I could comfortably in two months, (and I had the experience I now have to help me plan), this trip is the trip I'd take . . .

Days	Place	
?	London	Cheapest place in Europe to fly to, easiest place to adjust. From airport (easy RR or subway access from Gatwick or Heathrow) go to Victoria Station. Get ticket to Continent (Paris) at Sealink Office. Great tourist info office in Vic-

toria. Round London orientation bus tour from park in front of station, leaves all the time. Lay groundwork for your return to London (if ending trip there) — reserve good B&B, get tickets to the hottest play in town. Night train (N/T) and boat to Paris. 22:30 — 8:44.

4   Paris

Arrive in morning — easy to find budget one or two star hotel room. Don't look in famous tourist areas. Take subway to a place that sees no tourist. Use Paris subway. Three rides for a dollar anywhere in town. Walk — Latin Quarter, Notre Dame, St. Chapelle, Pont Neuf, self-serve lunch in Samartaine Department store, Louvre (take intro tour), Tuilieries Gardens, Champs Eylsees to the Arc de Triomphe. Ask hotel for small family-owned restaurant for dinner. Evening on Montmartre, soak in the spiritual waters of the Sacre Coeur, browse among the shops and artists of the Place du Tertre. Later be sure to enjoy Napoleon's Tomb, Les Invalides (Europe's best military museum), The Rodin Museum (The Thinker and Kiss), the Jeu de Paume (Impressionism), Pompidou Modern Art Gallery, a jazz club and Latin Quarter nightlife. Pick up "Pariscope" for an entertainment guide and remember most museums are closed on Tuesdays. ST (side-trip) #1 — Versailles, a must. Europe's grandest palace (subway to Invalids, SNCF train to end of line, Versailles R.G.) ST #2 — Chartres, great gothic cathedral, lectures by Malcolm Miller at 12:00 and 2:45.

2   Loire Valley

Make Tours your headquarters, Hotel de Orleans near station. Good all day bus tours of chateaux. If not really into chateaux, skip Loire. Consider ST from Paris to epitome of French chateaux, Chantilly. NT direct to Madrid, 21:00 — 9:00.

3   Madrid

Upon arrival reserve train out. Reservations on long trains are required in Spain (& Norway) even with Eurail. Taxi to Puerto del Sol for central budget room. Prado museum (Bosch, Goya, El Greco, Velesquez) and Royal Palace (Europe's most lavish interior) are musts. Bull-

		fights on Sunday and Thursday in summer, ask at hotel, buy tickets at arena. El Rastro (flea market), great shopping, Sundays, ST #1 — Toledo (whole city perfectly preserved, national monument, El Greco's home and masterpieces). ST #2 — Segovia, Roman aqueduct. Skip Avila. NT, Lisbon, 23:15 — 9:45.
3	Lisbon	Europe's bargain basement capital, see "Back Door." ST — Sintra (ruined Moorish castle), Estoril (casino nightlife) NT — Madrid, 21:10 — 9:35.
1	Madrid	Upon arrival, reserve NT to Barcy (22:20 — 8:10). Spend the day here, Night travel is best in Iberia — long distances, boring, hot, crowded, slow day trains. Beds (couchettes) are cheap on these trains.
2	Barcelona	Picasso's house (excellent), relax, shop, beach, NT — 19:00 — 8:00.
3	Rhone Valley or French Riviera	Avignon — (Papal Palace), Nimes and Arles (Roman ruins), Nice (where the jet set lays on rocks), Riviera (crowded, expensive, stressful, good modern art).
2	Cinqueterre	Great villages, coastal Italy at its best, see "Back Door." Accommodations tight.
2	Florence	Europe's art capital, packed in the summer, worth the headaches.
2	Hilltowns of Tuscany & Umbria	See "Back Door." Most neglected and under-rated side of Italy. Accommodations easy, leave Florence late, arrive Rome early.
4	Rome	Day #1 — Classical: Colosseum, Forum, Capitalino Hill (both museums), Pantheon. Eve — Piazza Navona (buy Tartufo ice cream at Tre Scalini). Day #2 — Vatican, St. Peter's, climb the dome, Sistine (rent headphone guide) and Vatican Museum (great market 100 yards in front of museum entry, picnic). Buy small black and white photo essay book on Pieta in bookshops and take advantage of the Vatican's Post, much better than Italy's. Day #3 — Ostia Antica, Ancient Rome's seaport (like Pompeii, but just a subway ride away from Rome). Bus from station to Tivoli (garden of fountains in

hills). Day #4 — National Museum (best art) in front of station. Piazza Barberini (Bernini fountain, Capuchin crypt, thousands of bones in first church on Via Veneto, Picadilly's best self-serve restaurant in Rome, subway stop). Explore Trastevere, old Rome alive today, good place for dinner. NT — Venice, 23:00 — 7:00.

2 Venice
Best intro — slow boat (#1) down Canale Grande. Sit in front and soak it in. Academy Gallery — best Venetian art. Doges Palace, St. Mark's and view from Campanile are musts, then wander, leave the tourists, get as lost as possible. Don't worry, you're on an island and you can't get off. NT 20:05 — 6:00.

2 Vienna
Paris' eastern rival. Grand capital of the mighty Hapsburg Empire. Lots of art history, and more old world charm and elegance than anywhere. Great tourist info under street in front of Opera. Consider ST to Budapest (#1) or Prague. NT — Switzerland.

6 Switzerland
Pray for sun. Most scenic train — Chur-Martigny (two non-Eurail segments). Best region — Bernese Oberland, south of Interlaken, see "Back Door." Best big city: Lucerne, lovely towns along Lake Geneva and in West (Murten and Friborg). Boden See (Meersburg castle town, tropical isle of Mainau, Lindau — Venice of North, Eurail covers boats on Swiss lakes.)

2 Tirol
Reutte ("Back Door" castle ruins), Innsbruck.

2 Bavaria
Fussen, Mad Ludwig's castles, Weis Church, villages.

3 Munich
Cultural capital, great palace, museums, Mathauser's Beerhall (Best, halfway between station and old town on right). Tourist info and room finding service in station. Lay groundwork for departure on Romantic Road bus tour upon arrival (make reservation, if necessary, confirm place and time of departure). ST — Salzburg, only 90 minute train ride away.

1 Romantic Road
Bus tour, free with Eurailpass (See "Back Door"). Munich-Weisbaden 9:00 — 20:00 with

		stops in Dinkelsbuhl and Rothenburg. Eve in Bingen.
3	Rhine/Mosel River Valleys	Cruise from Bingen to Koblenz (best castles, free with trainpass, get off stop before Koblenz to save long walk to station, great castle youth hostel in Bacharach). Mosel Valley (included cruises, Cochem town and castle, Trier-Roman town, Berg Eltz — long walk, great castle). NT Koln or Frankfurt — Copenhagen, 17:35 — 6:45.
1	Copenhagen	Leave bags at station, evening at Tivoli just across the street. NT — 23:49 — 8:44.
3	Stockholm	See "Back Door." Sleep on trains in Scandinavia — long, boring rides, capitals ten hours apart, hotels expensive. NT 22:05 — 8:25.
2	Oslo	See "Back Door." Consider ST to Bergen, very scenic train ride. NT 22:40 — 8:53.
1	Copenhagen	NT — 21:10 — 10:00, train goes right on to Puttgarten ferry.
4	Amsterdam	Many great side trips. Consider headquarters in small town nearby (Delft) as Amsterdam is getting awfully sleazy and seedy. Consider open-jaws return flight into London, out of Amsterdam, to avoid surface return to London ($40 and 12 hours). NT — 21:54 — 9:14.
?	London	Spend remaining time in English countryside, Bath, Cotswolds, Cambridge. Call to reconfirm flight home.

60 days scheduled on the Continent. Train times are old, use only as a rough guide. Eurailpass is good for two calendar months (i.e., the 15th through midnight on the 14th.) If you validated when you leave Paris and expire upon arrival in Amsterdam you spend 52 days leaving 8 days of trainpass time to slow down or add options.

Excursions you may want to add:

England — Oxford, Stratford, the Cotswold villages, Bath and more.

Geneva, Chamonix, Aiguille du Midi, Hellbrunner, Aosta (Italy).

Morocco and South Spain.

South Italy or Greece.

Finland or the Arctic.

East Europe or the USSR.

A day for showers and laundry.

Visiting and resting.

Travel days to avoid sleeping on the train.

A free day here and there. Every itinerary needs some slack.

The Whirlwind Tour includes fourteen nights on the train, saving over $100 in hotel costs and fourteen days for doing more interesting things than sitting on a train.

High Speed Town-hopping

When I tell people that I saw four or five towns in one day, they either say or think: "That guy must be crazy! Nobody can really see four or five towns in a day!" Many towns are very stop-worthy but take only an hour or two to cover. Don't let guilt feelings tell you to slow down and stay longer if you really are finished with a town. There's so much more to see in the rest of Europe! Going too slow is as bad as going too fast.

If you are efficient and use the High-Speed Town-Hopping method, you will amaze yourself at what you can see in a day. Let me explain with an example . . .

You wake up early in Town A. Checking out of your hotel, you have two or three sights to cover before your 10:00 train. (You checked the train schedule the night before.) Before getting to the station you visit the open-air market and buy the ingredients for your brunch.

From 10:00 to 11:00 you travel by train to Town B. During that hour you'll have a restful brunch, enjoy the passing scenery and prepare for Town B by reading your literature and deciding what you want to see. Just before your arrival you put the items you need (camera, jacket, tourist information) into your little rucksack and, upon arrival, check the rest of your luggage in a locker. (Every station has storage lockers.)

Before leaving Town B's station, write down on a scrap of paper the departure times of the next few trains to Town C. Now you can sightsee as much or as little as you want and still know when to catch your train. You are ready to go. You know what you want to see. You aren't burdened by your luggage. And, you know when the trains are leaving.

Town B is great. After a snack in the park you will catch the 2:30 train. By 3:00 you are in Town C where you will repeat the same procedure as you did in Town B. Town C just isn't what it was cracked up to be, so you catch the first train out after a walk along the waterfront and a look at the church.

By 5:30 you arrive in D, the last town on the day's agenda. The man in the station directs you to a good budget pension just two blocks down the street. You are checked in and unpacked in no time, and after "checking out" the bed for a few minutes, it's time to find a good restaurant and eat dinner. After a meal and an evening stroll you're ready to call it a day. Thinking back, it really was quite a day. You spent it Highspeed Town-hopping.

The Home-Base Strategy

The Home-base strategy is a clever way to make your trip itinerary smoother, simpler and more efficient. Set yourself up in a central location and use that place as a base for day trips to nearby attractions. Here are five advantages of using this approach to European travel:

1. The Home-base approach minimizes setting up time (usually over an hour). Searching for a good hotel can be exhausting, frustrating and time-consuming.

2. You are freed from your luggage. Being able to leave your luggage in the hotel enhances your mobility. You will enjoy yourself more without your luggage and with the peace of mind that you are set up for the night.

3. You will feel comfortable and "at home" in your Home-base town. This feeling takes more than a day to get, and when you are changing locations every day or two, you may never get the feel for a place.

4. The Home-base approach allows you to spend the evening in a city, where there is some exciting nightlife. Most small countryside towns die after 9:00 p.m. If you are not dead by 9:00, you will find more action in a larger city.

5. Europe's generally frequent and punctual train and bus systems make the Home-base strategy very practical. With a train pass, the round-trips are free; otherwise, the transportation is reasonable, often with reductions offered for round-trip tickets. Take advantage of the time you spend on the train. Use it productively.

Here are some of my favorite Home-base cities and some of their corresponding trips:

Madrid	Toledo, Segovia, Avila
Amsterdam	Alkmaar, The Hague, Haarlem, Scheveningen, Delft, most of the Netherlands.
Copenhagen	Lund, Malmo, Roskilde, Helsingor.
Paris	Reims, Versailles, Chartres, Fontainebleau, Chantilly
Bregenz, Austria	Lake Constance (Boden See) area, Lindau, Meersburg, Vorarlberg, Bregenzerwald, Feldkirch
London	Oxford, Stratford, Cambridge, Salisbury (Stonehenge), Bath
Avignon	Nimes, Arles, The Rhone Valley
Florence	Pisa, Siena, San Gimignano, Arezzo, many small towns
Munich	Salzburg: Berchtesgaden, Augsburg, Neuschwanstein, Linderhof, and Herrenchiemsee (three of King Ludwig's castles), many small Bavarian towns including Oberammergau.

Part Two

Thirty-four Back Doors

Thirty-four Back Doors

1 Hilltowns of Tuscany and Umbria *225*
2 Civita de Bagnoregio *228*
3 Italy's Cinqueterre *231*
4 Palermo *235*
5 Dingle Peninsula — A Gaelic Bike Ride *238*
6 North Ireland — A Terrible Beauty *241*
7 London — A Warm Look at a Cold City *245*
8 The Moors of England *252*
9 Bath, England — Elegant and Frivolous *254*
10 York Castle Museum —
    A Walk With Dickens *256*
11 The Romantic Road *259*
12 Castle Day *263*
13 Kleine Scheidegg and Gimmelwald —
    The Heart of Switzerland *267*
14 From France to Italy — Over Mt. Blanc *274*
15 Alsace —
    The French-Teutonic Land of Wine *278*
16 Brittany *283*
17 Carcassonne — Europe's Greatest Medieval
    Fortress City *286*
18 Versailles — Europe's Palace of Palaces *289*
19 France by Car *292*
20 French Cuisine *295*
21 Oslo *298*
22 Stalking Stockholm *301*

23   Eastern Europe   *304*
24   Ignored Bulgaria   *307*
25   Moscow After Dark   *310*
26   South Spain   *312*
27   A Day in Lisbon   *317*
28   Morocco — Plunge Deep   *321*
29   Yugoslavia   *326*
30   The Gorge of Samaria on The Isle of Crete   *330*
31   The Best Way From Athens to Turkey   *333*
32   Eastern Turkey   *337*
33   The Treasures of Luxor   *342*
34   Bad Towns   *348*

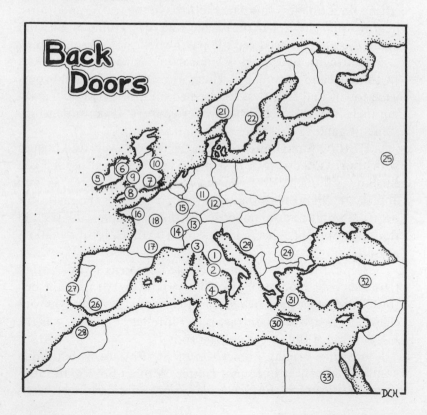

The Hilltowns
of Tuscany and Umbria

Too many people connect Rome and Florence with a straight line. If you break out of the Venice-Florence-Rome syndrome, you'll find the little Italy that the splash of Venice, the finesse of Florence and the grandeur of Rome were built upon.

The hilltowns of Tuscany and Umbria hold their crumbling heads proudly above the noisy flood of the twentieth century and offer a peaceful taste of what eludes so many tourists. I find the essence of Italy in this small town package, sitting on a timeless rampart high above the traffic and trains, hearing only children in the market and the rustling of the wind aging the already aged red tile patchwork that surrounds me.

Hilltowns, like Greek Islands, come in two basic varieties — touristy and untouristy. There are six or eight great touristed towns and countless ignored communities casually making their way through just another century. Take time to see some of each.

Historic San Gimignano bristles with towers and bustles with tourists. Tuscany's best preserved medieval skyline is a thrilling silhouette from a distance. It gets better as you approach. Nighttime's the right time to conquer the castle. Sit on its summit and imagine the battles these old cobbles and floodlit towers have seen. Even with crowds, San Gimignano is a must.

Siena, Florence's rival, is a city to be seen as a whole rather than as a collection of sights. Climb to the dizzy top of the bell tower and reign over urban harmony at its best. As you tour Siena, compare and contrast it to Florence. Florence was the big gun but it didn't call all the shots.

Assisi, a worthy hometown of St. Francis, is battling a commercial cancer of tourist clutter. A quiet hour in the awesome Basilica of St. Francis, some appropriate reading (there's

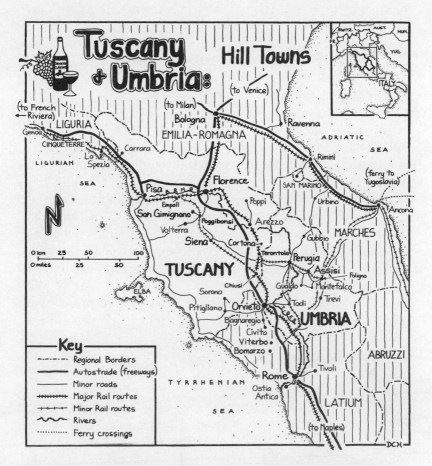

a great book store next door), and a meditative stroll through the back streets can still put you in a properly Franciscan frame of mind to dissolve the tour buses and melt into the magic of Assisi. Those who take advantage of this opportunity to get to know St. Francis remember Assisi as very special.

Orvieto is the typical tourist's token hilltown. It's a nice place with a fine cathedral but, in Tuscany or Umbria, nice isn't saying much. Enjoy Orvieto wine in Rome and its impressive hill-capping profile from the train or Autostrada, but your hilltown energy is better spent elsewhere.

Any guide book lists these and several other popular

hilltowns. But if you want to dance at noon with a toothless lady while the pizza cooks, press a hundred lira coin into the gooey ceiling of an Etruscan wine cellar for good luck, be introduced to a less than mediocre altar piece as proudly as if it was a Michelangelo, or have the local cop unlock the last remaining city tower and escort you to the top for a bird's-eye view of the town and the gawkers who just emptied out the barber shop below, stow your guide book, buy the best local map you can find and explore.

Perfect "Back Door" villages, like hidden pharaoh's tombs, await discovery. Photographers delight in Italian hilltowns. Their pictorial collections are far and away the best information source (e.g., "Italian Hilltowns" by Norman Carver). Study these, circling the most intriguing towns on your map. Debrief those who have studied Italy. Ask locals for their favorites. Most importantly, follow your wanderlust blindly. Find a frog and kiss it.

Gubbio, Volterra, Cortona and Arezzo are discovered but rarely visited. Civita de Bagnoregio, Sorano, Pitigliano, Trevi,

San Marino, just another magic Italian hilltown.

and Poppi are virgin hill towns. The difference between "discovered" and "virgin," touristically speaking, is "discovered" knows what tourism is and how to use it economically. "Virgin" is simply pleased that you dropped in. "Virgin" doesn't want to, or know how to, take advantage of you. It wants to enjoy you and you are free to enjoy it.

When you're planning your visit to Italy, include its hill-towns. Leave the train lines. Take the bus, hitch, or rent a car for a few days. Don't just chase down my favorites or your guide book's recommendations. Be fanatic, find the treasure — the cultural slumber of Umbria and the human texture of Tuscany.

Civita de Bagnoregio

Civita de Bagnoregio. People who have been there just say "Civita" with a special warmth and love. I hesitate to promote this precious chip of Italy which has somehow escaped the ravages of modernity. But it's so perfect — I have to share it. Please approach it with the same respect and sensitivity you would a dying relative, because — in a sense — that's Civita.

Eighty people live here. There's no car traffic, only a man with a donkey who works all day ferrying the town's goods across the long umbilical bridge that connects the town with a small distant parking lot and the rest of Italy.

Civita's sights are subtle and many tourists would not know what to do in a town without tourism. No famous sons, lists of attractions, orientation tours or museum hours. Just Italy.

Sit in the piazza. Smile and nod at each local who passes by. It's a social jigsaw puzzle and each person fits. Look above

at the old woman hanging out the window. She's in charge of gossip and knows all. A tiny hunchback lady is everyone's daughter and 2500 year-old pillars from an ancient buried Etruscan temple stick up like bar stools. The bar is gone as are most of the young people, lured away by the dazzle of today to grab their place in Italy's cosmopolitan parade.

A woman introduces you to a baby donkey as if it was her child and takes you through the church. Civita's church is the heartbeat and pride of the village. Festivals and processions start here, visitors are taken here and the town's past is honored here. Enjoy paintings by students of famous artists, relics of the local St. Bonaventura, a dried floral decoration spread across the floor, and a cool quiet sit in a pew. My friend uncovered a tiny dusty pump organ. She was proud to hear me play a Bach invention in her church. Playing it was like treading water and the music sounded submerged.

Civita is a pinnacle in a vast canyon. Erosion and the wind rule the valley and gnarled trees are time's eternal whipping boys. A lady, ignoring her eye-boggling view, took me into an ancient Etruscan cave to see her olive press. Even on a blistering day, those caves are always cool and an endless supply of local Civita wine is kept chilled awaiting future fun.

Civita has one restaurant. You can see its green door and handmade sign from the piazza. "Al Forno" (the oven) never had a menu. You eat what's cooking. Mom and Pop slice and quarter happily through the day. I've had plenty of memorable spaghetti, salad and wine on their patio, cuddled by Civita.

Civita is an artist's dream, a town in the nude, in full bloom with a surprise around each corner. Horses pose, the warm stone walls glow with personality, each stairway is dessert to a sketch pad or camera and the grand moat does its best to keep things that way. It is changing, however, as the aggressive present eats at the last strongholds of the past. Civita will be great for years but never as great as today.

You won't find Civita on any map. Take the train to Orvieto and catch a bus to Bagnoregio. From Bagnoregio you walk to Civita. Obviously, Civita has no hotel. Stay in Bagnoregio in a local "camera" or "bed and breakfast." Bagnoregio's only hotel is a 20-minute walk out of town. Ask for Boschetto di Angelo Catarcia. Angelo is a character who runs through life like a hyper child in a wading pool. Civita is past her prime but she smiles — and remembers.

Travelers in search of back-street treats.

Italy's Cinqueterre

"A sleepy, romantic and inexpensive town on the Riviera without a tourist in sight." That's the futile dream travelers chase in busy Nice and Cannes. Paradise sleeps just across the border in Italy's Cinqueterre.

With larger and larger tourist crowds drowning Europe's towns and resorts every summer, it's more important than ever to trade those long lines and "no vacancy" signs in on a more real and relaxed alternative. The Cinqueterre, just north of Pisa, is surprisingly untouristed.

Cinqueterre, meaning "five lands," is five pastel villages clinging to the rugged coast of the Italian Riviera. The villagers go about their business as if the surrounding vineyards were the very edges of the earth. An Italian syrup soaks every corner of this world and it's yours to sop up.

Each town is a character, Monterosso al Mare, happy to be appreciated, boasts a great beach and plenty of fine hotels

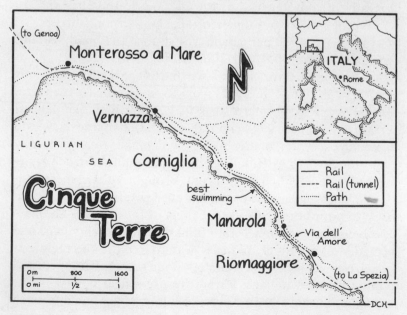

and restaurants. Its four little sisters are content to be over-looked and underbooked. Little Manarola rules its ravine and drinks its wine while its sun-bleached walls slumber on. Corniglia crowns its hill and beams, proudly victorious in its solitaire game of "king of the mountain." Most visitors are lured to Corniglia by the Cinqueterre's best beach and never climb the winding stairs to the actual town. Those who make the Corniglian ascent can expect to be rewarded by the Cinqueterre's finest wine and most staggering view — simultaneously. I ducked into a cellar with a grape-stained local. Furtively, we dipped long straws into dark kegs. Wine tasting drowns the language barrier. The Via dell'Amore (walkway of love) leads to Riomaggiore. With a beauty that seduced famed artists to live here, Riomaggiore is well worth a wander.

Vernazza is my favorite village. Its one street connects the harbor with the train station and meanders further inland, melting into the vineyards. Paths and stairways connect this watercolor huddle of houses with Main Street. Every day is a parade. A rainbow of laundry flags fly over barrel women wheeling fresh fish past the old men on the bench. Waves crash a steady breakwater beat as the Old World marches on.

Vernazza has but one pension, the Pension Sorriso. Sr. Sorriso charges $20 per person with dinner and breakfast, but is usually booked full with Italians (tel. 0187/812224).

The Cinqueterre is best seen on foot. An easy trail leads you through sunny vineyards from Riomaggiore to Vernazza. The hike on to Monterosso is in keeping with the general terrain — rugged. Flowers and an ever-changing view will entertain every step of any hike. As you make your sweaty way high above the glistening beaches and approach each time-steeped village, you'll be glad you brought your camera.

When you run out of time or energy simply catch a train back to your home base. While most of these towns are inac-cessible to cars, a tunnel-train blinks open at each village and provides a very quick and easy way to explore the region.

Given its lack of accommodations and the Cinqueterre's popularity with Italians, it's best to use a nearby city — like Lavagna, Levanto or Le Spezia as a home base and approach

Vernazza, Cinqueterre, Italy.

the Cinqueterre by train (50 cents, 30 minutes). Two nights nearby and a whole day to explore is ideal.

Five towns and rocky surf are all that interrupt the peaceful vineyard greens and Mediterranean blues of this Riviera. The tourists are looking for it, but have yet to find it. Discover Italy's Cinqueterre.

From the Journal

The weather was wild — blowing and almost raining. Bundled up, I walked down Main Street to the crashing waterfront. Spectacular is an understatement! Little varnished boats piled everywhere, waves beating mightily at and over the breakwater, taverns holding people like magnets holding tacks, lamp-lit side alleys climbing in every direction. I walked out to the weather-beaten point and just marveled at my spot.

Palermo

The European tourist boom can scarcely be heard in Sicily. It took me seven trips to get down past Italy's "boot," but I finally made it. The Sicilians (along with the Irish) are the warmest and friendliest Europeans I've met. (The Mafiosi are apparently all on our side of the Atlantic now.)

It's well worth the overnight train ride south from Rome or Naples to escape into this rich culture living peacefully oblivious to the touristic bustle that takes such a toll on Venice, Florence and Rome.

Eating and sleeping in high style at low prices is easy. From the Palermo train station, walk straight down Via Roma for your choice of many hotels. A reservation is not necessary. My favorite hotel is the Hotel Moderno, Via Roma 276. My double (Room 23) cost $20, was large, airy and included a rooftop patio with a view. The bathroom was bigger than some entire hotel bedrooms I've stayed in. The management was friendly and eager to share lots of tourist information.

Eating in Palermo is a real treat. Colorful street markets make shopping for picnics a joy. Pizzeria Bellini on Piazza Bellini, near the central "four corners" of Palermo, was my dinnertime hangout. Over the course of several meals, I ate my way through their menu, discovering for myself why Italians like to eat. Their fanciest pizza, "Quatro Gusti con Fungi" cost three dollars and is permanently etched on my palette.

Sightseeing, Palermo Style

One reason Palermo lacks tourist crowds is that it has very few tourist sights as such. It does have a way of life that, in its own way, offers the tourist more than any monument or museum ever could. Don't tour Palermo — live in it.

Thriving marketplaces abound. If you've ever wondered what it would be like to be a celebrity, go on a photo-safari through the urban jungles of Palermo. The warmth and excitement will give you smile wrinkles. Scores of merchants, housewives and children compete for your attention. Cries of "Photo!" come from all corners as you venture down busy alleys. Morning markets and eternal hawkers can be found in nearly any neighborhood.

Visit a vertical neighborhood. Small apartments stack high above the side streets. If you stop to chat, six floors of balconies will fill up, each with its own waving family. This is a great place for a zoom lens, but remember — if you take one family's picture, you'll be expected to honor the entire neighborhood equally. Proud mothers will hold up tiny babies, and you'll be showered with scraps of paper, each with an address on it. A fantastic energy fills the air, and saying goodbye hurts.

For a strange journey through an eerie cellar of the dead, visit the Catacombs of the Capuchin Monks. This dark and dreary basement has 8,000 clothed and very dead ex-monks hanging on its walls. A strange but meaningful habit.

For a more typical tourist attraction and a respite from the swelter-skelter of Palermo, bus inland to the soothing mountain town of Monreale. Inside Monreale's Benedictine church, you'll find a collection of mosaics that rival Ravenna. Dozens of Bible scenes, in mosaic, cover the walls of this church. Since I was wearing shorts, I was given a blanket to wear as a skirt. With my hairy, unholy legs covered, I worked my way, scene by scene, through the Bible.

Palermo has no "must-see" museum and nothing to compete with the tipsy Tower or Big Ben. But that's not why you'll visit Palermo, is it? Become a Sicilian. Move there for four or five days. Try it — you'll like it.

From the Journal

We had time for a morning stroll. Grabbing our camera stuff, we set out. At first we found nothing; then I noticed a wobbly stack of tenements facing one another, a faded rainbow with lots of laundry and people hanging out. One wave worked wonders. The whole place became like a giant, teeming pet store full of little creatures dying to be petted. We walked

A balcony of friends, Palermo, Sicily.

around, craning our necks upward and waving like victorious politicians to hordes of supporters. They called out for pictures and wouldn't let us go until we had filmed each window and balcony full of crazy people; mothers holding up babies, sisters posed arm in arm, a wild pregnant woman standing on a fruit crate, holding her bulging stomach, and an old, wrinkled woman, cheery in a paint-starved window frame. It's funny how you never know when you'll find yourself in an ideal picture-taking situation. After collecting addresses and many "Ciao's," we walked on, bought a half a watermelon and returned to our room. Out on our patio, we filled our plastic bidet with seeds and savored a Sicilian siesta.

Dingle Peninsula —
A Gaelic Bike Ride

Be careful — Ireland is seductive. In many areas the old culture seems to be winning its battle with the twentieth century and stress is a foreign word. I fell in love with the friendliest land this side of Sicily. It all happened in a "Gaeltacht."

A Gaeltacht is a national cultural preserve — where the government is actively fostering the continued survival of the old Irish culture. Shaded green on many maps, these regions are most common on the West coast of the Emerald Island. "Gaeltacht" means Gaelic-speaking. You will find the Gaelic culture alive, not only in the language but working the fields, singing in the pubs and in the weathered faces of the traditionally dark-clad Irish who live there. A Gaeltacht will give you Ireland in the extreme.

Dingle — green, rugged and untouched — is my favorite Gaeltacht. It is Ireland's western-most point, quietly living the way it wants to. While nearby Killarney and the famous "Ring

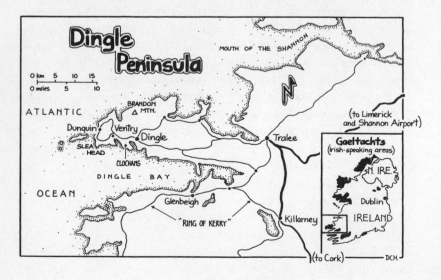

of Kerry" bustle with noisy tourists, Dingle Peninsula ages peacefully, offering an escape into the real Ireland.

Drive, take the bus or hitchhike to Dingle town. It's a good place to spend your first Irish night if you land at nearby Shannon Airport. From the town of Tralee, you'll pass over a ruggedly scenic mountain pass. Depending on the weather, you'll be dazzled by the lush views, or you'll creep slowly through milky fog, seeing nothing past the dark road's edge.

Dingle town has character. In a very Gaelic manner, it is quiet, salty and enjoyable. A weather-beaten friendliness will warm you, even on the coldest of wet mornings.

Find a good bed and breakfast. I enjoyed the hospitality of Mrs. Farrell's "Corner House" (tel. 06-51516). Any resident of Dingle should be happy and able to direct you to a good "B and B" like Mrs. Farrell's. A cozy bed, a huge breakfast and lots of tea shouldn't cost you more than $10. All across the British Isles, friendly ladies open their houses to travelers, providing bed, breakfast and an excellent look at the local lifestyle at a bargain price. Reservations are a needless security blanket.

After breakfast, find a bike to rent. (Your landlord can direct you to a bike rental place.) For a couple of dollars you will have wheels for the day. Pack a picnic, your camera and a raincoat, and you're on your way. The weather on this distant tip of Ireland is often misty, foggy and rainy. It's as wet as it is green — and I've never seen a greener land.

Bicycle around the peninsula. Follow the coastal road to the little town of Ventry. Chat with the "chatty" Irish you'll meet along the roadside. Those accents are priceless.

Continue along to Slea Head, the closest point in Europe to America. The rugged coastline stretches in both directions, offering magnificent views of the treacherous black-rock cliffs. Crashing surf, distant boats and the lush countryside complete this memorable picture. Sheep graze, bored by the quiet clouds constantly covering and uncovering the hills. An elfish black-clad Gaelic man might tell you of his arthritis, point out a landmark or sing you a song.

Be sure to explore some of the many "clochans," or bee-hive huts. These mysterious stone huts were built without mortar by seventh-century monks in search of solitude. They are especially exciting when it's just you and a hut in a desolate world of dark heavy mist.

Pedal on to Dunquin. For lunch, stop by Kruger Kavanaugh's Gaelic Pub and order something very Irish. Or, if the weather's nice, just down a Guinness at Kavanaugh's and find a quiet stream off the road a wee bit, and enjoy your picnic outside, sitting on a rock.

Now pedal up the hill and coast back down into Dingle town. You have finished your circle around the lovely Dingle Peninsula.

For your evening fun, find a "singing Gaelic pub." (O'Flaherty's is always a good time.) Here you will enjoy traditional music that has not yet been bastardized for the tourist. A tin whistle, a fiddle, a flute, goatskin drums and bad voices that sound great will awaken the leprechaun in you. The atmosphere will be as thick as the head on your pint of Guinness. Drink it all. If an Irishman buys you a drink, you might offer him a Gaelic toast. Lift your glass and say "SLOY tuh!" (spelled phonetically). Before you leave, be sure to thank him, by saying, "go rev MA ha gote." Live Gaelic music, plenty to drink and a robust local crowd can be a great way to end your day in Dingle.

Ireland will seduce you — let it . . . enjoy it . . . you may never be the same.

North Ireland —
A Terrible Beauty

Make your visit to Ireland complete by including Northern Ireland. Ulster, as the six counties of Northern Ireland are called, is only a two-hour train ride from Dublin and offers the tourist a very different and very Irish world.

The tourist information on Ireland doesn't recommend a visit to the "war-torn" North. The media blows the trouble all out of proportion, leading people to believe that nowhere in Ulster is there peace. That's exciting but false. These British-controlled counties of Ireland are a secret enjoyed and toured mainly by its own inhabitants.

Of course, people are being killed in North Ireland — about as many as are being killed in New York City. If you want trouble you can find it. But, with common sense, travel in Ulster is safe. You'll see many signs of the violence. Armored cars, political graffiti and bomb-damage clearance sales tell the story of the on-going troubles. Friends you meet will show you the remains of a bombed-out customs house or the flowers that mark the spot where someone was assassinated. But no tourist has ever been injured by "the troubles." I've been sending people who take my travel classes to Ulster for years and I get only rave reviews.

Here's a three-day plan that will introduce you to a capital city of 400,000 (occupied and guarded by the British army), the best open-air folk museum in Ireland, a once-prosperous and now rather sleepy beach resort and some powerful — if subtle — mountain beauty complete with villages, ancient stone walls and shepherds. At the same time you will get a firsthand look at "the Irish problem" — tragedy in an otherwise happy land.

Ulster lacks the dazzle of the Riviera but it charms more intimately. You'll meet some of the friendliest people on earth and learn first-hand about their struggle.

Pick up a map of North Ireland and Belfast at the Dublin

tourist office. Since trains leave from both cities several times a day, you could even make Belfast a day-trip from Dublin. (North Ireland is not covered by the Eurailpass. That segment of the journey costs about ten dollars each way.)

Belfast is dominated by a strange peace — and lots of police check points. The pedestrians-only "safe zone" in the city center bustles along oblivious to the problem. Many streets reek of the industrial revolution. Buildings that are a potential IRA target are protected by heavy metal screens. Religion is preached on billboards and through bullhorns. Promises of a better life through Jesus and pacing soldiers add to this strange urban stew. Only the visitor gawks at troops in bullet-proof vests. Before leaving the city center, pick up some information at the tourist office on High Street.

Enjoy the walk to Queen's University past the Town Hall with its massive exterior and impressive interior. Near the university, visit the Botanical Gardens and the Ulster Museum. The museum has some interesting traditional Irish and contemporary art and a good exhibition on the history of Ulster — from the North's perspective, of course.

Belfast is really just a busy industrial city (witness the world's largest cranes towering over the harbor). Plan to see

Belfast — barbed wire and national fire.

Belfast and get out by mid-afternoon, taking the twenty-minute bus ride to Cultra and the Ulster Folk Museum. Buses leave twice an hour from the Oxford Street Station, near the train station. Avoid Belfast at night. Unruly teenagers roam wild in the streets, and are more of a threat than the IRA.

The Ulster Folk and Transport Museum at Cultra is the best museum of its kind in Ireland, offering the closest look possible at old and traditional Irish lifestyles. Assembled in one huge park (like the open-air museums so popular in Scandinavia) are cottages and buildings from all over Ireland. Only here can you actually walk into an old schoolhouse, weaver's cottage, farmhouse — in fact, an entire old Irish village — with each structure traditionally furnished and warmed by a turf fire. Buy the guidebook, wander for three hours and you'll learn a lot about the culture of old Ireland. Any questions your guidebook doesn't answer can be answered by the man who attends each building. He'll talk about leprechauns or simply chat about the weather or photography. The neighboring Transport Museum specializes in turf sleds, horse-drawn carriages and old cars. When you've finished the museum, catch the same bus you came on and continue on into Bangor-town.

Formerly a stylish resort town, Bangor is a pleasant place to spend the evening. Take one of the bed and breakfast places ($12) right on the waterfront on Queen's Parade. I enjoyed the Roblyn House at #53. Mrs. Roblyn made certain I knew just where to find the pubs, the dancing and the outdoor gospel singing. I ended up discussing — and solving — the problems of the world with my hosts until 2:00 that morning. For an especially good look at the Irish, a touch of politics and a service you can understand, go to church on Sunday morning.

After Bangor, travel south down the Ards Peninsula alongside the Strangford Lough, a haven for migratory birds. At Portaferry take the little ferry across the bay and continue south to Castlewellen or Newcastle. You'll pass through Downpatrick where St. Patrick lies under a large but unimpressive stone.

Now you have reached the mysterious and beautiful Mourne mountains. Explore the villages and the soft, green rolling "mountains" of 3,000 feet. It's a land rich in folk history and tradition and equally rich in hospitality. Ask questions — the more you know about the Mournes, the more beautiful they become.

Newry and the border area between Ulster and the Republic of Ireland are two of the more dangerous spots, so pass quickly, heading southward to Dundalk, where a train will zip you back to Dublin.

Now you can send your family and friends a postcard announcing that you have toured North Ireland, had a blast — and survived.

London —
A Warm Look at a Cold City

I have spent more time in London than in any other European city. It lacks the grandeur of Rome, the warmth of Munich and the elegance of Paris, but it keeps drawing me back. Its history, traditions, markets, people, museums and entertainment combine to make it the complete city. The thrill just doesn't wear off.

Nobody needs to be told to see the Halls of Parliament or the Tower of London. Every visitor to London, however, could use some information that will make London a bit more intimate, less expensive and easier to enjoy.

London is huge and complex. Information is very important. *Let's Go: Britain* and Michelin's London guidebook are both great. Besides guidebooks, every visitor should have a map with bus lines, subway stops and major landmarks listed. "What's On" is a very good weekly entertainment guide to London. It's packed with up-to-date information on everything from rock concerts and the theater to "London for Children." Take full advantage of the helpful tourist information office in Victoria Station.

London is blessed with a great subway system. In such a large city, the "tube," as Londoners call their underground, is the most convenient way to get around. The tube is no longer as expensive as it used to be but, unlike the subways in Paris, the ticket prices are determined by distance traveled. Tickets start at about 50¢. If you plan to do a lot of sightseeing, consider purchasing a "Go As You Please" ticket. This ticket gives you unlimited travel on all of London's subways and buses. It's available in three-, four- or seven-day durations for $11, $17 or $22. If you are busy in London it can be a good value. A major advantage of traveling with this ticket is that you never have to brave the rush-hour ticket lines. You will probably see more of London since you have "free" rides everywhere. And, you can

245

do some joyriding on the double-decker buses (a great way to see the city). Remember, the fastest, easiest and cheapest way to get from Heathrow Airport into London is by subway. And, it is possible to buy your "Go As You Please" ticket at the airport to cover the trip into town.

Consider a one-day "Central Rover" pass and "cheap day returns" to keep your tube-ular bills down. Buses are cheaper and more scenic — but slower. Taxis are often the fastest, easiest and even cheapest way for a group of three or four people to travel. I generally enjoy a very informative and friendly conversation en route. I've never met a crabby cabbie in London.

London has been called the world's most expensive city. The best way to really keep your room and board costs down is to eat and sleep at one of London's youth hostels. While the hostels are nearly always full, it is easy to reserve a bed in advance. If I have a USA-London-USA plane ticket, I plan on

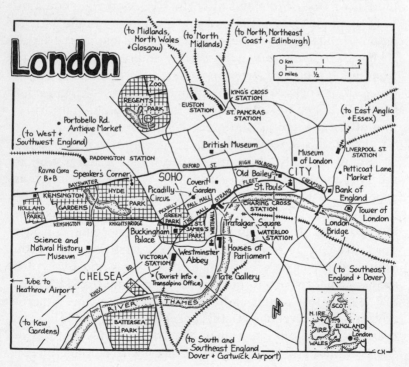

spending the last days of my trip in London. On the day I land, I pay for and reserve a spot in London's best hostel, the Holland House in Holland Park (tel. 937-0748). Then I know that, for $7 a night, I can spend the last part of my trip in a former Jacobean mansion. By cooking my own meals at the hostel or eating there in London's cheapest cafeteria, my shillings will go a very long way.

If big city hostels aren't your cup of tea, you can find many reasonable "bed and breakfasts" in the $10 to $15 per night range. Refer to your London guidebook, contact tourist information or try any of the "B & B's" on Cartwright Gardens near the Russel Square subway stop — or call my favorite, Ravna Gora near the Holland Park tube stop (tel. 727-7725).

It is very important to orient yourself in this great city. On the day you arrive, I'd advise taking the two-hour "Round London Sightseeing Tour." This is the best possible fast and cheap introduction to London. Buses leave hourly from Picadilly Circus, Marble Arch and Victoria Station. The tour is supposed to be "unescorted" but the driver usually gives a very entertaining commentary. From this double-decker bus tour you can see most of the major landmarks while getting a feel for the city.

On your first evening in London take yourself on a brief "London-by-night" walking tour. Your romantic image of London is best seen at night, when the busy 20th century gives way to quieter streets and floodlit monuments. It would be a pity to see London and not treat yourself to a golden Big Ben against a black night sky. Your walk should go from Picadilly Circus to Trafalgar Square and down Whitehall to Westminster where you can view the floodlit Halls of Parliament and "Ben" from the bridge over the Thames. With a little imagination, London will glow with this same evening charm in the days that follow. The bus tour and this London-by-night walk will provide the foundation for a very successful stay in one of the world's most exciting cities.

The list of sights in London is endless. The famous tourist attractions need no discussion here. I will mention a few parts of London that I think are particularly characteristic — yet are often overlooked by those who visit — with some ideas on how to enjoy them.

London is best seen and understood on foot. Several walking tours offer a fascinating and educational look at London. I thoroughly enjoyed the tours given by Alex and Peggy Cobban of "Discovering London." They escort several walks a day for the very reasonable price of about $3.00. "Shakespeare and the Historic Southbank," "The Great Fire and Plague," "Roman London" and "Jack the Ripper Murders" are just a few of the many walks that the Cobbans offer. Other walking tour companies include London Walks (tel. 882-2763) and Offbeat London Walks (tel. 762-7572). Check "What's On" for walking tour schedules.

London is, in many ways, a collection of villages. Even today, many of these corners of the city maintain their individuality. Chelsea is still very colorful. Often compared to Paris' Left Bank, this is London's Bohemian quarter. Soho, which lies north of Picadilly Circus, is a juicy and intoxicating combination of bustle, sleaze, markets, theater and people. It is London's Greenwich Village.

The most central square mile of London — and all of Britain — is the "City" of London. This is London's "Wall Street." You might want to take advantage of the interesting (and free) tours given at the Stock Exchange. Nearby, if you are interested in the traditional British system of justice, you can visit the Central Criminal Courts, nicknamed "Old Bailey." Powdered wigs, black capes and age-old courtesies make the public trials well worth a visit.

The Tate Gallery is a must. It has a wonderful collection of British painters (particularly Blake and Turner) and a modern collection including Picasso, Moore, Rodin, Van Gogh and nearly all the major Impressionist painters. Give yourself an art history lesson by taking one of the free tours available throughout the day.

History buffs shouldn't miss the Museum of London. It offers a very well organized chronological walk through Roman, Medieval, Renaissance and Modern London.

The British love their gardens, and their favorite is the peaceful and relaxing Kew Gardens. Cruise down the Thames or take the subway to Kew for a respite from the city and a good look at the British people. Don't miss the famous Palm House, built of glass and filled with exotic tropical plant life. A walk through this hothouse is a veritable walk through a jungle — in London.

Nearly every morning there is a market thriving somewhere in London. There are different markets for fish, fruit, antiques, clothing and plenty of other things. Petticoat Lane (miscellany, on Sunday mornings) and Portobello Road (antiques, Saturday mornings) are just a few of the many colorful markets that offer you just one more of London's many faces (but not much in the way of bargains).

After visiting Petticoat Lane's market on Sunday morning, I really enjoy an hour of craziness at Speaker's Corner in Hyde Park. By late morning there are usually several soapbox speakers, screamers, singers, communists or comics performing to the crowd of onlookers. (The Round London bus tour leaves from Speaker's Corner. If you catch it at 9:00 Sunday morning it will drop you off at 11:00 — prime time to witness the grassroots of democracy in action.) I enjoy Speaker's Corner so much that I make a special effort to be in London on a Sunday morning.

When you are in London (or elsewhere in England) you will have a great opportunity to make your own brass rubbing. The tourist information people (tel. 730-0791) can direct you to a "brass rubbing centre" where you will be taught how to make your own rubbing. You can choose from a selection of replica memorial brasses depicting knights and ladies from the distant past. You get all the necessary instruction and materials for only three or four dollars. Just cover the brass with your paper, grab your wax and rub away. In twenty minutes you'll have a meaningful souvenir that is suitable for framing.

I think one reason why I never grow tired of London is its great theater. The London visitor always has a stunning array of first-class plays to choose from. I have seen many memorable performances, including "Harvey" with Jimmy Stewart, "The King and I" with Yul Brenner, "My Fair Lady" and "A Chorus Line," just to mention a few. You get the quality of Broadway at a fraction of the cost.

Try to buy your tickets several days in advance. Avoid the $1.00 booking charge by buying your ticket at the theater rather than from a ticket office. This is easy since most of the theaters are located within a few blocks of each other in the area between Picadilly Circus and Trafalgar Square. You are more likely to get the best ticket selection by buying from the theater. I generally order one of the cheaper tickets. Most theaters aren't big enough to have bad seats. Many times I've found that the people just a row or two in front of me paid nearly twice what I did. If you don't like your seat, there are ways to improve your lot. I've been in London theaters that sound like a sifter as soon as the lights go down — the people with the cheaper seats move up, filling the unsold, more expensive seats.

If a performance is sold out (and many will be) you can nearly always get a ticket if you try. Ask the ticket salesperson how to get a "no-show ticket." It will generally involve a wait, but a few tickets are usually left unclaimed just before curtain time. You may also want to ask about the availability of "standing room only" tickets. A London play will probably cost anywhere from $5 to $15. I've chosen plays carefully, with the help of local recommendations, and have always felt that I got more entertainment than I paid for.

On Leicester Square there's a half-price-day-of-the-show ticket booth that is popular with budget tourists. I've never seen tickets to anything exciting on sale there and would happily avoid it and its savings to enjoy the play of my choice.

No visit to London would be complete without spending some time in one of London's colorful and atmospheric pubs. They are an integral part of the English culture. You'll find all kinds of pubs, each one with its own personality. My favorite is the Clarence, located on Whitehall, just a block from Trafalgar Square. Try the different beers (if you don't know what to order, ask the bartender for a half pint of his favorite), order some "pub grub," talk to the people — enjoy a "Public House." Enjoy London.

An atmospheric English public house — or "pub."

The Moors of England

The British are experts at milking every conceivable tourist attraction for all it's worth. "Land's End" is a good example. Even less worthy of your time and money are many well advertised places like "The Devil's Toenail." These private enterprises charge to park after psyching you up with many roadside announcements. After you pay to park and pay again to get through the turnstile, you hike to the bottom of the ravine to see, in this case, a rock the size of a truck tire that looks "just like the Devil's Toenail." England's moors are refreshingly untouristed.

Dartmoor is a wonderland of green and powerfully quiet, rolling hills just north of Plymouth. Crossed by only two or three main roads, most of the land is either unused or used only as a commons by the people of nearby villages. Dartmoor is best toured by car, but it can be explored by bus, thumb or on foot. The key here is to make a bed and breakfast headquarters in one of many small towns, or check into the youth hostel in Gidleigh. You'll feel like you're in one of the most remote corners of England. It's hard to believe that so many tourists so near are unaware of this inland retreat.

Dartmoor is perfect for those who dream of enjoying their own private "Stonehenge" sans barbed wire, policemen, parking lots and hordes of tourists. England is peppered with ancient stone circles and Dartmoor has several. Haytor Down and Gidleigh are especially interesting for those in search of England's mysterious ancient past.

An older Australian, doing the typical marathon Australian tour, told of the wonders that lurked just a bit deeper into the moor. Venturing in, I sank into the powerful mist-ical moorland. Ooo! Climbing over a hill, I was swallowed up. Hills followed hills followed hills — green, growing grey in the murk. Somewhere was a circle of stone 4,000 years old. You can get lost in the moor. Directions are difficult to keep. It is cold. Long-haired goats and sheep seem to gnaw on grass in their sleep. I found myself in a world of green, wind, white rocks and birds singing, but not present.

Then the stones appeared standing in a circle. They have waited for endless centuries — not moving — waiting for me to come. They still didn't move, but in stillness, they entertained. This is the way to see the puzzles left by civilizations past. Stonehenge won't quite make it.

From the Journal

The moor resists change, and Gidleigh is living proof. A castle loses itself in green overgrowth. A church grows shorter as tall weeds eat at the stone crosses and bent tablets that mark graves. A huge woman, who must be Mrs. Gidleigh herself, stands at the gate of her hostel, which is also the post office, and tells me to move my car far away. She instills fear and respect in those who come to her place; I feel lucky to get a bunk in the human half of the barn out back. The cows groan, the garden ripens and I make my bed.

From Gidleigh, I walked to a sleeping stone circle that had waited thousands of years for me to find it. Walking carefully into the empty moor, away from any roads and buildings, I found myself in a misty world all to myself that seemed to go on and on. It was a marvelous experience when the stone circle came into view. The circle was smaller than Stonehenge, but much more atmospheric.

Alone was an understatement. Sitting on a fallen stone, I let my imagination off its leash — wondering about the people who roamed England so long before written history was around to tell their story.

Grabbing the moment to write, I got out my journal, thinking about the moor, the town and this circle of stones . . .

Bath, England —
Elegant and Frivolous

Bath is the most underrated city in England — if not all of Europe. Two-hundred years ago this city of 80,000 was the Hollywood of Britain. Today the former trend-setter of Georgian England invites you to immerse yourself in its elegant (and frivolous) past — to enjoy a string trio over tea and scones. discover the antique of your dreams, and trade your jungle of stress for a stroll through the garden.

If ever a city enjoyed looking in the mirror — Bath's the one. It has more government protected buildings per capita than any town in England. The entire city is built of a warm-tone limestone it calls "Bath stone." The use of normal bricks is forbidden and Bath beams in its cover-girl complexion.

Bath is an architectural chorus-line. It's a triumph of the Georgian style, with its buildings as wrapped up in competitive elegance as the society they housed. If you look carefully you'll see false windows built in the name of balance and classical columns that supported only Georgian egos. The rich could afford to put feathered hats atop the three-foot hairdos of their women. The very rich stretched their doors and ground floors to accommodate these women. Today many families are nearly impoverished simply by the cost of peeling the soot of the last century from these tall walls.

Good-looking towns are not rare — but few combine beauty and hospitality as well as Bath. Bath makes everything easy. The town square is a quick walk from the bus and train station. (London is just a ninety minute ride away.) This square is a pincushion of tourist landmarks including the Abbey, the Roman and Medieval Baths, the royal "Pump Room" and a very helpful tourist information office.

Free walking tours leave from the square nearly every morning at 10:30. There are several guides. Some are real characters so make a quick survey and follow the most animated tour leader. These volunteers are as much a part of Bath as its architecture. A walking tour gives your visit a little more intimacy and you'll feel like you actually know a "Bather."

A good day in Bath would start with a tour of the historic baths. For two-thousand years this hot mineral water has attracted society's elite. Then enjoy a high tea with live classical music in the nearby **Pump Room** before catching the 10:30 city walking tour.

For lunch try the Crystal Palace Pub just down the street from the Abbey. A hearty meal served under rustic timbers or in the sunny courtyard will cost less than three dollars. "Pub grub" is so British it'll give you an accent. Blimey!

The afternoon should include a walk through three centuries of fashion in the Costume Museum. There's an entire room for each decade enabling you to follow the evolution of clothing styles right up to Twiggy, Charles, Princess Di and Blondie. The guided tour is excellent — full of fun facts and fascinating trivia. For instance, haven't you always wondered what the line, "Stuck a feather in his cap and called it macaroni" from "Yankee Doodle" means?

You'll find the answer (and a lot more) in Bath — the town whose narcissism is justified.

York Castle Museum — A Walk With Dickens

The York Castle Museum is the closest thing to a time-tunnel experience Europe has given me. York has much more to offer, but its museum alone makes the side trip from London worthwhile.

John Kirk (1869-1940) saw the old ways changing, and traditional bits and pieces from the past being discarded thoughtlessly. He amassed a giant collection of "bygones" at a time when they were considered junk by everyone else. The City of York converted a prison into a modern museum to house Kirk's treasures, and since the museum opened, Kirk has beamed over 18 million visitors out of the 20th century to walk through the England of Charles Dickens in York's Castle Museum.

Walls bridge centuries, and each room gives you an intimate peek into a period. Three centuries of Yorkshire interiors in the "Period Rooms" paint a cozy picture of life centered around the hearth with a peat fire warming huge brass kettles, and the aroma of fresh baked bread soaking into the heavy open-beamed ceilings.

Nearby, the Weights and Measures Gallery shows sets of standard measures since 1600. You never knew if your gold was all there without having it checked.

After walking through the evolution of romantic valentines, you can trace the development of farming, milling and brewing equipment. Early home lighting methods were fascinating, progressing from simple rush lights and candles through crude whale-oil lamps to more modern lamps and into the age of electricity. Imagine — electricity. An early electric heater has a small plaque explaining, "How to light an electric fire — switch it on!"

Musicians will enjoy many historical keyboard, brass and mechanical instruments. Everyone will enjoy the glass harmonica, a group of glass bowls you massage with wet fingers to make an eerie series of notes.

Kirkgate is the museum's most popular exhibit. As towns were being modernized in the 1930's, Dr. Kirk collected intact shops, all fully stocked, and reassembled them here. You can wander through a Lincolnshire butcher's shop, a Bath bakery, a coppersmith's shop, a toy shop and a barbershop. I never realized that the barber pole came from the days when a barber was a kind of surgeon. The pole's colors were symbolic of cutting, not hair, but skin: red for arterial blood, blue for venous blood and white for the bandage.

The original merchandise captured my attention more than the old buildings. A general store well stocked with groceries, candy, haberdashery and a sports shop with everything you'd need to fit in on a 19th century archery, cricket, skittles or tennis court. In the confectionary, you'll browse through mouth-watering "spice pigs," "togo bullets," "hum bugs" and "conversation lozenges."

York has had plenty of war in its past and that is evident as you walk through rooms and rooms of swords, centuries of firearms and many styles of armour and military uniforms.

The chronological orientation of the museum shows the progression of styles, tools and technology as people learned to cope with their world.

The costume collection walks you through the closets of the last three centuries showing each period's clothing styles incorporated into contemporary furniture and room scenes. Children of all ages are endlessly entertained by the toy collection. Dolls of the past come with porcelain heads, real hair and fine miniature clothing. You can hear the earliest baby squeak "Mama." Early games are on display including a ping pong set called "whiff-waff." Primitive steam and gas driven cars are permanently parked near ancient gravity-fed petrol pumps and an early garage.

The cells of this former prison used to house sheep thieves, Luddites (people who in 1812 revolted, trying to destroy the machines that were making their skills useless) and the famous highwayman, Dick Turpin. Now they guard dying crafts, and the visitor can browse through fascinating shops specializing in the making of combs, clogs, brushes, pipes, wheels, knives, books and candles.

When you visit England, plan on enjoying York and devoting the better part of a day to its walk into the past — the York Castle Museum.

The Romantic Road

The best way to connect the castles of the Rhine and the touristic playground of Bavaria is by traveling the unforgettable "Romantische Strasse." A car will give you complete freedom to explore this heartland of medieval Germany. The convenient Europabus tour (free with a Eurailpass) opens this door to small-town Germany to those without wheels.

The daily trip from Frankfurt to Munich, or vice versa, takes eleven hours. Four of those hours are yours to explore the fairytale towns of Rothenburg ob der Tauber and Dinklesbuhl.

This is one "back door" that is far from undiscovered. But, even with its crowds, this part of Germany is a must.

The daily 1984 schedule (March 20 — November 11) is: Wiesbaden (7:00 am) — Frankfurt (8:15) — Rothenburg (11:35 — 13:45) — Dinkelsbuhl (14:40 — 15:30) — Munich (18:55); and, in the other direction: Munich (9:00 am) — Dinkelsbuhl (12:20 — 14:15) — Rothenburg (15:15 — 17:00) — Frankfurt (19:55) — Wiesbaden (20:45). There is also a daily Fussen — Augsburg — Dinkelsbuhl — Rothenberg — Wurzburg tour (June 9 — Sept. 30). Any Frankfurt — Munich train ticket is good on this bus. Otherwise, the tour from Munich to Frankfurt costs $30 (the same as a second class train ticket). You can break your journey anywhere along the road and catch the same bus the next day. The bus company can even arrange hotel accommodations for you. Ticket reservations are free and a very good idea during peak season. Write to: Deutsche Touring GmbH, Am Romerhof 17, 6000 Frankfurt, West Germany (0611) 7903240 three days before the journey, indicating the date, journey and number of seats required.

Whenever you're traveling, it's wise to lay the groundwork for your smooth departure in advance. For instance, upon arrival in Munich (or Fussen near the castle of Neuschwanstein — see "Castle Day" Backdoor) ask at the train or tourist information office exactly where and when the bus leaves the next morning and if a reservation is advisable. Then, you'll wake up on departure morning and calmly step onto the bus that will ride you into one of the best days of your trip.

While the bus passes through many lovable little towns, the two-hour breaks in Dinkelsbuhl and Rothenburg are the day's highlights.

Dinkelsbuhl, a wonderfully preserved medieval town, is surrounded by old walls, towers and gateways. The peaceful green waters of the moat protect the many medieval jewels of architecture that lie within. You will have plenty of time for lunch at a typical restaurant (serving Frankonian specialties and Dinkelsbuhl beer) and for exploring, camera in hand, the old cobbled streets. Dinkelsbuhl celebrates the colorfully medieval Kinderfest (Children's Festival) in mid-July (see "Festival" chapter).

Back on the bus, you may have crazy Charlie Brown for a driver. I've had him for two Romantic Road tours and his act gets better and better. Wearing a black top hat and blowing his

whistle, he seems to know everyone he passes on the road. He waves and happily greets people all day long. At one point, his faithful canine friend, Snoopy, hops on the bus for a short ride. At Donauworth, as the bus crosses the Donau (Danube), Charlie slips in his cassette of "The Blue Danube Waltz." The group on board loosens up, and you have time to talk to and enjoy the other travelers and build some friendships. This isn't just any bus ride.

Rothenburg on the Tauber River is the other long stop. This is probably the most touristy town in Germany — and for

Rothenburg, Germany.

good reason. I have yet to find a better-preserved medieval town. Rothenberg is a joy even on the most crowded day. You can walk completely around the city atop the wall (best before breakfast), get lost among timeless, half-wooden gables and hear the turrets and clock towers. Rothenburg has two youth hostels, plenty of private zimmers and, of course, ample hotels, restaurants, and shops to accommodate the flood of visitors that invade each summer. Rothenburg is a good place to do your German souvenir shopping. Also enjoyable are several museums including one offering a fascinating look at medieval torture and punishment, a great puppet theater and many pleasant walks through the peaceful countryside. You may very well decide that the two-hour bus stop isn't nearly enough and break your journey here for a day or so. Those spending the night savor a fantasy of floodlit fountains and quiet cobbles.

The Romantic Road is a quick, comfortable, inexpensive and easy way to see two of Germany's most beautiful towns and one very romantic region, and the best way to connect the Rhine and Bavaria.

From the Journal

On the Romantic Road and especially just off it, where no unfamiliar car drives through unnoticed and flower boxes decorate the unseen sides of barns, I found what I came to see in Germany. Visitors can't help but exclaim, "It's so German!"

Church steeple-masts sailed seas of rich rolling farmland as I chased fragrant villages among the curves and hills. It was hard to believe that 65 million people called this Oregon State-sized country home.

At each village, ignoring the signposts, I'd ask an old woman for directions to the next town — just to hear her voice and enjoy the energy in her eyes. Thousands of tourists have passed through — few stop to chat.

Castle Day

Castles excite Americans. Since we have none in the USA, medieval castles are a popular European vacation target. From Ireland to Israel and from Sweden to Spain, Europe's endless castles await with dark nooks and dank crannies.

In Germany, the Rhine River is lined with castle-crowned hills on both sides. There is even a castle built in the middle of the river. These can be enjoyed conveniently by train, car or boat. To the south, Bavaria has many intriguing castles, including the fairytale castles of Mad King Ludwig II of Bavaria. His Neuschwanstein castle, near the town of Fussen, is straight out of Disneyland — or vice versa.

The Loire Valley is to France what the Rhine Valley is to Germany — the area with the most castles per mile. The chateau country of the Loire Valley gives you the chance to

"Mad" King Ludwig's Neuschwanstein Castle.

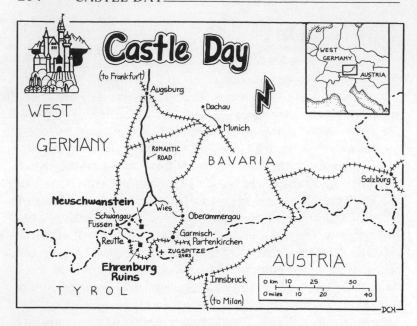

trace the development of castles, or chateaux, from the stark, defensive Middle Age castles (such as Chinon and Loches) through the "chateaux d'agrement," or pleasure castles, of the Renaissance (like Chenonceaux and Azay-le-Rideau), and the elegantly classical chateaux of the seventeenth and eighteenth centuries (Cheverny). Remember, many of these served as palaces away from home when a French King hit the road. The green Michelin guide to the Loire is a must.

Castles guard every corner of the Mediterranean. From Spain, France, Italy and Yugoslavia to the impressive Crusader castles of Rhodes and Acre, you will find a feudal fortress in every direction.

A real challenge to the castle-craving tourist is to find his own private castle, one that is accessible but without the rush of modern tourism and is still alive with winds from the past.

Europe hides countless forgotten castles unblemished by turnstiles, postcard racks and coffee shops. These are ignored by guidebooks. Just ask a local or your "zimmer-man" for a lead. My favorite is the brooding Ehrenburg ruins in Western Austria.

"Castle Day" takes you to three castles: the "modern," Disney-like Neuschwanstein castle and the much older Ehrenburg ruins.

Home-base in Fussen or the small Tyrolian town of Reutte. Reutte, situated very close to the German border is three scenic hours by train west of Innsbruck. Reutte is less crowded than Fussen and has ample accommodations, including a good youth hostel.

From Reutte, catch the early bus across the border to Fussen, the German town nearest to Neuschwanstein. Then take a local bus to King Ludwig's castle. This castle is one of Europe's most popular attractions. Get there early, line up and take the tour. The interior is enchanting. Ludwig had great taste — for a "mad king." Read up on this political misfit — a poet, hippy king in the age of "real politik." He was found dead in a lake, never to enjoy his castle dream come true. After the tour, climb further up the hill to Mary's Bridge for the best view. There is nothing quite like the crazy, yet elegant castle of Bavaria's mad king.

This is a busy day. After a lake-side picnic below Ludwig's place, catch the bus back to Reutte (you noted the time the bus returns upon arrival in Fussea) and you're ready for a completely different castle experience.

Pack a picnic and your camera and, with the help of some local directions, walk out of town to the Ehrenburg ruins. You will see two hills, one small and one larger, each crowned by a ruined castle.

The "Kleine Schloss," or small castle, is on the smaller hill. It is basically intact and wonderfully free of anything from the twentieth century — except for a great view of Reutte sleeping peacefully in the valley below.

The "Grosse Schloss," or large castle, is perched atop the biggest hill, eerily overgrown and very ruined. This is quite a hike above the small castle but worthwhile if you have time to get romantic. When I was there, a cloud shrouded the big hill, engulfing the faded castle in a spooky mist. This is especially thrilling if you've ever dreamed of medieval knights in armour, etc. You've got your own castle — let your imagination reign.

Back down in Reutte, a hearty dinner and an evening of local Tyrolian entertainment is a fitting way to end this memorable "Castle Day."

Tyrol's Ehrenburg ruins.

Kleine Scheidegg and Gimmelwald — The Heart of Switzerland

In Switzerland you will find Europe's most spectacular mountain scenery. There was a time when the only thing higher than those Alpine peaks was the prices you had to pay to see them. Switzerland has enjoyed a very low inflation rate and today it is no more expensive than its neighbors. Switzerland does suffer from tourist crowds, however, and you should keep this in mind when you choose your Swiss destination. How do you see the best of the Swiss Alps without enduring traffic jams and congested trails? The answer has two parts — Kleine Scheidegg and Gimmelwald.

Kleine Scheidegg — The Mona Lisa of Mountain Views

I had always considered Interlaken overrated. Now I understand that Interlaken is best used as a jumping-off point — it is the gateway to the Alps. No need to stop in Interlaken. Get an early start and catch the private train (not covered by your Eurailpass) to Grindelwald. Avoid the common mistake of making Grindelwald your final destination. Take advantage of its very helpful tourist information office. Browse through the expensive tourist shops, if you like. Stop at the Co-Op Grocery Store and buy what you need for a first-class mountain picnic. Then ascend into a wonderland of powerful white peaks by taking the train to Kleine Scheidegg or even higher to Mannlichen.

Now you have successfully run the gauntlet of tourist traps and have reached the ultimate. Before you towers the greatest mountain panorama that I have ever enjoyed. The

Jungfrau, the Monch and the north face of the Eiger boldly proclaim that they are the greatest. You won't argue.

Kleine Scheidegg, an hour's hike from Mannlichen, has a lodge and an outdoor restaurant. People gather here to marvel at tiny rock climbers — many of them quite dead — dangling by ropes halfway up the icy Eiger. If money is not something you are trying to conserve, you can take the ride from here to the towering Jungfraujoch. It's impressive, but I couldn't have asked for a more spectacular view than what Kleine Scheidegg gave me.

From Kleine Scheidegg, you begin your hike into the next valley, the less-touristed Lauterbrunnen Valley. The hike is not difficult. My gear consisted only of short pants, tennis shoes and a tourist brochure. If you have packed light, and all your luggage is on your back, then you have the good feeling that it doesn't really matter where you spend the night. If you left your luggage in your Interlaken hotel, today's trip must be circular;

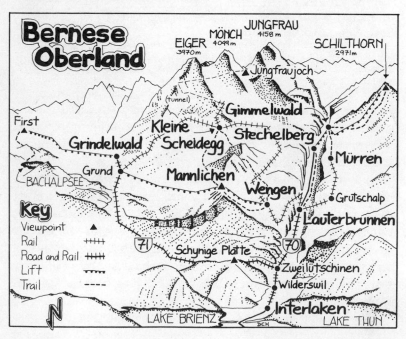

a train or bus will take you down the Lauterbrunnen Valley and back to Interlaken.

It's lunch time as you hike into your own peaceful mountain world. Find a grassy perch, and your picnic will have atmosphere that no restaurant could match. Flowers, the sun and the view all make your picnic taste "magnifique."

Continuing downhill, you may well be all alone and singing to the rhythm of your happy footsteps. As the scenery changes and new mountains replace the ones you've already seen, you enter the traffic-free town of Wengen. Avoid the steep and relatively dull hike from Wengen to Lauterbrunnen by taking the $2 train down to the valley floor. The roar of Staubbach Falls draws you near, but keep your distance. This mighty waterfall throws stones. I witnessed an unwary tourist take a bloodying blow to the head — a mistake he'll make only once.

Gimmelwald — Where Heidi Lives

The real gem of this valley is the sleepy town of Gimmelwald. Gimmelwald is a small village with more bell-ringing cows inhabiting it than people. Since it allows no cars, you'll hike into it from the town of Murren. Take the Lauterbrunnen-Grutschalp funicular — a small train — up the steep wall on the way to Murren. Murren has several good hotels, but I would recommend spending the night at Gimmelwald in its special little youth hostel. This Swiss Alp chalet is the craziest, dirtiest, loosest and friendliest hostel I've ever seen. A big Alp-happy family will instantly adopt you and fill you with spaghetti and mountain stories. Strangely, your concerns about the messy kitchen have vanished — you're high in the Alps. The hostel has a few drawbacks, but with a million-dollar view for $2 a night, it's hard to complain. I forgot all about my busy itinerary and just moved in for awhile. I learned why they say, "If heaven's not what it's cracked up to be — send me back to Gimmelwald."

For friendly — if somewhat more subdued — budget

accommodations, check out the Hotel Mittaghorn, just up the hill from the hostel. (Call Walter at 036-551658.)

From Gimmelwald you can make several hikes, or you can take the cable car to the summit of the Schilthorn. When you're ready to rejoin the rest of the world, hike down to the valley floor (or take the lift) and catch a bus back to Interlaken.

If you are interested in the heart of Switzerland, it's best seen from Kleine Scheidegg. If you're looking for Heidi and an orchestra of cow bells in a Switzerland that most people think exists only in dreams and storybooks — spend some time in Gimmelwald.

From the Journal

Climbing slowly, I came to the top of the valley wall and made my way through farms and meadows to Gimmelwald. The sun was low in the sky; it had been raining off and on. Thunder, waterfalls, birds and cow bells were the sounds I heard. Sturdy old Swiss men climbed the hills to milk their cows, and I was happy to see that I had found a Switzerland that still looked and lived the way every traveler dreams it might.

A Talk With a Swissman

If Carter and Reagan were in a boat and it sank, who would be saved? "The country." At least that's what a Swissman told me.

A traveler who doesn't talk to the local people is like a farmer who doesn't milk his cows. A local person gives you a special insight to his country. He may also show you yours from a new perspective. I can't visit Switzerland without having breakfast with Fritz Moser — he won't let me. Here is the cream of one of my conversations with Fritz, a fifty-year-old teacher from Interlaken.

What's the most common mistake made by visitors to Switzerland?

They go only where they're told — to the famous touristy places. You won't find the truth in Interlaken or Lucerne.

Where is the true Switzerland hiding?

It exists but you won't find it yodelling on a cassette tape. You must linger longer. The traditional Swiss people are not as bold as their mountains. They tense up in front of strangers. Find a small village and stay there for a few days. Soon, even the farmer's wife will remember her schoolbook English.

Where are the traditions most alive?

Without a doubt, in the old cantons of Schwyz, Uri and Appenzell. This is the "Old Switzerland," or "Urschweiz." The people still practice the ceremonial town meeting called the "Landsgeminde." Here, all the men of the community gather to vote by raising their family sword. Many men, especially in Appenzell, still wear the traditional black hat, tie and coat. Each old-timer puffs proudly on his pipe, undoubtedly "the most ornate in the valley."

How can a visitor best understand Switzerland?

You must realize how our nation has grown from three cantons (or states) to 23. Our first loyalty is to the canton, then to Switzerland. I am Bernese first, then Swiss. You will find a special mentality in each canton. Our country has four linguistic groups, German (74%) in the north and east, French (20%) in the West, Italian (4%) in the south, and Romansh (1%) in the southeast. These people think like they speak — differently.

You must also understand that we are a small nation between giants, with almost no raw materials. World War II was our natural situation in the extreme — isolation, dependence on others for natural resources, and neutrality.

What is the local opinion of the Germans?

My generation remembers World War II and for us the

German is the bad man. I know it's dangerous to generalize but I will. The Germans make a comparison and then declare, "We do this better."

Americans don't say, "We do it better." They say, "We do it this way and it's up to you to choose which is better." But the Germans say "We do it like this and this is better." There is a difference.

What is the Swiss opinion of Americans?

The general opinion is, "Americans will buy anything."

Are there too many tourists in Switzerland?

That depends on who you ask. Those who earn money from the tourists would like to see more. Most of us think we have enough tourists. Really, we have lost our country. On Sunday we stay home. The Swiss people go to other countries now.

Alps close-up from the Schilthorn, 10,000 feet.

When is Switzerland the most crowded?

In July and August. On July 14th the French go on holiday. The Germans have holidays in August. The August invasion is worst.

How would you feed and entertain a very important foreign guest?

We would go to a small town or village restaurant. Big city restaurants have lost much of the local flavor. A "country theatre" provides unbeatable local entertainment. Here, the villagers put on a traditional play or musical and it's always great fun. Remote valleys and small villages is where the Swiss savor their Swissness.

From France to Italy — Over Mt. Blanc

Loading into a tiny gondola, Ken and I were launched into our own glacial dreamworld. For forty minutes, we silently floated several miles over France's Mt. Blanc 'massif.' Hanging our heads out the window, exploring every corner of our view, we were sailors in a new sea.

Let me suggest an exciting way to cross the French-Italian border. This border crossing will take you from the best of the French Alps into a quiet and remote valley in the north of Italy: from Chamonix to the Valle d'Aosta via 12,600-foot-high Aiguille du Midi.

Chamonix is a very convenient overnight train ride from Paris (10:30 p.m. — 8:30 a.m.). As you near the town of Chamonix, you'll be staggered by the mountain wall that faces you. This is the Mont Blanc "massif" and, topping it off, is Mont Blanc itself. At 15,781 feet, it's the highest point in Europe.

Chamonix is a resort town, expensive and crowded. Most of its visitors have one thing on their minds — mountains. The town has many expensive hotels as well as several chalets offering dormitory accommodations at very reasonable prices. The youth hostel, formerly the barracks housing the diggers of the Mont Blanc Tunnel, is a good place to stay for three dollars a night.

From Chamonix there are enough hikes and cable car rides to keep you busy for a long time. If you came only to take the ultimate ride, get on the telepherique to the Aiguille du Midi. This expensive lift (about $20 round trip) is Europe's highest and most spectacular. If the weather is good, it's worth whatever they charge. (The youth hostel gives 25% discount coupons.) Afternoons tend to cloud-up so try to take the ride in the morning.

A good plan to save a little money and enjoy a hike at the same time is to buy a ticket all the way up, but only halfway back down. This gives you a chance to look down at the Alps and over at the summit of Mont Blanc from your lofty, 12,600-foot lookout. Then you descend to the halfway point where you are free to frolic in the glaciers and hike back to Chamonix at your leisure. Wear warm clothes for the trip because, even when the valley is warm and sunny, the weather on the summit is cold.

From the top you can return to Chamonix or continue over the mountain to Italy. If you decide to leave France from the Aiguille du Midi, you climb into a small, red "gondola for two" and dangle silently for forty exciting mintues high over a glacier. Slowly, you glide across the Mont Blanc "massif" to Hellbrunner Point, where you meet the Italian border guards at 11,000 feet.

The descent from Hellbrunner Point takes you into the Valle d'Aosta. This is Italy with a French accent. A dash of France and a splash of Switzerland blend with the already rich

Alps from atop the Aiguille du Midi, 12,600 feet up.

Italian flavor to create a truly special character.

Try to catch a ride with a fellow cable car passenger who has a car parked in Entreves, where you will land. Ride with him (or take a bus) to the next town, Courmayeur, or better yet, straight to the main city of the valley — Aosta.

Historic Aosta is the best place to spend the night — and maybe the next day. "The Rome of the Alps," as Aosta is called, has many Roman ruins. I enjoyed Pension Rosini (Via D'Avisa 4, tel. 44-2860). The Ulisse Restaurant at Via Ed. Aubert #58 is a popular local place with great pizza and better prices. You'll notice that on the south side of the Alps your travel dollars become more like the Italian cheese — they

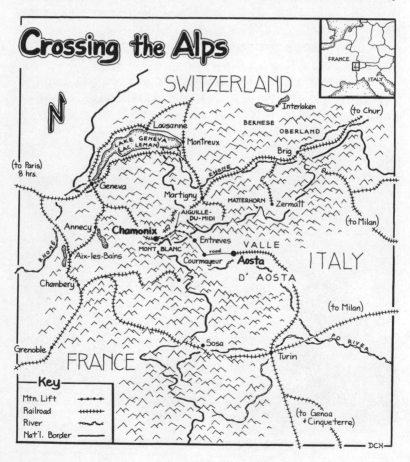

Crossing the Alps

stretch farther. From Aosta, the train will take you to Milan and the rest of Italy.

Chamonix, Aiguille du Midi, and the Valle d'Aosta — surely a high point on anyone's European vacation.

From the Journal

In the gondola, we climbed and we climbed. Chamonix shrank behind us as the trees thinned below us. Rocks sailed by, replaced by snow and ice. After nine minutes, we stopped, wandered around and caught part two of the journey. This was serious. We rose spectacularly above everything to 12,600 feet!

Ken and I were high — running around, enjoying every inch of the altitude. On the very top we looked over at Mt. Blanc, caught a glimpse of the distant Matterhorn, took pictures, squinted into the glaciers, tried to keep our fingers warm in the below-freezing weather and savored the scenery. Then, to top it all off, a class of French girls were feeling the altitude and dancing the Halfway-to-Heaven Tango. Visitors were welcome to cut in.

Just keep telling yourself, "It'll make it one more time."

Alsace — The French-Teutonic Land of Wine

The French province of Alsace stands like a flower-child referee between Germany and France. Bounded by the Rhine river and the softly rolling Vosges mountains, this is a lush land of villages, vineyards, ruined castles and an almost naive cheeriness. Wine is the primary industry, topic of conversation, dominant drink, the perfect excuse for countless festivals and a tradition that provides the foundation for the rest of the Alsatian folk culture.

Because of its location, natural wealth and naked vulnerability, too many Alsatian generations have weathered an invasion. A thousand years as a political pawn between Germany and France has given it a hybrid culture. This Gallic-Teutonic mix is seen in many ways. Restaurants serve sauerkraut with fine sauces and sausage with French bread behind half-timbered Bavarian gables. If you listen carefully you'll notice that Alsatian French is peppered with German words. Most locals who swear do so bilingually and many of the towns have German names.

Alsace's wine road or the "Route du Vin" is an asphalt ribbon tying 90 miles of vineyards, villages and feudal fortresses into an understandably popular tourist package.

Alsace's dry and sunny climate has made it a wine center since Roman days. As you drive through 30,000 acres of vineyards blanketing the hills from Marleheim to Thann you'll realize that this is really a *vinocentric* society combining time-honored traditions with unbounded love of the vine to produce some of France's finest wine.

During the October harvest season the whole Alsatian Plain erupts into a carnival of colorful folk costumes, traditional good-time music and Dionysian smiles. I felt as welcome as a local grape picker and my tight sightseeing plans became as hard to follow as a straight line.

Wine-tasting is popular throughout the year. Roadside "degustation" signs invite you into the wine "caves" where a local producer will serve you all seven Alsatian wines from dry to sweet with educational commentary if requested. "Cave-hopping" is a great way to spend an afternoon on the "Route du Vin." I generally buy a bottle of my favorite wine at each stop. The more expensive wines cost nearly $3 a bottle. Who ever thought French wine-tasting could be a poor person's sport?

The small caves are fun but be sure to tour a larger wine co-op. Beer-drinking Germans completely flattened many Alsatian towns in 1944. The small family-run vineyards of these villages were resurrected as large, modern and efficient cooperatives. Little Bennwihr has a co-op of 211 people. They are proud to show you their facilities which can crush 600 tons of grapes a day and turn out 14,000 bottles an hour. No tour finishes without taking full advantage of the tasting room. Bennwihr has a wine tradition going back to Roman times. Its

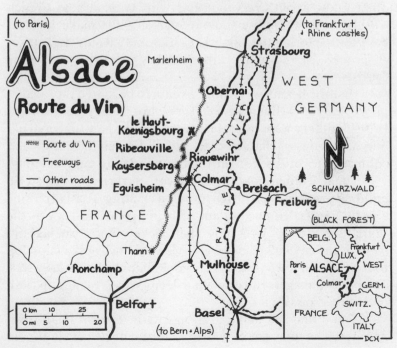

name is from the Latin "Benonis Villare" or Beno's estate —
and Beno served up a great Riesling.

If you can pick grapes you can get a job in October. For a
hard day in the vineyards you'll get room and board, $20 to $30
and an intimate Alsatian social experience lubricated liberally,
logically, by the leading local libation.

There's more to Alsace than meets the palate. Those centuries of successful wine production built prosperous and
colorful villages.

Alsatian towns are historic and unique mosaics of gables,
fountains, medieval belltowers and gateways, cheery old inns,
churches and ancient ramparts. Geared for the tourist trade
they offer plenty of budget one- and two-star hotels ($10 to $15
per double) and ample opportunity to savor the Alsatian cuisine. Colmar is the best home-base town and Riquewihr, Ober-
nai, Riveauville, Kaysersberg and Equisheim are just a few of
the storybook towns you'll be sure to enjoy.

Colmar is one of those great towns that Americans just
don't know about. Very popular with German and French
travelers, this well-preserved old town of 70,000 makes an ideal
base for exploring the villages, castles and "Route du Vin" of
Alsace. Its dry and sunny climate makes good wine and happy
tourists.

Historic beauty was a poor excuse to be spared the ravages
of World War II. But it worked for Colmar. The American and
British military were careful not to bomb the half-timbered old
burghers' houses, characteristic red and green tiled roofs and
cobbled lanes of Alsace's third largest and most enjoyable city.

Today Colmar not only survives — it thrives with historic
buildings, impressive art treasures, an exciting Alsatian cuisine
and that special French talent of being great but cozy at the
same time. School girls park their rickety horse carriages in
front of the city hall ready to give visitors a two dollar clip-clop
tour of the old town. Antique antique shops welcome browsers,
and hotel managers run down the sleepy streets to pick up fresh
breakfast croissants.

You'll find the sights of a big city in a warm small-town
package. The town got its wall in 1220 and its rich old houses in

the centuries that followed. The wonderfully restored tanners' quarters is full of tall narrow "cob-walled" dwellings. The half-timbered walls are a mix of straw and clay and the roof tops are confused and erratic, struggling to get enough sun to dry their animal skins. Nearby is "La Petite Venice" complete with canals, a pizzeria, and a handy laundrymat.

For maximum local fun remember Colmar goes crazy during its August winefest and for two weekends in September called the "Sauerkraut Days." Feasting, dancing, music and wine — Alsatian style.

Colmar combines its abundance of art with a knack for showing it off. Grunewald, Schongauer and Bartholdi all called Colmar home.

Before Frederic Bartholdi created our Statue of Liberty one hundred years ago he adorned his hometown with many fine statues. Don't miss the little Bartholdi museum offering a good look at the artist's life and some fun Statue of Liberty trivia.

Four hundred years earlier Martin Schongauer was the leading local artist. In 1473 he painted his masterpiece the "Virgin of the Rose Garden." Many travelers over-dose on the Virgin and Child theme. Give this one a chance. Looking fresh, crisp and new, it's set magnificently in a Gothic Dominican church. I sat with a dozen people silently as if at a symphony. Schongauer's Madonna performed solo on center stage, lit by 14th century stained glass, with a richness and tenderness that could only come from another age — a late-Gothic masterpiece.

The Unterlinden museum is one of my ten or twelve favorites in Europe. Housed in a 750 year old convent (formerly a center of Rhenish mysticism), it's the best collection of art and folk treasures in Alsace. Exhibits range from neolithic and Gallo-Roman archeological collections to the modern art of Monet, Renoir, Braque and Picasso. You can lose yourself in Alsatian folklore exploring the Gothic room, a Renaissance home, a 17th century Alsatian wine cellar complete with presses, barrels and tools, and an 18th century peasant's home.

The highlight of the museum is Grunewald's gripping Isenhein Altarpiece. This is actually a series of sculptures and paintings on hinges that pivot like shutters. One of the most powerful paintings ever. Stand petrified in front of it and let the agony and suffering of the crucifixion drag its gnarled fingers down your face. Just as you're about to break down and sob with those in the painting turn to the happy ending — a glorious psychedelically colorful resurrection. It's like stepping from Goya's "dark stage" right into the Yellow Submarine. We know very little about Grunewald except that, through his painting, he's played tether ball with human emotions for five hundred years.

Colmar has a helpful tourist information center providing city maps, guides and accommodations help. They can also suggest side trips around Alsace's "wine road," into Germany's Black Forest and nearby Freiburg, or even a tour of the Maginot line.

Finding a room should be easy. My favorite is Hotel-Restaurant Le Rapp, downtown at 16 Rue Berthe Molly (tel 416210). Bernard is the owner and the closest thing to the perfect French gentleman you'll ever find. He offers doubles for $10 to $15 and classy Alsatian cuisine in an elegant dining hall. Named after a hometown boy who became one of Napoleon's top generals, Le Rapp — like Colmar — is hard to beat.

Brittany

Brittany, France's scenic western tip, is Celtic not French. According to a recent Gallup poll, 80% of its people are loyal to Brittany, not France, and many of those actually want to create an independent country.

If every secessionist group in Europe had its way Europe would crumble into a pile of bickering little nations and the United Nations would have to add a new wing. While most of these groups have little chance of success, the tourist should understand that the map is not as stable and simple as your atlas indicates. The Breton struggle is just one example of the pent up nationalistic frustrations in Europe and around the world today.

Jane Danic has had the night shift in my favorite one-star Paris hotel for years. Before I can grab my key and escape to bed she reviews the past and won't let me call it a day until I'm up to date on the latest developments in the struggles of the Breton people against "French Imperialism."

"In 381 Brittany was founded by her Irish ancestors. In 845, Count Nevenhoe was chosen to lead Brittany against the French. Since his private land was on the border, it was thought that he would put up the strongest defense." As if it happened yesterday, Jane tells me, "In 1532, Queen Ann of Brittany married Charles the 8th of France on the promise that Brittany would remain independent." From the days of Napoleon until the days of Jane's youth even the word "Brittany" was illegal. Jane had to call her countr᷉   ⁷est France" or risk a stint in jail.

When asked how she would describe her people she explained, "Breton people are fighters — for the pleasure alone. They like violent sports — 90% of the young men wrestle or play football (soccer). 'Gaelic football' was outlawed by the French government. The number of broken legs was incredible! We are individuals and love to be different at any price. Even the Celtic fish look different. You can recognize a Breton

283

by his or her prominent brow and the little distance between the eyeballs and the brow."

I asked why she is called Jane and not a Celtic name. "We are forbidden Celtic names and my parents wanted no trouble. Jane is 'Chann' in Celtic or Breizh (pronounced "Braizh"). According to France, people with a Celtic first name are 'non-existing.' Now it's fashionable to have a Celtic first name and fight the French state in the international court in The Hague. One family had eight Celtic-named children. None of them 'existed.' They won their court battle and received international passports as citizens of Breizh. In our language the word for French and foreigner is the same — "Galleg."

"Even with French names our children are Bretons at heart. When asked what language they'd like to study in school, 80% answered 'mine,' meaning Celtic. The second choice was English followed by French."

When asked about the present state of the Breton movement, Jane said, "No one knows. Information is misty. Nothing is precise. We are great administrators and many important French bureaucrats and civil servants are Breton nationalists. But the movement is fragmented. Remember we like our independence and must be different so groups grow, then split. I know of at least six serious movements. There are only about 10,000 militant nationalists, the rest ask only for reasonable local autonomy — but that is a seed that can grow. We have a magazine called 'Breizh.' It's allowed because it's only 'cultural,' but if you look between the lines you can see nationalism on every page."

Jane explained that Mitterrand's recent concessions to Corsica were not good news to Breton nationalists. "He told us we cannot have the same status as Corsica. He did not say why but it doesn't matter. Corsica's so-called autonomy is a joke. The French state wants to remain united."

To get an intimate feel for Brittany as a Celtic nation, leave the coast. The Celtic culture is most pronounced inland and along the eastern border region where the struggle has accentuated the differences. Meet the people. Militant bookshops called "Breizh Livre" are gathering places for nationalists. These are usually near the church and welcome visitors. You'll find cultural guides, calendars of local festivals and plenty of Celtic friends here. The most colorful festivals are the annual "pardons." Each village honors its patron saint with a festival that starts religiously somber and formally ritualistic and grows into a wild party. The most extravagant pardons are in Treguier (mid-May), Ste. Anne d'Auray (mid-July), Perros Guirec (mid-Aug) and in Josselin (mid-Sept).

The Celtic language is heard in the winter while French is more common during the tourist months. Celtic is often spoken at home. To actually live with a local family you can stay in "Gites Ruraux" or "Maison de la Bretagne." Local tourist bureaus can direct you to these Bed and Breakfast-type accommodations.

As you visit Brittany your tourist information will direct you along the scenic and rugged coast and to the many picturesque fishing villages like St. Malo, Concarneau and Dinan. Make a point to go inland where tour buses are scarce, English menus become rare and the Celtic flavor of the local people saturates the bleak architecture, stark moors and peaceful farmland. You'll learn that France is not all French.

Brittany's Celtic people have a mind of their own.

Carcassone — Europe's Greatest Medieval Fortress

*Before me lives Carcassonne, the perfect medieval city.
Like a fish that everyone thought was extinct, somehow
Europe's greatest Romanesque fortress-city has survived the
centuries.*

*I was supposed to be gone yesterday but here I sit —
imprisoned by choice — curled in a cranny on top of the wall.
The wind blows away the sounds of today and my imagination
"medievals" me.*

*The moat is one foot over and one-hundred feet down.
Small plants and moss upholster my throne.*

Twelve-hundred years ago Charlemagne stood below that
wall with his troops — besieging the town for several years. A
cunning townsperson saved "La Cite" just as food was running
out. She fed the town's last bits of grain to the last pig and
tossed him over the wall. Charlemagne's forces, amazed that
the town still had enough food to throw fat pigs over the wall,
decided they would never succeed in starving the people out.
They ended the siege and the city was saved. Today the walls
that kept Charlemagne out open wide for visitors.

After the packed beaches and touristic merry-go-round of
the French Riviera and the intensity of Paris, Carcassonne is
like jumping into the "Herbal Essence waterfall." Located in
the unspoilt Languedoc region of southwest France near the
boring little country of Andorra, it is well-served by trains and
just off a major highway.

Carcassonne is a thirteenth-century Disneyland of towers,
turrets, and cobbled alleys. It's a castle and a walled city — a
Windsor Palace and a Rothenburg — rolled into one. If you
need cherries on top, Carcassonne offers museums, art exhibits
and concerts as well.

In my relentless quest to experience the entire spectrum of

travel styles, I spent nights in the cheapest and most expensive places within the medieval walls — the youth hostel ($3) and the Hotel de la Cite ($30). Both were great values.

The new and perfectly central hostel had plenty of room when I arrived at 10:00 P.M. in mid-July. I shared a room with a 55-year-old Australian who gave me tea and raisins, and a 30-year-old German who approved of my "Nuclear Power — No Thanks" pin (a good idea these days for those flying the American flag on their luggage).

After breakfast (one dollar with unlimited coffee and company from around the world) the hostel warden carefully made sure I knew how to enjoy Carcassonne to the fullest.

It was tough to leave but I decided that, "in the name of research," I'd check into Carcassonne's best hotel, the Hotel de la Cite — where $30 buys Old World ecstasy. This was a small price to pay to be king for a day. Each room was different but all were royal. The place had a special warmth — the lamps weren't bolted to the tables. There was no T.V., I just pulled my chair up to the window and dreamed at the floodlit castle. I saw at least two musketeers.

In general European tourism is down and, unless you go

to the most touristy places at the most touristy times or insist on a specific popular hotel, reservations shouldn't be necessary. I booked into this hotel (like most of my hotels) without reservations. This was in mid-July, when I'm told, "All of France is on vacation and things are impossible."

Your dinner expenses are up to you. I spent $22 for a lavish feast in the romanesque dining hall of the hotel one night and $2 for ravioli, melon, bread and tea at the hostel the night before. Restaurant meals in Carcassonne range from $4 to $30. And, of course, there are the peasants who munch bread, cheese and wine among the ramparts, while tossing crumbs to moat-birds and thinking of Charlemagne.

Versailles —
Europe's Palace of Palaces

Versailles is the Palace of Palaces. If you visit only one palace in Europe — make it Versailles.

The home of France's most splendid "divine monarchs" is an easy one-dollar 12-mile train ride from downtown Paris.

Louis XIV built Versailles. He was the epitome of an absolute monarch, a deputy of God, and the trend-setter for European royalty to follow. He was, in his opinion, the King of Kings. Many great European palaces were obvious attempts to match the unmatchable splendor of Versailles.

To appreciate Versailles give yourself a pre-trip history lesson. Versailles is just one busy century of French history, from 1682-1789. Some background in Greek mythology will be helpful in appreciating the palace art since much of it tells symbolic stories of Zeus and his Olympian family. Louis XIV called himself the "Sun King." Apollo was also the Sun King. The art style of the palace is baroque, controlled exuberance. You'll find much of that exuberance just barely controlled on the ceilings in magnificent paintings — most dealing with mythological subjects. The triumph of Hercules was a painted illustration of the King's power.

For an expert's opinion, I interviewed a palace historian and guide. She recommended this basic strategy. Buy a guidebook at the entrance. The small two dollar book is fine. A book is important because you're on your own to explore most of the palace. The book will give you plenty of information on the state rooms and the Hall of Mirrors. The King's Rooms are a must and are shown only with a special guided tour that you can pick up inside the palace. Be sure to see the more intimate Queen's apartments and the Royal Opera as well.

My guide was quick to answer my questions about the tourists' most common mistakes: "They go too fast. They aren't prepared. And they don't know how to look. Forget about the present — really see things by losing yourself in the history. Soak it in. Soak in it. Be influenced. Be sensitive to what pleases you. Too many people walk through the palace reading their guide book — they forget to look! Sit outside, read the book, then enter and look — absorb."

The guides are historians and educators. My guide told me, "We are not merely people who have learned what to say in each room. When the people are really interested we are very happy and can enjoy the tour. English and American visitors are our favorites. They really get excited about Versailles — and so do we."

The grounds surrounding Versailles are a sculptured forest, a king's playground. Explore the backyard. Marie Antoinette's little hamlet (le Hameau) will give any historian or romantic goosebumps. This is where the queen (who eventually laid her head under the "national razor" during the Revolution) would escape the rigors of palace life and pretend she was a peasant girl, tending her manicured garden and her perfumed sheep. She was sort of a "back-to-basics" queen.

Versailles can have horrifying crowd problems. I've survived waking nightmares when tour bus crowds crushed in and

If you're not careful, you'll be at the end of this line — Versailles.

Marie Antoinette's little Hamlet, Versailles.

hysteria broke out. People were screaming, separated forcibly from their children — and not enjoying Versailles. It made a pre-Rolling Stones concert crowd look like monks in a lunch line. The palace is packed on Tuesdays when most Parisian museums are closed. Versailles is closed on Mondays. Thursdays and Fridays are best. Beat the crowds by arriving before the 9:45 opening time. It is easiest to reach Versailles by taking the train from the les Invalides station in Paris to Versailles R.G., the end of the line. The palace is just three blocks from the station. Bring a picnic.

You'll understand why they call Versailles the "Palace of Palaces" and Louis the "Sun King."

France by Car

Take a week in the French countryside with a rental car and a couple hundred dollars. You'll thank yourself. I lived a month in ten days with a little rented Fiat. What I learned couldn't be taught in a classroom. Intensified living and cultural broadening — that's travel. The sights of France are well covered in the guidebooks. Let me just relay some tips that will make your visit easier, cheaper, and more fun.

Driving from Paris to Avignon is as tricky as driving from Seattle to Portland. France is laced with super highways differing from ours only in that they charge tolls and the average speed is 80 mph. The country roads are a breeze but city driving can be an "ache de la head." Traffic on the right gets priority. The freeway's left lane is used strictly for passing.

When navigating through cities I stow the map and follow the signs. "Centre Ville" means to the town "centre" and "Toutes Directions" means anywhere else. For starters, that's all you need. Park near the city square (usually under the church's spire) where you'll find the helpful tourist information office. Don't be timid about parking. Observe. If everyone seems to be ignoring regulations — follow suit.

From 12:00-2:00 everyone is lunching, most sights and shops are closed and the roads are quiet. This is when I put a sandwich and a hundred miles under my belt. For the same reasons, evenings are also a good time to travel. Even in mid-July evening room-finding was easy with the obvious exceptions of touristy towns like Nice and St. Tropez.

My car, the cheapest on the list, cost about $200 per week with unlimited mileage. Large companies charge more but allow you to drop the car at any of their French offices. Not knowing where I'd be after ten days, I enjoyed this flexibility. Be sure to pay extra for zero deductible (CDW) insurance. Without it one dent could cost you $400. With it you can drive more European (aggressive) — and probably safer. Ask your travel agent for car rental specifics.

If Marco Polo was alive today he'd take advantage of Michelin's yellow maps (1/200,000 for $1) and their Green Guides ($8) to each part of France. English editions are available in the USA for more, in France for less.

Most American travelers think the French are rude. Many leave France feeling like the "Elephant Man" — uncomfortable. Those who look for rudeness have no trouble finding it. If you're militantly polite, fanatically optimistic and leave your Yankee-panky home you'll become one of the lucky elite who enjoy France AND its people.

Learn the polite phrases. Overuse them and smile a lot. Try to speak French. English has become the world's "lingua franca" and the French don't like it. It's true that many French refuse to understand anything short of perfect French. A "Maurice Chevalier accent" will work wonders and "thing-a-ma-jigs" are called "le truc" or "le machin."

Don't treat the French as objects. Be human, genuinely interested. Their bureaucracy can be frustrating, especially when the problem's compounded by "la barrier de language." Get personal, make a friend and the bureaucracy often melts away. "Liberty, Equality and Fraternity" is more than a dusty slogan to the people of France.

The French take a good meal seriously. The miserable sandwiches you'll find in kiosks everywhere are a soggy punishment for not eating properly. A French phrasebook and a guide to restaurants like, Michelin's Red Guide, are handy tools for those planning to sample France's high cuisine.

Truck stops around the world are good eateries. If you're running on empty in France remember that restaurants displaying the "Relais Routier" plaque have been approved by the French truck drivers' union.

Traveling allows two cultures to lay naked side by side. Differences are unveiled, often creating problems. Learning overcomes these problems. Exploring France on your own, you'll learn that their comma looks like our decimal point and their decimal point has a tail. (A dollar and a half is 1,50 and there are 5.280 feet in a mile.) You can buy postage stamps at a "Tabac" shop but they shouldn't be trusted for exact postal rates. If you don't like the long hard pillow-log ("un traversin") on your hotel bed, you can usually find our softer kind ("un oreiller") in the closet. I also learned that French pharmacists are first aid experts who dole out advice as well as medicine. Most minor medical problems are handled at the pharmacy, without a doctor.

Polite Paris

Let's explore this "mean Parisian" problem.

The French, as a culture, are pouting. They used to be the "creme de la creme," the definition of high class. Their language was the "lingua franca" — everyone seemed to speak, or want to speak, French. There was a time when the Tsar of Russia and his family actually spoke better French than they did Russian. Those were glorious days for the French.

Today they are reeling, lashed by Levis, crushed by the Big Mac of American culture and depressed by a wet noodle economy. Their franc has lost half its value against the U.S. dollar in the last four years. Last year the French government had to drastically limit the amount of money its people could take out of the country, which ended many French dreams of international vacations.

Understand that most of us see Paris in the height of hot busy summer when the Parisians see their home town flooded with insensitive foreigners who butcher their language and put ketchup on their meat. That's tough to take smiling.

If you expect rude coldness in Paris, you'll find it. I don't believe Paris is made up of millions of mean people. If you look for warmth and friendliness, you'll find it. I refuse to recognize anything as inexcusably bad. At worst, the Parisians I meet are people struggling to be human in an oppressively large city that used to rule the world culturally. It's tough adjusting to a lesser position on our planet's totem pole of aggressive cultures.

Have fun with the French.

French Cuisine

Cultures express themselves differently around the world. Switzerland is savored in the mountains. Music is Austria's forte and Italy immerses you in great art. Japan tunes you in to the beauties of sensuality and simplicity, and France is the world's great taste treat.

A visitor to the Alps needs a book of hikes. Those going to Italy will find an art history book handy. And, if you're going to France, you should have a list of regional culinary specialties. While this chapter may not be great writing, I'm sure it's tastier than anything I've written so far.

Here is a check list of each region's most exciting dishes, cheese and wines. Consider each item a local art form that should be experienced during your visit.

Provence (The Rhone Valley) and the Cote d'Azur (French Riviera) are famous for Bouillabaise, a fish and shellfish stew in white wine, garlic, saffron and olive oil. Other popular dishes include the onion and anchovy tart with black olives called Pissaladiere; a tomato, pepper, onion, garlic and eggplant stew served hot or cold called Ratatouille; and Brandade de Morue, a blend of pureed fish with olive oil and spices. Banon cheese is made locally from goat or cow milk. (Try it, ewe like it.) A popular sweet is Nougat, made from sugar and almonds. The most important regional wines to sample are Cotes de Provence (rose), Tavel (rose), Cotes du Rhone (red, rose or white), and Chateauneuf du Pape (red or white).

The Basque country, straddling the French-Spanish border on the Atlantic coast eats, speaks, and lives its own way. The "Poulet Basquaise," chicken in a hot pepper sauce, and the Jambon de Bayonne, a raw, slightly salty ham are local specialties, as are duck and goose pates. The Basques are proud of their Fromage de Pyrenees, made from cow's milk, and their popular local wine, Jurancon.

In Bordeaux, of course, you have fine local wines and truffles. Also, try Entrecote Bordelaise, a rib-eye steak in a

mushroom, red wine, shallots and local marrow sauce. North of Bordeaux is Cognac. You know what to drink there.

In Bourgogne, southeast of Paris, you'll picnic in class with escargots (snails), Foie Gras (goose liver pate with truffles), Burgundy wines, and of course, hot Dijon mustard.

After a long day of chasing chateaux on the Loire, find a cozy restaurant and treat yourself to Andouilles, a spicy tripe sausage (don't look tripe up in the dictionary, just eat it), Anguilles (eels), a Tarte Fromagere (cheese tart) and macaroons for dessert. The Loire is famous for its wines. Try Vouvray, Muscadet and Sancerre.

In the French Alps and Savoie, Fondue and Raclette are two melted cheese specialties. Arbois-Jaune is the wine to try.

In Normandy, the adventurous glutton will want to try Tripes "a La Mode de Caen" (tripe cooked in the oven with calve's feet, vegetables and apple brandy) — a meal in itself. The more timid tasters are sure to enjoy crepes here and the locals wash these tasty thin pancakes down with cider (usually alcoholic). Before turning in have a glass of Calvados, a very powerful apple brandy.

In Brittany sample the seafood, shellfood and "Far," a sweet cake made with prunes and brandy. Crepes are also popular here. Purists go for "crepe beurre et sucre"(just butter and sugar).

In the north of France, the people eat a slimy sausage called "Ouillette" and "Frites/Moules"(French fries and mussels). Wash everything down with local beer.

Alsace, on the German border, has an exciting cuisine of its own. Many dishes have a German twist, like Choucroute Garnie (sauerkraut with ham, bacon and sausage). Try the onion tart and the rhubarb tart as well as the powerful munster cheese. Alsatian wine is world famous. Explore the "Wine Road" and taste them all. I like the Gewurztraminer and the Riesling.

In nearby Lorraine, real men eat quiche. The people of Lorraine turn small yellow plums into a dandy brandy (Mirabelle) and a tart tart (Tarte aux Mirabelles).

To the west is Champagne (and plenty of it) and even further west is Paris, famous for its onion soup and Brie cheese.

This "list" is far from complete, but it's a good start. Remember, the French eat lunch from 12 to 2 and so should you. In evening time, eight to nine is the time to dine. Tips are included in the price unless otherwise indicated (service non-compris), and you call a waiter with a polite "garcon s'il vous plait," or "mademoiselle." To ask for the bill, just scribble on your palm with an imaginary pencil and ask "l'addition?"

The Michelin Red Guide is the ultimate guide to French restaurants, and the most serious Francofoodophiles don't leave home without it. Any restaurant displaying a "Relais Routiers" recommendation is an excellent choice.

With more than eight francs in a dollar, now is an excellent time to eat your way through France. Bon appetit!

Oslo

Oslo is fresh, not too big, surrounded by forests, near mountains and on a fjord. Oslo's charm doesn't stop there. Norway's largest city, capital and cultural hub is a smorgasbord of history, sights, art and Nordic fun. An exciting cluster of sights is just a fifteen-minute ferry ride from the City Hall. The Bygdoy area reflects the Norwegian mastery of the sea. Some of Scandinavia's best preserved Viking ships are on display here. Rape, pillage, and — yah sure ya betcha — plunder was the rage a thousand years ago in Norway. There was a time when much of a frightened Western Europe closed every prayer with "and deliver us from the Vikings." Gazing up at the prow of one of those sleek time-stained vessels, I could imagine the thrill and the horror of those raids.

Nearby, Thor Heyerdahl's balsa raft, the Kon-Tiki and the polar ship Fram exhibit Viking energy channeled in more productive directions. The Fram, serving both Nansen and Amundsen, ventured further north and south than any other ship.

Just a harpoon-toss away is Oslo's open-air "Folkemuseum." The Scandinavians were leaders in the development of these cultural parks that are so popular around Europe now. 150 historic log cabins and buildings from every corner of the country are gathered together in this huge folk museum. Many houses have a person in local dress who's happy to answer questions about traditional life in that part of Norway. Don't miss the 1100-year-old Gol stave church. Each of the Scandinavian capitals has a similar open-air folk museum.

Downtown Oslo is dominated by its avant-garde city hall. The Norwegians are justifiably proud of their "Radhuset." Built 35 years ago, it was a collective effort of Norway's greatest artists and designers. Take a tour of the interior. Over 2,000 square yards of bold colorful murals are a journey through the collective mind of modern Norway.

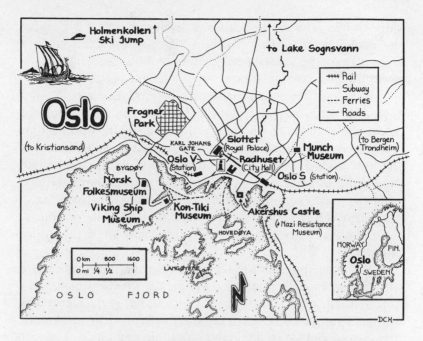

Norway has given the world two great modern artists, Edvard Munch and Gustav Vigeland. After visiting Oslo, many tourists become Vigeland fans — or even "Munchies." Frogner Park, behind the royal palace, features 150 bronze and granite sculpture groups representing 30 years of Vigeland creativity. The centerpiece of this Nordic sculpture garden is the impressive 60-foot tall tangle of bodies known as the "Monolith of Life." This and the nearby Vigeland museum are musts on any list of Oslo sights.

Oslo's Munch museum is one of Europe's most enjoyable art galleries. Like Amsterdam's Van Gogh museum, the Munch museum is small, displaying an impressive collection of one man's work rather than stoning your powers of absorption with art by countless artists from countless periods. You leave the Munch museum with a smile, feeling like you've really learned something about one artist, his culture and his particular artistic "ism" — Expessionism. Don't miss "The Scream" which captures the fright many feel as the human "race" does just that.

You can explore 700 years of local history in Oslo's Akershus Castle. The castle houses a fascinating Nazi resistance museum. The "Freedom Museum" shows how one country's spirit cannot be crushed regardless of how thoroughly it is occupied by a foreign power. Well worth a visit. Oslo has been called Europe's most expensive city. I'll buy that. Life on a budget is possible only if you have plenty of information and take advantage of money-saving options that are available. Arthur Frommer's *Scandinavia on $25 a Day* is the best book for this region. Remember, budget tricks like picnicking and sleeping in dormitory-type accommodations offer the most exciting savings in the most expensive cities — like Oslo. Oslo is more expensive because you get more. Second-class Norwegian-style is first-class in many other countries.

Language problems are few. The Norwegians speak more and better English than any people on the Continent. My cousin attends the University of Oslo. In her language studies she had to stipulate: English or American. She learned American — and can slang me under the table any day.

Stalking Stockholm

If I had to call one European city "home" it would be Stockholm. Green, clean, efficient and surrounded by as much water as land, Sweden's capital is under-rated, landing just above Bordeaux, Brussels and Bucharest on many tourist checklists.

While progressive and frighteningly futuristic, Stockholm respects its heritage. Throughout the summer mounted bands parade daily through the heart of town to the royal palace announcing the changing of the guard and turning even the most dignified tourist into a scampering kid. The Gamla Stan (Old Town) celebrates the Midsummer festivities (June 21, 22) with the down-home vigor of a rural village, forgetting that it's the core of a gleaming twentieth-century metropolis. Stockholm grabs the future but clings to its past.

Stockholm is a place to "do" as well as see.

The culture and vitality of Sweden is best felt at Skansen, an island park of traditional and historic houses, schools and churches transplanted from every corner of the country, live folk music, dancing, pop concerts, a zoo, restaurants, peasant-craft workshops and endless amusements — a smorgasbord of cultural thrills enjoyed by tourists and locals alike. To call Skansen "Europe's Disneyland" is an understatement.

Nearby is the Wasa, the royal flagship that sank ten minutes into her maiden voyage, 350 years ago. While not a good example of Viking seaworthiness, the Wasa is incredibly intact in her super-humidified display house and a highlight on any sailor's itinerary.

The "Carl Milles Garten" is a striking display of Sweden's favorite sculptor's work. Strong, pure, expressive and Nordic, Milles' individual style takes even the most uninterested by surprise. Hanging on a cliff over-looking the city, this sculpture park is perfect for a picnic.

A sauna is Sweden's answer to support hose and a face lift. It's as important as a smorgasbord in your Swedish experience.

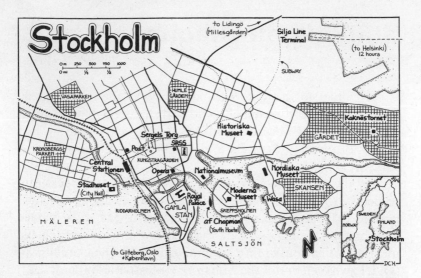

"Simmer down" with the local students, retired folks and busy executives. Try to cook as calmly as the Swedes. Just before bursting, go into the shower room. There's no "luke cold" and the "trickle down theory" doesn't apply — only one button bringing a Niagara of liquid ice. Suddenly your shower stall becomes the Cape Canaveral launch pad and your body scatters to every corner of the universe. A moment later you're back together. Rejoining the Swedes in the cooker, this time with their relaxed confidence, you now know that exhilaration is just around the corner. Only very rarely will you feel so good.

Consider a few side trips from Stockholm. Just a subway-ride away is Farsta, a trip into the future — if many urban planners get their way. You arise in the hub of this ultra-ordered suburb. Apartment complexes circle you in careful formation. Department stores, parks, transportation facilities and schools are placed conveniently and all the people know just where to go — like worms after the rain. It makes you wonder if such scientific packaging is the only answer as our continually more advanced society deals with ever-larger crowds.

While most visitors make sidetrips to the enjoyable but overrated towns of Upsalla and Sigtuna, a quick visit to Helsinki is more exciting. Finland's capital, just an overnight boat-ride away, is Scandinavian only by geography. Its language is completely unrelated, and culturally there's nothing "yah sure ya betcha" about Finland.

Getting to Helsinki is a joy. The daily or nightly ships ($20 or free with a Eurailpass) feature lavish smorgasbords, dancing and the most enchanting island scenery in Europe.

Stockholm's floating youth hostel.

Eastern Europe

Europe has an eastern half — a whole different world filled with 120 million people and as much culture as the West. Most tourists get within two or three hours of the East — but few venture in. Those who do find a uniquely modern side to Europe and, in some places, more old Europe than they dreamed possible.

Eastern Europe is a challenge to the independent Western tourist. The bold price list behind my hotel's reception desk put me into the "capitalist" category — paying more than "socialist" guests and getting less respect. German is the handiest second language, spoken to some extent by most who were in school during the Nazi years. English is the language of the young educated people who thirst for exposure to Western thoughts. Everyone learns Russian but no one speaks it. Individuality is a vice and the masses matter most. That translates to service first to group tourism and leftovers at best to the single adventurer. If I was a Bulgarian hotel clerk you would be a temptation, a language problem and a hassle to me and your business means nothing. I wouldn't work to accommodate you.

Fear permeates this society where children are bribed to inform on their parents and the government has its clumsy fingers on everything. The only rock concert of the year conflicts with the Easter church service, and to get meat for a visitor a woman will stand in line half a day and still pay a local fortune for a lousy sausage. ("The biggest animal in the world is a Bulgarian pig. Its body is in Moscow and its head is in Bulgaria.")

Travel in Eastern Europe is a package deal with rewards and pitfalls. The wonders of 120 million people making do as part of a huge mercantilistic Soviet world can't help but impress and forever broaden the visitor. You'll find an incredible strength and warmth surviving under a crust of fearful subservience when you explore East Europe.

The East is as rich culturally as Europe's West. It's much less flashy and, frankly, less appealing to the average American tourist. The new society is almost by definition dreary, gray and stone-faced. Officially, niceties are "bourgeois" frivolities to be enjoyed only by officials. Only people on society's lowest rung can be openly warm and close to a Western visitor. I was told, "They have nothing more to lose."

Americans have a hard time believing that foreign mail is screened and spies actually follow tourists around. It happens all the time. I won't let this chapter degenerate into a spy thriller, but on several occasions I've had local friends point out the same lurking spy day after day.

A visit to Eastern Europe requires patience and flexibility. You can travel freely through most of these countries staying where you like and doing pretty much exactly as you please. Most of these countries require a visa and have a minimum daily expenditure requirement. These policies change with the political tide so check with your travel agent before departing. Visas can be purchased in the USA, in any European capital (it can take a couple of days) or often at the border. Local tourist information is basically propoganda — designed to steer you into areas each government would like you to see. Be sure to take in a guide book from the West — one with the guts to tell you how to function and not be manipulated.

I've always felt completely safe in Eastern Europe, the risk and consequences of any cultural exchange is willingly borne by the subjects of these governments. A lunch with you is a fresh mountain stream flushing the communist cobwebs out of a mind struggling to remain free.

Demographically, Eastern Europe is a mess. There is no homogeneous country. Political, racial and linguistic boundaries only vaguely resemble each other, but the related problems have taken a back seat to new ones since the Soviet army "liberated" these people from the Nazis in 1945. Every city in every Warsaw Pact country will have a central monument glorifying the current rulers of Eastern Europe.

As you travel through Eastern Europe try to find the most remote villages and regions. The same places that most successfully resist the modern world have been least affected by the current government. Any country has far reaches where life goes on and, to these people, the governmental tune is always the same — only the musicians change. Visit a university and make yourself approachable. I did and found myself being interviewed for a campus newspaper article. Approach very young and very old people and those on society's bottom rung. These folks are not worried about social acceptance. Break the ice. We are fairytale people living in a skyscraper world speeding to a Hollywood beat and unknowing victims of our passionate materialism. Locals will look at you and wonder about the sexual revolution, drive-in restaurants, and how we can go anywhere if our whole world is "private property."

Ignored Bulgaria

Have you ever been to Bulgaria? Known a Bulgarian? Received a letter from Bulgaria or ever known someone who's been to Bulgaria? Why not? There are five million Bulgarian people all struggling to be happy just like you and me.

I stumbled into Bulgaria and returned each summer for the next five years. It grabs you in a strange melodramatic happy/sad way. The most subservient people of Eastern Europe, mind-clutched by Mother Russia, and saddled with a bureaucracy that makes my post office line seem speedy, welcome the Western visitor with curious glances.

Most people see Bulgaria from the window of the Istanbul Express. They pay $25 for a transit visa and transit. A tourist visa is free, requiring you to stay at least three days and spend $10 per day. Take time to smell this country's breath. As a tourist, you'll experience the same frustrations that Bulgarians do as citizens. You'll see firsthand a society that looks East and dreams West.

Sofia is the Paris of Eastern Europe. A quiet capital of monuments, huge churches and wide yellow-cobbled boulevards. The streets just separate the sidewalks. There aren't many cars.

Sofia is the "big time" in Bulgaria. Notice the fashions, the style of this society's elite, browse through the department stores, sip coffee in the most elegant cafe you can find. Wander through the university. Listen to the men talking sports in the park and notice gypsies and country people gawking just like you. Under the big red star lies George Dimitrov, the local Lenin, pudgy and waxed under glass and open to visitors most days.

Plovdiv, Bulgaria's most historic town, is just a two hour train ride away. The stark "Stalin Gothic" of Sofia takes a back seat to mellow wooden balconies drooping over coarse cobbled streets. Plovdiv is cozy. Its computerized fountain pulsates to the beat of watered-down pop music as the young gather around doing their gangly best to be decadent. The center of town is a walking mall. People browse silently, talk in hushed tones, and vicariously enjoy impossible luxury goods in window displays. It's a sad society of healthy birds — with clipped wings.

Take a bus ride into the hills. Find the farms and villages where people are closer to the earth and the government fades. Restaurants fill with rough hewn lumber-jack types, smoke and folk music. This bawdy brew is a Breugal painting come to life. In the countryside you walk with dancing bears, clap to gypsy bands and find people more relaxed, open and easy-going. For vacation Bulgarians are dumped into a funnel and land on the Black Sea coast. Each socialist country has its premier resort area and none can hold a candle to the resorts of the West. As a visitor, you are interested in the country and not its escape. Skip the beach.

Gubrovo is a Bulgarian Knott's Berry Farm offering the best peek into what's left of the rich local folk culture. Here the folk crafts are honored as endangered species and the visitor is free to wander, observe, learn, and, of course, buy.

Every culture has its comic scapegoats. Indians laugh at the Sikhs, Americans poke fun at Poles, and Norwegians at Swedes (for good reason). Bulgarians joke about stupid, cheapskate Gubrovians, who, to save money on sweeps, let a cat down the chimney. ("Where is your wedding ring?" "My wife is wearing it this week.")

Without a local friend most of Bulgaria will be misunderstood. You are a precious window to the West and if you're approachable you'll never be lonely. People will stalk you for hours to establish a friendship. They collect Western comic books and rock albums, listen regularly to the Voice of America and hope only to play this game of freedom in their minds. Many Bulgarians have been to London so many times in their dreams that they talk about it like they once lived there. But they know a trip to the West can only be a fantasy.

While Americans would make lousy pawns, it is a valuable experience to spend a few days in a land where there is no alternative. Bulgaria is a battleground of old and new, East and West, full of people handling life's dilemmas realistically in a land of denial.

Moscow After Dark

In a Moscow bakery a stranger tenderly tucked a small wad of folded paper into my hand and vanished. Thrilled, I hid my hand in my pocket. Later, I read the note . . .

"I am a student and young artist. I want to meet you and speak with you. Our meeting will be interesting for you and for me. We must learn each other best. I'll wait you tonight near old church on the bench at 22:00 o'clock. I ask you don't show this paper russian peoples because many peoples (they work in hotel, maybe driver or guide . . .) serve in police, and police don't allow us to speak with you because it is the 'influence of West.' And they do all bad things with purpose to prevent meetings soviet and foreign peoples. They say you that all young soviet peoples, which want to meet you are very bad and dangerous for you. But it is not truth. I ask you don't come with many friends because police notice at once us and it will be very badly for me. You can come with one or two friends. I'll tell you about what you want to know. We'll have a good time I am sure. Please, believe me. (My little friend gave you this paper, maybe I.)"

When taking a tour of Russia it's refreshing to talk to a rebel — someone not programmed to paint a rosy-red picture of the USSR. If you're interested in a stimulating discussion of contemporary issues and problems, stray from your tour flock. Your keys to freedom from the group are local money and a city map. Away from your group the locals will find you much more approachable.

To the local man on the street you are a walking dream — a mystery. Most will ignore this forbidden fruit but many will seek you out. Just to talk of Western things is, to many Russians, the next best thing to being there. I'll never forget the Russians discreetly filling my ear with juicy bits of the "free world" as they shuffled off a city bus. One woman delicately whispered "Led Zeppelin" and at the next stop a uniformed

man muttered "free love." They were visibly thrilled by their
ability to be decadent.

I went to church at 10:00 and out from the onion-domed
shadow stepped Victor. He had adrenalin-perked eyes and
politics on his breath. He said it's safer if we walk. In Russia, two
people meeting without authorization is an "illegal assembly."
We walked . . . and talked.

Victor witnessed to me, powered by a born-again determi-
nation to keep his mind unshackled. He was frustrated by the
Western world's insensitivity to and misunderstanding of the
plight of the muted people of the USSR. Victor had lots to say
including these quotes: "The government is against religion but
has made Lenin into a Jesus Christ to the Russian people. The
next war will not be between the USA and the USSR, but
between China and Russia. What the government says, the
Chinese do. The Russian people just live and die. Anyone who
is loud is made quiet by the police. Our national newspaper,
Pravda (which means 'truth'), is a collection of lies. Thinking
Russians listen to the Voice of America. This conversation is
dangerous for me but not you. If I am informed on, the police
will wait. But someday soon I will disappear."

People's Art, USSR
It's not all propaganda.

South Spain

When people head south from Madrid, it's generally with Granada, Cordoba, Seville or the Costa del Sol in mind. These three cities have lots to offer — as big cities. The Costa del Sol, in my mind, is a concrete nightmare, worthwhile only as a bad example. The most Spanish thing about the south coast is the sunshine — but that's everywhere. For something different and a bit more authentic, try exploring the interior of Andalusia. Make this an exercise in going where no tourist ever went.

I spent several days driving rather aimlessly from town to village on the back roads of Southern Spain, enjoying a wonderfully untouched Spanish culture. All you need is time, a car and a willingness to follow your nose, winning some and losing some. My goal was to elude the tourist centers so common in this part of Europe. In doing so, I realized that the farther from the tourist trade you get, the more difficult it is to find basic tourist needs like room and board. I found some great towns and learned some valuable lessons.

Good information on Andalusia is as rare as it is important — very. While the tourist centers enjoy plenty of information, there just isn't much written about the towns of the interior. This area is unvisited, so there aren't a lot of facilities for tourists. The Michelin Guide, which is usually invaluable, skips the Andalusian countryside. Get the best map you can find, look for locally printed books as you're traveling and ask the people you meet for touring suggestions.

Accommodations in these remote parts are meager. Use a middle-sized town as a base to do your village-hopping. Spain has a very carefully controlled hotel industry. Each establishment is rated by the government and displays its classification on a blue plaque near the door. The categories are, in roughly descending order of luxury and price, H (hotel), HS (hostal), HsR (hostal-residencia), P (pension), CH (casa de huespuedes), and F (fonda). Hotels and hostales are further distinguished by ratings of one to five stars (five being best). While prices correspond to the blue plaque, standards of cleanliness and comfort may vary. It is not uncommon to find an "HsR" that is more desirable (and cheaper) than a one-star "H." Shop around. Ask to see the room before accepting. Consider heat and noise problems. Establish the complete price. If there's a need to complain, ask for the government-required "libro de reclamaciones" (complaint book). Your interest in this book alone will generally clear up any problem. In towns with no formal accommodations available, ask around for a "casa particular" (a room in a private house). Accommodations, relative to the rest of Europe, are very cheap.

For the traveler who stubbornly refuses to adapt to Spanish eating habits, meals will be one ordeal after another. Eat when the locals do — roughly between 1:00 and 3:00 and from 9:00 to 11:00 in the evening. If the restaurant is empty, you're probably too early. For between meal snacks (tapas), go to a bar for a tortilla (omelet) or a bocadilla (sandwich).

English is spoken only rarely and a few phrases of Spanish are more valuable than ever when you leave the tourist centers.

Travel partners should spend driving time quizzing each other on the phrase book.

The siesta rules the early afternoon. It stretches as you sink south. Banks generally close for the day at 1:00 or 1:30. Plan accordingly.

This Andalusian adventure is best by car. The roads are fine, traffic is light. Car rental is inexpensive and public transportation is pretty bad. Gas, while expensive, is easy to get, and the people are friendly. Hit the back roads and find that perfect village.

Half the towns I visited were worth remembering. Noteworthy towns are not hard to find, so don't worry about missing some of these. South of Cordoba, Aguilar de la Frontera and Puente-Genil are nice. Aguilar has a pleasant square, outdoor dancing and people who are fascinated by tourists with hairy legs.

My most prized discovery in Andalusia is Estepa. Except for the busy truck route that skirts the town, peace abounds. Situated halfway between Cordoba and Malaga, Estepa hugs a small hill. The hill is crowned by the convent of Santa Clara, worth five stars in any guidebook but found in none. Enjoy the territorial view from the summit, then step into the quiet, spiritual perfection of this little-known convent. Just sit in the chapel all alone and feel the beauty soak through your body. The evening is prime time in Estepa. The promenade begins as everyone gravitates to the central square. Estepa's spotless streets are shined nightly by the feet of ice cream-licking strollers. The whole town strolls — it's like "cruising" without cars. Buy an "ice cream bocadillo" and follow suit. There's a great barber — a real artist — located right on the square. Estepa's only drawback is its lack of decent accommodations. I found only one place, and its location on the truck route made sleeping impossible. I ended up sleeping under the stars on the porch of Santa Clara's convent. It was a beautiful night and the police were very understanding.

To the south is hill-capping Tepa, where the people go into hysterics when you take their picture. Menzanares and Carratraca are also worth a stop. The Michelin guide raves about the

Chorro Gorge. Skip it — it's not worth the drive unless you're a real gorge-ophile.

I can't say too little about the Costa del Sol. If you've read the book this far, you know my travel style and that style is not pink-tourists-sipping-Cokes-on-beaches-in-the-shadows-of-high-rise-hotels-filled-with-groups-taking-package-holidays-in-the-sun.

Don't miss Ronda. Straddling an impressive gorge and with lots of history spicing its cobbled streets, it's a joy. Nearby are the Pileta Caves. Follow the signs past groves of cork trees to the desolate parking lot. A sign says (in four languages) to "call." That means scream down the valley, and the old man will mosey up, unlock the caves, light the lanterns and take you on a memorable, hour-long, half-mile journey through the caves. He is a master at hurdling the language barrier, and you'll get a good look at countless natural formations as well as paintings done by prehistoric "hombres" 25,000 years ago. (That's five times as old as the oldest Egyptian pyramid!) The famous caves at Altamira are closed, so if you want to see Neolithic paintings, this is a must.

From Ronda, the road to Arcos de la Frontera is great. Driving in Arcos is like threading needles with your car. Its setting over a vast plain is impressive. The bell tower affords a great view and an ideal place to enjoy a picnic lunch. (Cover your ears at the top of the hour).

This style of travel, which I just applied to Andalusia, can be applied to travel anywhere. There is sightseeing and there is lifeseeing. Sightseeing is easy to report on as most guidebooks do. In Andalusia, there aren't a lot of sights, but there's so much life. Go find it.

From the Journal

Estepa was my Spanish treasure chest. Below a hill crowned with a castle and a convent spread a freshly washed and very happy town that fit my dreams of Southern Spain.

The evening promenade was on and everyone was washed and dressed just right, gravitating to the "ciudad centro" and the town square. I would never have survived the ridicule in my shorts, so after a quick shower, I dressed as Spanish as I could and joined the parade. We still were treated like we were walking around in the nude. We tried and tried to figure out what it was — our hair, my beard and glasses, our shoes, our walk, our odor, our aura? We were even stared at in the dark disco and from a distance in our car!

After much celebrity status, things cooled off enough so that we could just sit and observe this amazing social scene. Night after night, the town's people don't sit in front of the TV alone, they congregate and enjoy each other's company, young and old, outside under the stars.

Estepa, south Spain.

A Day in Lisbon

Can you keep a secret? Lisbon is the cheapest and one of the most exciting cities in Europe — without tourist crowds! Portugal is Europe's bargain basement. Lisbon's budget pensions in the Avenida de Liberdade neighborhood charge $15 for a double. For a little more money, you can live regally. Rooms are priced according to the facilities they provide. A new hotel with all the modern conveniences will cost much more than an older no-frills pension. Public transportation in Portugal's capital city is convenient and cheap. One fare takes you anywhere on the trolleys and buses. Taxis can be very reasonable as well. In fact, for three people traveling a short distance, a taxi ride could cost less than three bus tickets. For speed, ease and comfort, I took advantage of the affordable taxi service on all but the longer rides.

Portugal is unsung and uncrowded. This is refreshing after braving the peak season crowds of France and Germany. Geographically, Lisbon is far from Europe's tourist-beaten

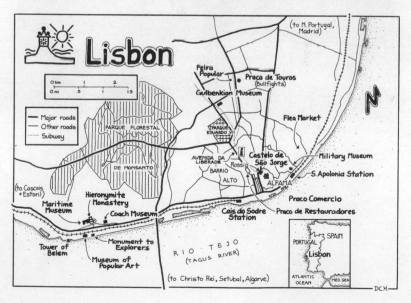

track — ten hours by train from Madrid, twenty-four from Paris. When traveling by train to Lisbon, stay on the main train line (Paris-Madrid-Lisbon). Take the overnight train from Madrid to Lisbon. Rich rewards await those who make this trip.

Follow me through a day in Lisbon . . .

Ask your landlady to wake you early with breakfast. (Many room prices include a light Continental breakfast served in your room, since most pensions have no dining room.) Then catch a taxi to the foot of the Alfama, near the waterfront.

Fish market in Lisbon's Alfama.

The Alfama, Lisbon's old sailor's district, dates back to Visigothic times. The Alfama is Lisbon's living past — to me, its highlight. A tangle of cobbled and confused alleys and bent, red-roofed houses, it's sure to enchant you. Spend the morning exploring the fish and produce market at the foot of the Alfama. This is just one of this area's many faces, a field day for the photographer and a refreshing contrast to the orderly American supermarket.

Then wander deeper into this urban jungle. The roads are squeezed to mere concrete pathways, houses comfort each other in their romantic shabbiness and the air drips with laundry and the smell of clams and fish. You'll probably get lost but that doesn't matter — unless you're trying to stay found. Poke aimlessly, sample ample grapes, avoid rabid-looking dogs, peek through windows and greet people who sit on thresholds. Punctuate their boredom. Let their smile be a warm Portuguese rubdown. The buildings, spiced by their inhabitants and sliced by cobblestone paths, make a neighborhood unlike any other.

Gradually, work your way up the castle-crowned hill until you reach a little green square called Maradouro de Santa Luzia. Rest here and enjoy the lovely view of the Alfama below you.

By now it's noon, and you should be quite hungry (unless you took more than pictures in the Alfama market). Across the street from Maradouro de Santa Luzia is a busy little, unnamed, working-class restaurant full of babble and hungry Portuguese. Treat yourself to a huge plate of boiled clams and cockles (the house specialty) and anything else that looks good. Three dollars will buy you a feast.

If you climb a few more blocks to the top of the hill, you'll find the ruins of Castelo Sao Jorge. From this fortress, which has dominated the city for almost fifteen hundred years, you will enjoy a commanding view of Portugal's capital city.

Your day is entering its second half as you grab a taxi and ask to be taken to Torre de Belem (the Belem Tower). Here you will find a cluster of Lisbon's top tourist attractions.

The Belem Tower is a small but imposing fortress with a

Gothic interior and a Renaissance exterior. Just down the street the huge Monument to the Explorers reminds us of the days when Magellan and Vasco de Gama made Portugal a world power. Across the street is the Hieronymite monastery which has, in my opinion, Europe's finest cloisters and is the best example anywhere of Manueline-style architecture. In this same area you will also find the Coach Museum and a fascinating naval museum.

The evening is best spent at the "Feira Popular" (popular fair) on Avenida da Republica. Every night from May through September, the fair bustles with Portuguese at play. Join the crowds and have a hearty chicken dinner, complete with wine, for a couple dollars. A visit to the "Feira Popular" is a fitting way to end your day in Lisbon.

Lisbon's salty sailor's quarter, the Alfama.

Morocco — Plunge Deep

Walking through the various souks of the labyrinthian medina, I found sights you could only dream of in America. Dodging blind men and clubfoots, I was blasted with a collage of smells, sounds, sights and feelings. People came in all colors, sizes, temperaments and varieties of deformities. Milky eyes, beggars, stumps of limbs, sticks of children, tattooed women, weather-aged old men with a twinkle behind their bristly cheeks, grabbing salesmen, inviting craftsmen, enticing scents, half-bald dogs and little boys on rooftops were reaching out from all directions. Ooo! Morocco!

Morocco is maximum thrills per minute and dollar. Slices of Morocco make the Star Wars bar scene look bland. And it's just a quick cruise from Spain. You can't, however, experience Morocco in a day-trip from the Costa del Sol. Plunge deep and your journal will read like a Dali painting.

While Morocco is not easy traveling, it gets rave reviews from those who plug this Islamic detour into their European vacation. Here are some tips and a suggested itinerary.

Skip Tangiers and the Moroccan "Tijuanas" of the north coast. Tangiers is not really Morocco; it's a city full of con men, who thrive on green tourists. Take the boat from Algeciras, Spain to Tangiers, where you will find the quickest connections south to Rabat. Power your way off the boat through the shysters to the nearby train station. They'll tell you anything to get you to stay in Tangiers. Believe nothing. Be rude if you have to. Tangiers can give you only grief, while the real Morocco lies to the south.

Rabat is a good first stop in Morocco. This most comfortably European city in Morocco lacks the high-pressure tourism of the towns on the north coast. Stay at the Hotel Splendid (8 Zanqat Ghazza, tel 232-88) which is a favorite of the Peace Corps workers.

Taxis are cheap and a real bargain when you consider the comfort, speed and convenience they provide in these hot, dusty and confusing cities. Eat and drink carefully in Morocco. Bottled water and bottled soft drinks are safe. I had "well-cooked" written in Arabic on a scrap of paper and ordered meat cooked that way for safety. The Arabs use different number symbols. Learn them. Morocco was a French colony so French is more widely understood than English. Travel very light in Morocco. You can leave most of your luggage at your last Spanish hotel and spend a night there upon your return from Africa.

After Rabat, pass through Casablanca (the movie was great — the city is not) and catch the "Marrakesh Express" south. You'll hang your head out the window of that romantic old train and sing to the passing desert.

Marrakesh is the epitome of exotic. Take a horse-drawn carriage from the station downtown where you can find a hotel near the Djemaa el Fna. Djemaa el Fna is the central square of Marrakesh. This is where the action is. Desert musicians, magicians, storytellers, acrobats, snake charmers, gamblers and tricksters all perform, gathering crowds of tribespeople who have come to Marrakesh to do their market chores. As a tourist, you'll fit in like a clown at a funeral. Be very careful, don't gamble and hang onto your wallet. This is a trip into another world — complete with pitfalls.

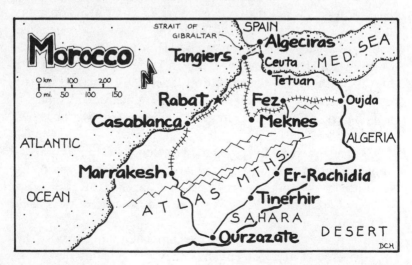

You can spend an entire day in the colorful medina, or marketplace. Wander aimlessly from souk to souk (there is a souk for each area of trade, e.g., the dyers' souk, the leather souk, the carpet souk).

In the medina you'll be followed — or "guided" — by small boys who claim to be "a friend who wants to practice his English." They are after money — nothing else. Make two things crystal clear: you have no money for them and you want no guide. Then completely ignore them. Remember, while you are with them, these boys get commissions for anything you buy.

The market is a shopper's delight. Bargain hard, shop

around and you'll come home with some great souvenirs. Government emporiums usually have the same items you find in the market, priced fairly. If you get sick of souks shop there and you'll get the same price — haggle-free.

From Marrakesh, catch the bus south, over the rugged Atlas Mountains, to a region that no longer faces the Mediterranean. This is Saharan Morocco. Explore the isolated oasis towns of Ouarzazate, Tinerhir and Er-Rachidia.

These towns each have a weekly "market day" when the tribespeople gather to do their shopping. Unless you enjoy goats' heads and honeydew melons, there isn't much more than pictures that a tourist would want to take. Stay in Tinerhir's Hotel du Todra and climb to the roof for a great view of the busy marketplace below.

Venture out of town into the lush fields where you'll tumble into an almost Biblical world. Sit on a rock. Dissect the silence. A bearded old man in a white robe and turban might clip-clop slowly past you. He seems to be growing side-saddle out of his weary donkey and his eyes are as wide as yours. Suddenly, six Botticelli maidens flit like watercolor confetti across your trail and giggle out of sight. Stay tuned. The show goes on.

The bus rides in this part of Morocco are real trips. I could ramble on for pages about experiences I've had on Moroccan buses — mostly bad — but I don't want to spoil the surprise. Just ride them with a spirit of adventure — and your fingers crossed.

From Er-Rachidia, if you're ready to return to our world, take the bus over the Atlas Mountains to Fez or Meknes. Fez, along with Marrakesh, is a must. Both of these towns give you royal and big-city Morocco at its best.

From Fez you can catch the air-conditioned train back to Tangiers. If you bought a round-trip boat ticket from Spain you can just walk onto the boat. Without a ticket, you'll have to buy one at the Tangiers ticket office — no easy matter. If they will only sell you a ticket for a later boat (to prolong your stay in lovely Tangiers) you'll have to buy it. Try using that ticket for the next boat out. It will probably get you on.

After your trip you'll always remember that swing through Morocco as the adventure that bumped the rest of your world a couple of rungs up the ladder of normalcy.

Morocco in a rented bus. Why not?

Yugoslavia

Yugoslavia (the union of the South Slavs) has seven distinct peoples in six republics who speak five languages, have three religions, two alphabets (Latin and Cyrillic) and one government. The only thing these people have in common is a dislike for each other.

It's a fascinating place and was at one time one of Europe's undiscovered tourist paradises. Now it's discovered and the Dalmatian Coast is a popular tourists' playground. But for each noisy resort there's a quiet town or sleepy beach nearby.

When the "Iron Curtain" was dropped Americans filed Yugoslavia right next to Bulgaria in their mind. Things have changed and these days Yugoslavia is closer politically and economically to West Europe than to its eastern neighbors. Traveling there is no more difficult than traveling in Italy, and it can be every bit as enjoyable. Yugoslavia is a great off-beat tourist target.

The Plitvice National Park, south of Zagreb, is one of Europe's greatest natural wonders. There's nothing like this grand canyon of sixteen terraced lakes laced together by waterfalls. Countless cascades and strangely clear and colorful water make this park a misty natural wonderland.

You can enjoy a whole day picnicking, rowing, exploring behind "bridal veil" falls and climbing stone stairways that are losing their battle with the busy Plitvice waters. Children love Plitvice and it tends to bring out the kid in Mom and Dad as well. Public buses serve Plitvice from many cities, including Zagreb.

Dubrovnik is Yugoslavia's number one tourist attraction. George Bernard Shaw called Dubrovnik "the pearl of the Adriatic, a paradise on Earth." I call it the most romantic place this side of Kashmir.

Dubrovnik handles its tourist crowds very well and they don't really detract from its wonderfully preserved, traffic-free atmosphere. It can be expensive however and the budget traveler should avoid modern hotels in favor of the private accommodations that offer double the culture for a fraction of the cost. I'll never forget being met at the bus station by fifteen women all begging me to come home with them — a rare thrill! Drive a hard bargain, and you should get a very reasonable rate — for "bed and breakfast."

Dubrovnik is best seen from its wall. Circle the city. Every view is different. Once a part of Venice's empire, Dubrovnik bubbles with Venetian flavor. Picnic on nearby Lokrum Island, where an enjoyable midday break can include a swim. Then savor a classy dinner downtown, followed by dancing in a moonlit medieval courtyard.

Evenings are well spent promenading up and down the main street. The peace of "pedestrians only" is especially evident after dark when Main Street is quietly crammed with happy people.

A trip by bus through Montenegro and Macedonia will take you through Europe's Appalachia. This Titograd to Skopje ride is long and exhausting, but you'll be rewarded with

spectacular mountain scenery and a chance to see some time-passed towns like Pec, Pristina and Decani.

Titograd is so dull that it's interesting. This bleak symbol of Tito's modernization of Yugoslavia is the gateway to the hairiest bus ride in Europe. Since that bus leaves early, an overnight in Titograd is unavoidable. The hotels aren't cheap and your only alternative is the bus station or the park (which is permissible).

As your bus climbs higher into the mountains, the twen-

tieth century fades. You'll see people doing their laundry on rocks that were grooved by their ancestors' dirty socks. Those people seem to live their entire lives up there — stranded in the past. They are Albanians. Americans aren't allowed in Albania, but one third of all Albanians live in Yugoslavia — in the area you'll see through the window of your Titograd-Skopje bus.

After twelve hours the bus stops in Skopje, the capital of Macedonia. It's a strange city, still bewildered by the twentieth century. The people, even in their modern "Moscow-style" mass housing, will look at you as if you were something extraterrestrial.

These three highlights of Yugoslavia — Plitvice, Dubrovnik and the bus ride — can be part of your trip from Central Europe to Greece, or vice versa. Most people take the boring marathon train ride through Yugoslavia via its capital, Belgrade. While this is the fastest way to Athens (short of flying) it will seem like a million years. A more interesting plan would be to: Take the train from Central Europe to Zagreb. Spend the night there and travel to Dubrovnik by bus, possibly spending some time in Split and Korcula (a mini-Dubrovnik and the birthplace of Marco Polo). From Dubrovnik, take the bus to Titograd where, the following day, you will venture by bus to Skopje. From Skopje you can catch a train to Athens. This trip can also be done in the opposite direction. Whichever way you do it, you can say you've seen the best of Yugoslavia.

The Gorge of Samaria
on the Isle of Crete

Hordes of tourists flock to the Greek island of Crete. Many leave disappointed. Their problem was that they failed to leave the crowded cities behind and get away from the tourists. One sure-fire escape is to take the ten-mile hike through the Gorge of Samaria. Here is a day that you're sure to enjoy . . .

Your home-base for this circular excursion is Khania (pronounced "HAWN-yuh"), a city on Crete's north coast which is serviced frequently by the overnight boat from Athens. Catch the earliest bus from Khania past Omalos to Xyloskala. By 7:00 a.m., after a very scenic 25-mile bus ride, you'll be standing high above the wild Gorge of Samaria. Xyloskala is a small lodge, the end of the road — and the beginning of the trail. The bus will be full of hikers; no one else would come here at this early hour. The air is crisp, the fresh blue sky is cool and most of the gorge has yet to see the sun. Before you lies a downhill, ten-mile trek through some of the most spectacular scenery anywhere in Greece. This four to six hour hike down Europe's longest gorge is open from May 1 to October 31.

Pack light for this hike, but bring a hearty picnic lunch. Water is no problem, since you will follow a pure mountain stream through most of the gorge. Food can't be bought in this wonderfully wild gorge. Wear light clothes, but bring a jacket for the cool morning at the top of the gorge. Come prepared to swim in one of the stream's many refreshing swimming holes. Photographers will go through lots of film.

You will descend to the floor of the gorge down steep switchbacks for about an hour until you come to the stream, a great place for your picnic. A leisurely meal here will do three things: bolster your energy, lighten your load, and bring you peace, as this break will let most of the other hikers get ahead of you.

Between you and the Libyan Sea on Crete's southern shore are about eight miles of gently sloping downhill trails. You'll pass an occasional deserted farmhouse, and a small ghost town with a well. In the middle of the hike, you'll come to the narrowest (and most photographed) point in the gorge where only two or three yards separate the towering cliffs. The cool creek trickles at your feet, reminding you that a little farther downstream you can take a refreshing dip in one of the stream's natural swimming holes — it feels great! Keep your eyes peeled for the nimble cliff-climbing agrimi, Crete's wild mountain goat.

Finally, by mid-afternoon, after a leisurely ten-mile walk, you arrive at the coast. There, in a flood of oleander flowers, you'll find a tiny community with a small restaurant and a few cheap places to stay. The town, Ayia Roumeli, is accessible only by foot or by boat. Three times a day, a small boat picks up the hikers and ferries them to Kora Sfakion. (Know when the last boat leaves before you begin your hike, so you can plan accordingly.)

While you're waiting for the boat (after you buy your ticket), take a dip in the bathtub-warm, crystal-clear waters of the Libyan Sea. The black sand beach is beautiful, but it absorbs the heat, so wear your shoes right to the water's edge. A free shower is available on the beach. The hour-long boat ride to Khora Sfakion connects with a bus which will return you to Khania. In crossing the island of Crete, the bus goes through some lovely land and several untouched villages inhabited by high-booted, long-mustachioed, espresso-drinking Cretans. I wanted to get out and explore, but my bus was direct. By 8:30, I was back in Khania.

This day was, in every sense of the word, gorge-ous.

From the Journal

After a drink we walked on and came to the narrowest part of the gorge. Soon the gorge shrank to barely three yards across, with the stream carving it ever deeper and mountains towering on both sides of it. It was the hottest part of the day, and I found a natural pool that wasn't full of other hikers. Dying for a swim, I jumped into my own little tub, complete with a waterfall and wonderfully refreshing. There's nothing like a swim in a mountain stream when you're hiking on Crete. We had a snack, laid on a hot rock and then, after one more dip, we headed on.

The ten miles (sixteen kilometers) passed fast and soon signs of Greek civilization were peeking at us through the bushes. A ghost town was inhabited by the two goats who greeted us as we passed through. Then we got to the coast. Above us sat a ruined castle, behind us was the gorge, and in front of us was the deep, blue, placid Libyan Sea. Africa was out there somewhere, and we were about as far south as you can get and still be in Europe.

The Best Way
From Athens to Turkey

The best thing about Athens is the boat to Turkey. While so many people get as far east as Athens, very few realize how accessible and exciting Turkey is. My feeling is that every trip to the Greek Islands should include a visit to the west coast of Turkey. If you're looking for cultural thrills, remember Turkey is farther from Greece culturally than Greece is to the USA.

Turkey is the last frontier of European tourism, appealing to travelers for many reasons. Most importantly, Turkey provides a rich and very contrasting culture, something that modern Europe is losing. Turkey is much cheaper than any European country. Its lira has dropped in value over the last several years from six American cents to less than a penny. Turkey offers some of the finest classical ruins to be found anywhere. And, Turkey is not overrun by tourists the way most of Greece is.

The best way to get to Turkey from Athens is to sail. Athens is one of Europe's most notorious tourist traps. It is very crowded. See what's important — and leave! Catch a boat to the island of Samos. The 13-hour boat ride arrives in the morning. You can buy a sleeping berth or sleep free, under the stars or inside. (Be quick to stake out a couch to sleep on.) A third-class ticket will cost about $12. It's a good idea to pack a picnic for the ride (Piraeus, Athens' port town, has a good market near the harbor). Food purchased on board is expensive.

Samos (180 sq. mi., 60,000 people) is my favorite Greek island: green, mountainous, diverse and friendly. It is crowded with tourists, but not as bad as many other Greek islands. Bus transportation on the island is fine. Try to stay in Vathi, a charming town of narrow, winding lanes creeping out of the sea and up the hillside. Many streets are too narrow for cars, which preserves the quiet Greek atmosphere. Learn to play backgammon with the locals — they'll love you for it.

Rent a motor bike to explore Aesop's island. You can see the desolate Temple of Hera, one of the Seven Wonders of the Ancient World; Pythagorian, the hometown of Pythagoras; untouched mountain towns like Pandhrosen, and forgotten old monasteries. Wild fig trees beg to be tasted, and old Greeks lead grape-laden donkeys down empty country roads. There are plenty of good beaches and local restaurants to enjoy as well. A motorbike is a worthwhile ten-dollar splurge.

Now you've reached the end of Greece; the brown mountains of Turkey dare you to cross the narrow channel, to trade the grapes of Samos for the more exotic fruits of Turkey.

Greeks and Turks mix like Christians and Moslems.

Border crossings are more difficult and expensive than they have to be. The Greek government levies a heavy tax on each ticket sold, to discourage this easy exit from the country. They would rather the tourist backtrack through Athens, contributing still more money to the industry that is Greece's number one source of foreign revenue — tourism.

There is a daily boat from Vathi to Kusadasi in Turkey. The two-hour ride costs around twenty dollars which, while unfair, is still worth it. You will land very close to my favorite Greek ruins — Ephesus (Efes). It would be a crime to be in Samos and miss the home of the Ephesians, even if you aren't particularly interested in classical ruins.

Another convenient way to get to Turkey is from the island of Rhodes. Rhodes is well worth a visit. This Crusader city takes you back into medieval Europe as well as any place in Europe. From Rhodes you can take a small Turkish boat to the enjoyable resort town of Marmaris on the southwest tip of Turkey. From here (or Kusadasi), modern buses can take you anywhere in Turkey (including Istanbul, where trains leave daily for Germany and Western Europe).

If you're going to the Greek islands, go to Rhodes or Samos, and for some real spice, include a side trip into Turkey.

From the Journal

Turkey is a rich land. I need it in each trip — but not too much of it. A week or ten days is just right, but then it's nice to leave.

Turkey is enjoyable because it's different enough to be exciting and interesting, but not so different that it's hard to be comfortable and relaxed. The people, while most wear a Western facade in clothes, are definitely Turkish in mind, and there still is a flavor about these people that makes them special. I don't know if they're bored or happy or apathetic or what, but the entire country — at least the male population, which is what the traveler sees — is "into" certain things like: worry beads; disdain for American capitalism, imperialism and fascism; drinking tea and spending a great part of their lives playing cards, dominoes or backgammon; smoking; stepping on the heels of their shoes (wearing them bent down); being about two days unshaven; keeping pictures of Ataturk on their walls; and hanging around together.

Eastern Turkey

Most tourist maps of Turkey show plenty of places in the western half but an empty void in the east. From the looks of the map, there's nothing there. But the only thing that Eastern Turkey has virtually nothing of is tourists. It's a wild and fascinating land that very few people even consider visiting. It's a land where even the simplest activities become games or adventures. A walk down the street or a visit to the market becomes an exotic journey. Each meal is a first, every person an enigma, every day an odyssey. Consider a visit.

Eastern Turkey presents the visitor with challenge after challenge. Communication is difficult. English is rarely spoken. Since many Turks have worked in Germany, German is the most valuable European language in Turkey. Distances are great and transportation, while cheap, is quite rugged. Most western women are comfortable here only in the company of a male partner. Modern accommodations are virtually nonexistent; there just isn't enough demand to support tourist hotels. You will be an oddity, the constant center of attention. People will stare and follow. Privacy will be found only in your hotel room — if you have drapes.

Nevertheless, exploration of Eastern Turkey is a special travel thrill and those who visit scheme to return. The people are curious and perhaps immature at times, but basically friendly and helpful. Communication requires creativity. A Turkish vocabulary of twenty or thirty words is essential. Bus companies with modern Mercedes-Benz buses offer frequent and very cheap transportation to all corners of Turkey. Smaller buses called dolmuses will take you anywhere the larger buses won't. Erzurum, Eastern Turkey's major city, is a $12 bus ride from Istanbul. This 24-hour marathon ride drops you in a land that makes Istanbul seem normal.

Hotels and restaurants, in modest Turkish style, abound and it's impossible to spend much money.

If you're looking for excitement and a very different cul-

337

ture, Eastern Turkey's rewards far exceed the costs associated with traveling there. There are few tourist sights as such (museums, tours, famous buildings, etc.). Yet, everything about Eastern Turkey combines to sweep you into a whole new world. You are given a close look at the traditional Moslem culture in towns with more horse traffic than cars. The streets are the man's domain while unliberated women appear in public only as walking gunny sacks. A photographer will go through a lot of film.

Some Hints to Make Your Visit Easier

By all means, locate some literature on Eastern Turkey, research the area and know what interests you. Take a good map with you.

Eat carefully. Find a clean-looking restaurant and venture into the kitchen. Choose your food personally by tasting and pointing to what you like. Establish the price before you eat. Joke around with the cooks — they'll love you for it. Purify your water with iodine, Halazone or by boiling it. Bottled soft drinks and boiled chai (tea) and coffee are cheap and safe everywhere. Watermelons are a great source of safe liquid. If you order a glass of tea, a teahouse will be happy to "process" your melon and give it to you peeled and in little chunks on a big plate.

Learn to play backgammon before you visit Turkey. Backgammon, the local pastime, is played by all of the men in this part of the world. Join in. It's a great way to make a lot of friends in a teahouse, the local hangout.

Really get away from it all. Take a minibus, or dolmus, ride into the middle of nowhere. Get off at a small village. (If the men on the bus think you must be mistaken or lost to be getting off there, you've found the right place.) Explore the town, befriend the children, trade national dance lessons, be a confident extrovert. Act like an old friend returning after a ten-year absence — you'll be treated like one.

Venture onto the property of a large family. You'll be greeted by the patriarch, who is very proud to have a foreign

visitor. Join him cross-legged on his large, bright carpet in the shade. The women of the household will bring you tea, then peer at you from around a distant corner. Shake hands, jabber away in English, play show-and-tell, take pictures of the family, and get their addresses so you can mail them a copy. They'll never forget your visit — neither will you.

People will be staring at you all day long. To maintain your sanity, be crazy. Keep a sense of humor. Joke with the Turks. Talk to them, even if there's no hope of communication. One afternoon, in the town of Ercis, I was waiting for a bus and writing in my journal. A dozen people gathered around me, staring with intense curiosity. I felt that they needed entertainment. I sang an old Hoagy Carmichael song, "Huggin' and a-Chalkin'." When the bus came, my friend and I danced our way on board, waving goodbye to our cheering fans. From then on I entertained (with a terrible voice) most of Eastern Turkey.

This is an exciting land — and a tremendous way to spice up your trip. Never again, in your mind, will you associate Turkey with cranberries.

From the Journal

The town — I never saw a name — had one wide dusty road, and on each side for about 200 or 300 yards were houses of mud brick with wooden poles for support. Cow dung, dried into innocent-looking, large, rough loaves, was piled into neat mounds in every yard. Geese, ducks and chickens roamed around like they owned the place, while women loaded two pails of water onto their balancing sticks at the wells. Oxen pulled huge wagons of hay, and every few minutes, a proud horseman would gallop, bareback, down the street. This town had no electricity, no paint or advertisements on the walls, no cars or trucks and only one small general store.

We were definitely big news. Boldly, like victorious but humane generals, we sauntered through the town, greeting people from house to house, shooting pictures, shaking hands and acting quite sure of ourselves. Throngs of villagers

*gathered around us, and Carl and I were moved to entertain.
We sang and danced, becoming the village stars. A cute little
girl caught my eye and she became my very embarrassed friend.
We had our picture taken together and then moved on.*

*Carl found a wonderfully spunky old lady who was
dressed very colorfully and was the epitome of good health.
She invited us into her spotless house and soon, half the village
had crowded in after us. The window filled with faces struggling to get a look at the visitors. Our friend brought us
homemade honey, still in the waxy comb; bread; stringy, powerful and delicious cheese, and tea. I was visibly tickled, I'm
sure. It was fun to pick out especially beautiful girls and
embarrass them with just a glance. They were all super-shy and
very curious. By popular demand, I danced, dragging in the
laughing old lady, to the delight of the house full of Turks.*

The Treasures of Luxor

Egypt seems distant, but it is actually quite accessible. From Athens it's just a ninety-minute flight or a day at sea and you're in a whole new world. Economy or student boat and plane tickets from Athens to Egypt are reasonable at about $100 each way. For the best possible price, buy your ticket in Athens. These tickets are not advertised outside of Greece.

If you visit Egypt, Luxor is a must. The train ride from Cairo to Luxor is posh and scenic — a fun experience itself. A second-class air-conditioned sleeping car provides comfortable two-bed compartments, fresh linen, a wash basin and wake-up service. Make a reservation for this ride at least three days in advance, both ways. In the crazy Cairo ticket office, be patient and persistent, and tip (bribe) if necessary.

In the cool months (peak season) hotel reservations are a good idea. Off season, in the sweltering summer months, there are plenty of empty rooms. Air conditioning is found only in the luxury hotels, and these rooms, at about $40 per double, are relatively expensive. Modest hotels with a private shower, fan and balcony offer doubles for less than $15. A cot in the youth hostel, for less than a dollar, is rock bottom in price — and comfort. The Hotel Horus' central location (Maabed El Karnak Street, tel. 2165), showers, fans, good clean restaurant, friendly and helpful management, and priceless (i.e. safe to drink) cold water machine make it a real bargain (double rooms for under $15). Hotel Horus is just across the street from the impressive Temple of Luxor and a three minute camel ride from the Nile.

Luxor is not a place where you should save money at the expense of comfort and health. Your dollar goes a long way in Egypt, and a little extra expense will bring a lot of comfort.

Eat well and carefully. With the terrible heat, your body will require plenty of liquids. Water from drinkable sources is safe (e.g., that which is served in restaurants). Pepsi and the local cola, Sico, are safe and very cheap. Watermelons are

342

cheap, safe and quite quenching. Keep your melon cool in your hotel's refrigerator. Choose a clean restaurant. Hotels generally have restaurants comparable to their class and price range.

Transportation in and around Luxor is a treat. The local taxis are horsedrawn carriages. These are very romantic but, as usual in Egypt, you must drive a hard bargain and settle on a price before the driver "moves 'em out." The Egyptians will overcharge anyone who will overpay.

You can cross the Nile from dawn until late at night on the very old Nile ferry. The "Tourist Fary," as the sign reads, costs only pennies. Sit on the roof and enjoy the view with the local crowd, or sit inside and wonder how the old engine, which is kicked into gear by the pound of a large rock, keeps running.

A fun way to become mobile is to rent a bicycle. For less than two dollars a day, you can bike through Luxor and the surrounding villages. The bicycle is also useful in creating your own cool breeze and for quick getaways from unwanted followers (beggars).

Transportation on the West Bank of the Nile (across from Luxor) consists of donkeys, bicycles and automobile taxis. Donkeys can be rented for the romantic approach to the tombs and temples of West Thebes. The desert heat will melt the romance, and you may feel like a first-class ass sitting on your

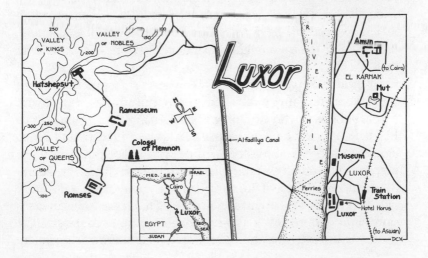

dusty donkey. Bikes, for the cheap and hardy, are a possibility for touring the ruins and tombs. An automobile taxi is the quickest and most comfortable way to see the sights of West Thebes. A taxi can be rented for about $15 for the day. The "day," because of the heat, generally lasts from 5:00 am until 12:00 noon. When split between four tourists, the taxi is a very reasonable way to go. To save money and make friends, assemble a little tour at your hotel. You will enjoy the quick and easy doorstep service of the taxi, and in one day, you will adequately cover Luxor's West Bank sights.

Survival on the Nile during the heat of summer is easier if you follow a few hints. The summer heat, which often exceeds 120 degrees, is unbearable and dangerous after noon. Begin each day by 5:00 a.m. Those early hours are prime time: the temperature is comfortable, the light is crisp and fresh, and the Egyptian tourist hustlers are still sleeping. Spend the afternoon indoors or in the shade. Wear a white hat (you can buy them there) and carry water. An Egyptian guidebook is a shield proving to unwanted human guides that you need no "help."

You must be constantly on the budgetary defense. No tip will ever be enough. Tip what you believe is fair by local standards and ignore the inevitable plea for more. If you ever leave them satisfied — you were ripped off. Carry candies or little gifts for the myriad of children constantly screaming "Bakshish!" ("Give me a gift!") Hoard small change in a special pocket so you will have tip money readily available. Getting change back from your large bill is like pulling teeth — on a duck.

Luxor deserves a lot of time. There is so much to do. I spent more time in Luxor than in any European small town, and I could have stayed longer. The primary tourist magnet is the ancient ruins. The East Bank offers the tourist two famous temple sites: the Temples of Amun, Mut and Khonsu at Karnak, one mile north of Luxor, and the Temple of Luxor which dominates the town of Luxor.

Because of an ancient Egyptian belief, all the funerary art, tombs and pyramids were built on the West Bank of the Nile — where the sun sets. Across the Nile from Luxor is an area rich in tombs, temples and ruins. Be selective, buying tickets for the most important sights at the ticket office near the ferry landing. The Temple of Queen Hatshepsut, Deir el-Medina, the Ramesseum, the Colossi of Memnon, and the Valleys of the Kings, Queens and Nobles are just some of the many monuments from Egypt's ancient past that await you. You will become jaded sooner or later, so don't waste your powers of absorption on anything less than important. Some of the best values in local crafts are sold by people outside of each ruin.

Luxor town itself has plenty to offer. Explore the market. You can get a very inexpensive custom-made kaftan with your name sewn on in arty Arabic, if you like. A trip out to the camel market is always fun (and you can pick up a camel for half the USA price). Take an evening cruise on the Nile in a felucca, the traditional sailboat of this area, for just a few dollars an hour. Relaxing in your private felucca in the cool beauty of a Nile sunset is a very romantic way to merge day and night.

Finally, the villages that surround Luxor, expecially those on the other side of the river, offer a fascinating escape into the past. Rent a bike to explore Luxor's most unappreciated attraction — the villages. The people are tremendous. Be bold — make things happen. You won't be sorry.

Five Days in Luxor

Day 1 Your train from Cairo arrives at 5:00 a.m. Even though it's too early to check in, leave your bags at a hotel, telling them you'll return by midmorning to inspect their rooms. Take a horse carriage to the temples at Karnak while it's still cool. The cool of these precious early hours should never be wasted. Check into a hotel by midmorning. Explore Luxor town. Enjoy a felucca ride on the Nile at sunset.

Day 2 Cross the Nile and rent a taxi for the day. (It's easy to find other tourists to split the transportation costs.) If you are selective and get an early start, you should be able to see everything you want at a relaxed tempo by noon. That is a lot of work, and you'll enjoy a quiet afternoon back in Luxor.

Day 3 Arrange an all-day minibus trip through your hotel to visit Aswan, the Aswan Dam and the important temples south of Luxor. With six or eight tourists filling the minibus, this day should not cost over ten dollars.

Day 4 Rent bikes and explore the time-passed villages on the west side of the Nile. Bring water, your camera and a bold spirit of adventure. This could be your best day in Egypt.

Day 5   Enjoy Luxor town. Tour the excellent Luxor museum. Take advantage of the great shopping opportunities here. Catch the overnight train back to Cairo.

From the Journal

Afternoons along the Nile are sluggish, to say the least. Dogs lie still, Arabs curl up in the shade, streets steam quietly and boats sit as if carved out of the sleepy river. I don't do much either. Today had a good six hours of sightseeing, and I deserved the afternoon snooze I took.

This evening, Pam and I rented bikes and enjoyed a great new feeling of mobility and freedom. We pedaled through the town, happily blowing in the breeze, catching cool shade and leaving little bakshish beggar kids in the distance. In the cool of the evening, we left the city life behind, taking the old boat across the Nile to the other side . . . in search of village life. I like this side. The Nile gives it a lush, green foliage, and poking up among the reeds, sugar cane and date palms are mud huts and villages — untouched by the touristic bustle of Luxor. We ventured down a long dirt road bounded by sugar cane, following an irrigation ditch that led to a village.

We were big news to this little village. People scurried, grabbing their families to come and see the Americans who were visiting their town. It was really a royal welcome. They would have given us The Key to the Village — but there were no locks. We had the town's attention, and smiles, lit by glittering eyes, kept the sunset lingering. It was a precious evening.

Badtowns

It's generally not considered "in good style" to write negatively about tourist destinations. It is helpful, however, to have advice on which places to skip, and I never claimed to have "good style" anyway, so I'd like to give you one man's very judgmental view of Europe's dullest cities.

Zurich is Switzerland's largest city, and it's a crime to be there instead of in the mountains on a sunny day. The average person on the street can name only one Swiss city, Zurich, and name familiarity is a rotten reason to go somewhere. It's a nice place to live but I wouldn't want to visit.

Bordeaux must mean boredom in some ancient language. If I was offered a free trip tomorrow to that town, I'd stay home and clean the fridge. People go there for the wine. Bordeaux wine country and Bordeaux city are two very different things. There's a wine tourist information bureau in Bordeaux which, for a price, will bus you out of town and into the more interesting wine country nearby.

Andorra, a small country in the Pyrenees Mountains between France and Spain is as scenic as any other chunk of those mountains. People from all over Europe flock to Andorra to take advantage of its famous duty-free shopping. As far as Americans are concerned, Andorra is just a big Spanish speaking Radio Shack. There are no great bargains there for us. We enjoy unbeatable prices on stereo and photographic equipment right here.

Germany's famous *Black Forest* disappoints more people than it excites. If that's all Germany offered, it would be worth seeing. Locally, any large forest in a country the size of Oregon with 65 million people is a popular attraction but I'd say the average visitor from the Pacific Northwest would prefer Germany's Romantic Road and Bavaria to the east, the Rhine and Mosel country to the north, the Swiss Alps to the south and France's Alsace region to the west — all high points that cut the Black Forest down to nubs.

348

Nuremberg enjoys fame and attracts tourists for what it was in the past and is no more today. Germany has many sights more worthy of your sightseeing time. The best thing about Nuremberg is the train to Munich.

Bucharest, the capital of Romania has very little to offer. Its top selling post card is of the Intercontinental Hotel. *Belgrade,* Yugoslavia's capital is another stop that is best not started. It's one of the few things I can think of that are more boring than the long train ride through the center of Yugoslavia. Stay on board until you're in Greece or meander down Yugoslavia's Dalmation coast.

If you're heading from Yugoslavia to Greece, skip *Thessaloniki,* which deserves its chapter in the Bible but not in travel guidebooks, and don't linger too long in Athens.

Athens, while well worth visiting, is probably the most over-rated city in Europe. One-hundred years ago, Athens was a sleepy town of 8,000 people with a pile of ruins in its backyard. Today it's a giant mix of concrete, smog, noise and tourists. See the four major attractions (the Acropolis, the Agora, the Plaka and the great National Museum of Archeology), spend an evening at the delightful Dafni wine festival on the edge of town (second Saturday in July through first Sunday in September) and get out to the islands or countryside.

Probably the most common serious mistake people make in their itinerary planning is squeezing a week of Greece into their busy trip. It takes four days of traveling to get from Rome to Athens and back. It's not worth rushing your whole itinerary and four days of hot travel for three days in Athens. Greece is the most touristed but least explored country in Europe. It's worthwhile but it takes time — and that time is best spent away from the noise and bustle of Athens.

The towns I've mentioned here are worth skipping only because they are surrounded by so many places more worthy of the average traveler's limited vacation time. If you have a villa in Bucharest or a cuckoo clock shop in the Black Forest, no offense is meant. I just don't like your neighborhood.

Appendix I —
A Checklist of Sights

This list is very arbitrary and by no means complete. The places mentioned are just some of my favorites that I would recommend to you.

Museums and special places that have impressed me . . .

ITALY

Rome
Pantheon
Piazza Navona, night life
Castel Sant Angelo
Campidoglio Hill, Museo Capitollino, city history
Forum
Colosseum
Mamertine Prison, St. Peter's Prison
Santa Maria della Concezione, Cappuchin crypt, bones
St. Peter's Cathedral
Vatican Museum, Sistine Chapel
National Museum, near station, ancient art
Museo Etrusco
Baths of Caracalla, open-air opera
Tivoli, Villa D'Este
Tivoli, Hadrian's Villa
Ostia Antica, ancient port town

Milan
Duomo, cathedral, roof top
Santa Maria delle Grazie, Leonardo's Last Supper

Venice
Grand Canal
Basilica of San Marco
Doge's Palace
Campanile, bell tower
Basilica del Frari, Donatello's St. John the Baptist
Peggy Guggenheim Collection, modern art
Burano, lace town

Florence
Duomo, baptisery
Bargello
Palazzo Vecchio
Uffizi Gallery
Santa Croce
Accademia
Pitti Palace

San Gimignano

Siena

Assissi
Basilica di San Francesco

Orvieto
Duomo
bus to Bagnaregio, walk to Civita di Bagnaregio

Naples
Pompeii
Herculaneum
National Archeological Museum

350

Paestum
Greek Temple Site, in Italy

Palermo
Monreale Cathedral mosaics

Agrigento
Greek ruins

Syracuse
Greek ruins

GERMANY

Munich
Marianplatz
Residenz
Alte Pinakothek
Deutsches Museum
Mathaser's Beerhall
Dachau

Oberammergau
Die Weis Church, Bavarian Baroque

Fussen
Neuschwanstein, Mad King Ludwig's castle

Berchtesgaden
Salt Mine tour

Rothenberg
Rathaus tower view
Folterkammer, torture museum

Bodensee
Meersburg, town and castle
Tropical island of Mainau
Lindau, Venice of the North

Aachen
Charlemagne's Cathedral

Koln
Cathedral

Moselle Valley
Cochen Castle and town
Berg Eltz
Trier, Roman town

Rhine Cruise
Bingen to Koblenz
St. Goat, walk boat to castle

Bonn
Beethoven's Haus

Hamburg
St. Pauli, red light district

Berlin
Museum of the wall (escape attempts), at Checkpoint Charlie. East Berlin over Checkpoint Charlie
Pergamon Museum (E.B.)
Brandenburg Gate

AUSTRIA

Wien (Vienna)
Tourist Info near Opera
Hofburg
Schloss Schonbrunn
Kunsthistorisches Museum
Grinzing
Rathauskeller, City Hall restaurant

Salzburg
Castle
Hellbrunn Castle, trick fountains
Baroque cathedral
Mozart's birthplace
Music festival, late July through August

Graz
Laudeszeughaus, medieval armory

Reutte
Ruins of Ehrenburg castle

SWITZERLAND

Zurich
Kunsthaus, modern art
Swiss National Museum

Luzern
Medieval covered bridges

Berner Oberland
Best Alps, south of Interlaken

Murten
Walled Town

Lake Geneva
Chateau de Chillon

Geneva
Walking tour

ENGLAND

London
Houses of Parliament, tour

Westminster Hall, oak ceiling
#10 Downing Street
Trafalgar Square, museums
Piccadilly
Soho
British Museum
Victoria and Albert Museum
Hyde Park, Speaker's Corner
St. Paul's Cathedral
"The City"
Stock Exchange
"Old Bailey" Courthouse
Tower of London, tour, jewels
Museum of London
Tate Gallery, modern art
The Theaters, near Shaftsbury
    Ave.
Kew Gardens
Greenwich Maritime Museum and
    ships
Antique Markets
City walking tours, listed in
    "What's On"
Brass Rubbing

Canterbury
Cathedral

Cinque Ports
Rye

Dover
Castle

Battle
Battle (of Hastings) Abbey
Bodiam Castle

Brighton
Royal Pavilion
Palace Pier and promenade

South Downs
Beachy Head

Arundel
Castle

Salisbury
Cathedral
Stonehenge
Avebury stone circles

Bath
Roman and Medieval Baths
Pump Room, tea and scones
Royal Crescent, Circus
Assembly Rooms, Costume Museum

Bath Abbey
Scrumpy
Walking Tours, free

Wells
Cathedral

Glastonbury
Abbey

Tintagel
Castle, hostel, King Arthur

Oxford
University, walking tours
Blenheim Palace

Cotswald Villages
Stanton, Stanway — cutest
Stow-on-the-Wold, headquarters
Cirencester, Roman city, museum
Ironbridge Gorge, Industrial Rev-
    olution

York
Walled City, walking tours
Minister
York Castle Museum, outstanding

Hadrian's Wall, near Haltwhistle
Once Brewed, hostel, museum

Cambridge
University, walking tours
King's College Chapel

Edinburgh
Castle
Royal Mile, Robert Burns, Walter
    Scott, Robert Louis Stevenson
National Modern Art Gallery
Folk music in pubs

WALES

Cardiff
St. Fagan's Open Air Folk Mu-
    seum
Caerphilly, Europe's 2nd largest
    castle
St. David's Cathedral, Welsh
    speaking
Aberystwyth

Caernarfon
Castle

Snowdon
National Park

IRELAND

Dublin
National Museum
Trinity College
General Post Office
Hurling Match, Dog Racing

Rock of Cashel

Gaeltachts
Gaelic Pubs

Belfast
Ulster Museum and Art Gallery
Cultra Folk Museum

DENMARK

Copenhagen
Tivoli May 1-Sept. 17 amusement
park
Christiania, commune
National Museum
Nazi Resistence Museum
Carlsberg Brewery Tour
Louisiana, modern art, north

Helsingor
Hamlet's Castle

Roskilde
Viking Ships
Cathedral

Odense
Hans Christian Andersen land

NORWAY

Oslo
Radhuset, city hall tour
Nazi Resistance Museum, Aker-
shus
Bygdoy — Viking ships, Fram
Kon Tiki, Ra, Open Air Folk
Museum
Munch Museum
Frogner Park, Vigeland Sculp-
tures

Bergen
Bryggen
Hanseatic League Museum
Mt. Floien
Fantoft Stave Church
Troldhaugen, Edvard Grieg
Gamla Bergen

Trondheim
Nidaros Cathedral
Music Museum

Tonsberg
Historic town

SWEDEN

Stockholm
Sverigehuset (Sweden House,
tourist info)
Gamla Stan, old town
Djurgarden, Wasa
Skansen, Grona Lund, open air
folk museum
Historiska Museet
Kulturhuset
Sauna
Millesgarden, Carl Milles sculp-
ture
Planned suburbs

Lund, Malmo

FRANCE

Paris views:
Tour Eiffel
Tour Montparnasse
Arc de Triomphe, museum and
view on top
Notre Dame
Sacre Coeur
Pompidou Center

Ile de la Cite
Notre Dame
Ste.-Chapelle, stained glass
Conciergerie

Left Bank
Sorbonne University
Latin Quarter
Les Invalides, military museum,
Napoleon's tomb
Rodin Museum
Les Egouts (sewers tour)

Right Bank
Galeries Lafayette, shopping
American Express Co., mail
service
Jeu de Paume, Impressionism
Palais du Louvre, greatest art
museum

Palais de Tokyo, Post-Impressionism
Pompidou Gallery of Modern Art
Sacre Coeur, Place du Tetre
Musee de Cluny

Side Trips
Versailles, greatest palace
Le Hameau
Fontainebleau, Napoleon's Palace
Chantilly, great chateau
St. Denis, 1st Gothic church
Chartres, Malcolm Miller tours, greatest Gothic church

Rouen
well-preserved town

Bayeau
Tapestry, Battle of Hastings
Cathedral
Arromanches, D-Day landing museum

Mont. St. Michel

Carcassonne
Europe's greatest medieval fortress city

Avignon
Palais des Papes

Arles, Nimes
great Roman ruins

Nice
Museums of Matisse and Chagall

Loire Valley
Chateaux country
Tours — home base
Chambord, Chenenceau, Azay-le-Rideau, Chinon

Strasbourg
Cathedral, view
Route du Vin, Alsacian wine road, "degustation" — tasting
Riquewihr, Colmar

Reims
Champagne caves
Cathedral, gothic, Chagall stained glass

BELGIUM

Brussells
Grand Place

Musee d'Art Ancien, Flemish masters
Place du Jeu de Balle, flea market
See Brussels and Die . . . Laughing
Local Student Guide, excellent

Brugge
Markt, Belfry view
Groeninge and Gruuthuse museums, Flemish art
Begijnhof, peaceful old "nunnery"

Antwerp
Cathedral
Rubens' house

NETHERLANDS

Amsterdam
Rijksmuseum, Rembrandt
Van Gogh museum
Ann Frank's House, Nazi Resistance
Beginhof
Red Light District
Leisdeplein, nightlife

Alkmaar, Edam
cheese

Zaandijk
windmills

Den Haag
Peace Palace
Madurodam, mini-Holland
Torture Museum
Scheveningen beach resort town

SPAIN

Madrid
Prado Museum, Bosch, Goya
Puerto del Sol
Palacio Real, royal palace
Plaza Mayor, night life
Rastro, Sunday flea market

Segovia
Aqueduct, Roman
Alcazar, castle
Cathedral

Salamanca
Plaza Mayor, Spain's best square

Toledo
El Greco's House and museum
Museo de Santa Cruz, Santo Tome

Seville
Alcazar
Cathedral, Giralda
Piazza d'Espana
Weeping Vigin alterpiece

Ronda
Pileta Caves

Estepa
Convent's hilltop chapel, excellent

Cordoba
Moorish architecture

Granada
Alhambra, Generalife

Barcelona
Gaudi architecture
Ramblas

PORTUGAL

Lisbon
Alfama, sailor's district
Castelo Sao Jorge
Belem Tower
Hieronymite Monastery
Monument to Explorers
Coach and Maritime Museum

Sintra
Moorish castle ruins

Obidos
walled town

GREECE

Athens
Acropolis, temples, museum
Agora, Temple of Hephaistos
Plake, old town, shopping, night-
life
National Archeological Museum

Near Athens
Temple of Poseidon, Cape Soun-
ion
Daphne wine festival, monastery,
Byzantine mosaics
Delphi ruins

Peloponnese
Old Corinth
Mycenae
Nafplion
Epidauros

Islands
Mykonos, Delos
Crete, Palace and Museum of
Knossos, Gorge of Samaria
Rhodos, crusader city, boat to
Turkey

Appendix II — European Festivals

Each country has a "4th of July" celebration. A visit to a country during its national holiday can only make your stay more enjoyable.

Austria	Oct. 26	Morocco	March 3
Belgium	July 21	Netherlands	April 30
Bulgaria	Sept. 9	Norway	May 17
Czechoslovakia	May 9	Poland	July 22
Denmark	April 16	Portugal	April 25
Egypt	July 23	Romania	Aug. 23
Finland	Dec. 6	San Marino	Sept. 3
France	July 14	Spain	Oct. 12
East Germany	Oct. 7	Sweden	April 30
Greece	March 25	Switzerland	Aug. 1
Hungary	April 4	Turkey	Oct. 29
Ireland	March 17	USSR	Nov. 7
Italy	June 2	West Germany	June 17
Luxembourg	June 23	Yugoslavia	Nov. 29
Malta	Dec. 13		

EUROPEAN FESTIVALS

Austria
Salzburg Festival, July 26-Aug 30. Greatest musical festival, focus on Mozart

Belgium
Bruges, Ascension Day. Procession of Holy Blood. 3 p.m. (40 days after Easter). 1,500 locals in medieval costume.

"Adriaan Brouwerfeesten," last Sat & Sun in June. Beer festival in Oudenaarde, nice town 35 mi W of Brussels.

"Ommegang," 1st Thurs in July. Brussels' Grand Place. Colorful medieval pageant.

Denmark
Tivoli, May 1-Sept. 15. Always a festival. Copenhagen.

Midsummer Eve, June 23 & 24. Big festivities all over Scandinavia, bonfires, dancing, burning of tourists at the stake.

Roskilde Rock Festival, last weekend in June or 1st in July. Annual European Woodstock, fairground atmosphere, big acts. Roskilde, 20 mi W of Copenhagen.

Hans Christian Andersen Festival, mid July-mid Aug in Odense. Great family entertainment. Danish children perform fairy tales.

England

Jousting Tournament of Knights, last Sun & Mon in May at Chilham Castle near Canterbury. Medieval pageantry, colorful.

Allington Castle Medieval Market, 2nd or 3rd Sat in June in Maidstone (30 mi SE London). Medieval crafts and entertainment.

Druid Summer Solstice Ceremonies, June 20 or 21. Stonehenge, Hoods and white robes, rituals from midnight to sunrise at about 4:45 a.m.

Ainwick Medieval Fair, last Sun in June to next Sat. Medieval costumes, competition, entertainment. Ainwick, 30 mi N of Newscastle.

Haslemere Early Music Festival, 2 Fridays before 4th Sat in July. 16th-18th c. music on original instruments. 40 mi S of London.

Sidmouth Int'l Folklore Festival, 1st to 2nd Fridays of August, 300 events, 15 mi E of Exeter.

Reading Rock Festival, last weekend in August. England's best. 40 mi W of London.

Nottingham Goose Fair, 1st Thurs-Sat in Oct, one of England's oldest and largest fairs. Nottingham.

Guy Fawkes Day, Nov. 5. Nationwide holiday.

France

Fetes de la St. Jean, around June 24, 3 days of folklore and bull running in streets. St. Jean de Luz (on coast, S or Bordeaux).

Tour de France, first 3 weeks of July, 2,000 mile bike race around France ending in Paris.

Maubeuge Int'l Beer Festival, Thursday before July 14 for two weeks. Great entertainment and beer in largest beer tent. In Maubeuge near Belgian border.

Bastille Day, July 13 & 14. Great National Holiday all over France. Paris has biggest festivities.

Great Festival of Corouaille, 4th Sun in July, Huge Celtic folk festival at Quimper in Brittany.

Alsace Wine Fair, 2nd & 3rd weekends in Aug in Colmar.

Festival of Minstrels, 1st Sun in Sept. Wine, music, folklore, etc. in Ribeauville 35 mi S of Strasbourg.

Fete d'Humanite, 2nd or 3rd Sat and Sun of September. Huge communist fair color festivities — not all red. Paris.

Germany

Der Meistertrunk, Sat before Whit Monday. Music, dancing, beer, sausage in Rothenburg o.d.T.

Pied Piper's Procession, Sundays, 1:00 p.m. all summer, Hamlin (where else?).

Ayinger Volksfest, 2nd thru 3rd weekend in June. White bear, concerts and Maypole dancing at Aying, 15 mi SE of Munich.

Freiburger Weinfest, last Fri thru following Tuesday in June. Wine festival in Black Forest town of Freiburg.

Kinderzeche, weekend before 3rd Mon in July to weekend after. Festival honoring children who saved town in 1640's. Dinkelsbuhl.

Trier Weinfest, Sat to 1st Mon in Aug. Trier.

Gaubondenfest, 2nd Fri in Aug for 10 days. 2nd only to Oktoberfest. Straubing 25 mi SE of Regensburg.

Der Rhein in Flammen, 2nd Sat in Aug. Dancing, wine and beer festivals, bonfires. Koblenz to Braubach.

Moselfest, last weekend in Aug or 1st in Sept. Mosel wine festival in Winningen.

Backfischfest, last Sat in Aug for 15 days. Largest wine and folk festival on the Rhine in Worms.

Wurstmarkt, 2nd Sat, Sept, through following Tuesday. And 3rd Fri through following Monday. World's largest wine festival in Bad Durkheim, 25 mi W of Heidelberg.

Oktoberfest, starting 3rd to last Sat in Sept through 1st Sun in Oct. World's most famous beer festival, Munich.

Greece

Epidaurus Festival, approx 1st of July to 1st of Sept. Greek drama and comedy. 2,500 yr old amphitheatre. Epidaurus, 100 mi SW of Athens.

Rhodes Wine Festival, 1st Sat in July through 1st Sun in Sept. Great variety of Greek wines. Arts, handicrafts, music, dancing. Rhodes.

Dafni Wine Festival, 2nd Sat in July through 1st Sun in Sept. Many varieties of wine, music, dancing, restaurant. Nominal cost. Special bus from Koumoundourou Square. 5 mi from center of Athens.

Ireland

Pan Celtic Week, 2nd through 3rd weekends in May. Singing competitions, bagpipes, harps, stepdancing, wrestling, hurling. Killarney.

Fleadh Cheoil na h-Eireann, last weekend in Aug. Ireland's traditional folk musicians. National festival, locale changes yearly.

Italy

Sagra del Pesche, 2nd Sunday in May. One of Italy's great popular events, huge feast of freshly caught fish, fried in world's largest pans. Camogli, 10 mi S of Genoa.

Festa de Ceri, May 15. One of the world's most famous folklore events, colorful pageant, giant feast afterwards. Gubbio, in hill country, 25 mi NE of Perugia.

"Palio of the Archers," last Sun of May. Re-enactment of medieval crossbow contest with arms and costumes. Gubbio, 130 mi NE of Rome.

"Palio," July 2 and Aug 16. Horse race which is Italy's most spectacular folklore event. Medieval procession beforehand. 35,000 spectators. Siena, 40 mi SW of Florence.

Joust of the Saracen, 1st Sun of Sept. Costumed equestrian tournament dating from 13th c. Crusades against the Muslim Saracens. Arezzo, 40 mi SE of Florence.

Historical Regatta, 1st Sun of Sept. Gala procession of decorated boats followed by double-oared gondola race. Venice.

Human Chess Game, 1st or 2nd weekend in Sept on even-numbered years. Medieval pageantry and splendor accompany re-enactment of human chess game in 1454. Basso Castle in Marostica, 40 mi NW of Venice.

Netherlands

Kaasmarkt, Fridays only from late April to late Sept. Colorful cheese market with members of 350 yr old Cheese Carriers' Guild. Alkmaar, 15 mi N of Amsterdam.

North Sea Jazz Festival, weekend of 3rd Sun in July. World's greatest jazz weekend. 100 concerts with 500+ musicians. Den Haag.

Norway

Constitution Day, May 17. Independence parades and celebration. Oslo.

Midsummer, June 23-24. "Jonsok Eve" celebrated with bonfires, beer, open-air dancing, boating, Nationwide.

Horten Festivalen, 1st Sun in July. Small festival features all kinds of music, esp rock. Located 50 mi S of Oslo in Horten and reached by train & bus from the Oslo West station.

Portugal

Popular Saints Fair, June 12, 13; 23, 24; 28, 29. Celebration of 3 favorite saints. Parades, singing, dancing in streets, bonfires, bullfights. Lisbon.

Feirade Santiago, July 25-Aug 8. Celebration for patrons saint featuring feast day, cultural events, folklore, bullfights. Setubal, 20 mi SE of Lisbon.

Romaria de Senhor da Nazare, 2nd weekend in Sept. 3 colorful processions in picturesque fishing village. Daily bullfights, market, nightly folk music, dancing. 70 mi N of Lisbon. Nazare.

Scotland

Beltane Festival, approx 3rd week of June. Ancient festival dates from Celtic sun worship festival and is combined with annual Common Riding. Peebles, 25 mi S of Edinburgh.

Inverness Highland Gathering, 2nd Sat in July. Athletes in kilts, bagpipers, traditional dancing. Inverness, 160 mi NW of Edinburgh.

Edinburgh Festival, 3rd to last Sun in Aug through 2nd Sat in Sept. World's most comprehensive performing arts festival. Edinburgh.

Argyllshire Highland Gathering, 4th or last Thurs in Aug. Athletics, dancing, piping competition. Oban, 95 mi NW of Glasgow.

Cowal Highland Gathering, last Fri and Sat in Aug. One of the largest Highland Gatherings. Complete highland festivities. Dunoon, on coast west of Greenock and 25 mi (via ferry connection) NW of Glasgow.

Braemar Royal Highland Gathering, 1st Sat in Sept. Largest and most famous highland gathering with Royal Family in attendance. Braemar, 60 mi W of Aberdeen.

Spain

Int'l Music and Dance Festival, approx early July. Classical music and ballet in courtyard of the Alhambra. Leading performing arts festival in Spain. Grenada.

Running of the Bulls, July 6-14. World-famous "encierros," (running of the bulls), accompanied by religious observances, processions, jubilant festivities. Pamplona.

St. James Fair, approx July 15-31. Festivities, fireworks, fairs, cultural events. Santiago de Compostela, 390 mi NW of Madrid.

El Encierros de Cuellar, last Sun in Aug through following Wed. Spain's oldest running of the bulls event. Dances, bullfights. Cuellar, 35 mi N of Segovia.

Sweden

Midsummer, Fri and Sat nearest June 24. Dancing, games, music during height of summertime when days are longest. Nationwide, and throughout Scandinavia.

Asele Market, 2nd or 3rd weekend in July. Laplanders' most important folk festival for 200 years. Asele, 400 mi N of Stockholm.

Ancient Gotland Athletic Games, Sat and 2nd Sun in July. Ancient sports contests between Norsemen. Stanga (Gotland) 25 mi SE of Visby.

Switzerland

Landsgemeinda, 1st Sun in May. Largest open-air parliamentary session. Glarus, 40 mi SE of Zurich.

Montreux International Jazz Festival, 1st through 3rd weekends in July. Comprehensive annual musical events featuring top artists. Montreux.

William Tell Plays, 2nd Thurs in July through 1st Sun in Sept. Dramatic presentations retelling the story of William Tell. Open-air theatre. Interlaken.

Swiss National Day, Aug. 1. Festive national holiday! Parades, concerts, bell ringing, fireworks, yodeling, boat rides. Nationwide.

Yugoslavia

Hay Making Day, 1st Sun. in July. Competition in hay making, horseracing, stone throwing. Folk costumes. Kupres, by bus from Banja Luka (55 mi), Split (65 mi), or Sarajevo (75 mi).

Zagreb International Folklore Festival, next to last Sun through last Sun in July. One of Europe's largest folklore revues. Zagreb, 230 mi NW of Belgrade.

These are just a few of Europe's countless folk and music festivals. Each country's National Tourist Office in the USA will send you a free calendar of events. The best book I've seen for a listing of the great festivals of Europe is Playboy's *Guide to Good Times: Europe*, $2.95. ISBN 0-872-16819-0.

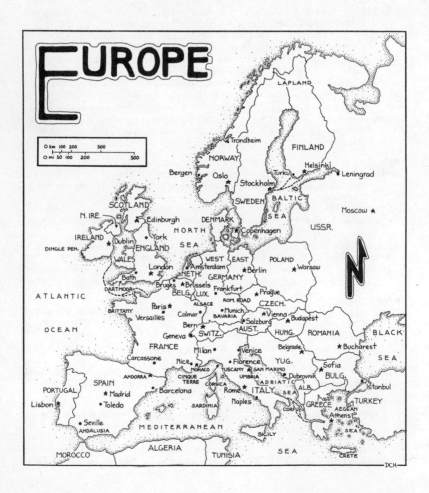

Appendix III – Sample Train Trips

SAMPLE EUROPEAN TRAIN TRIPS

How long they take and how much they cost in 1984.

From . . . . To		2nd Class (One Way)	Journey Time (Hours)
Amsterdam	Brussels	$19	3½
	Frankfurt	42	6
	Copenhagen	72	12
	Munich	74	12
	Paris	42	5½
	Vienna	96	15
	Zurich	78	11
Athens	Munich	94	39
	Beograd	43	20
Barcelona	Marseilles	38	8
	Madrid	38	8
	Rome	81	20
	Paris	79	12
Berlin	Hamburg	22	3½
	Brussels	64	10
	Warsaw	32	9
	Paris	85	14
Brindisi	Rome	25	7
	Patras	75	17
Kopenhavn	Koln	69	11
	Oslo	53	10
	Rome	155	31
	Paris	107	14
	Stockholm	44	8
Madrid	Lisbon	30	9
	Seville	30	6
	Paris	93	16
Oslo	Trondheim	50	8

Paris	Stavanger	52	9
	Bergen	45	7
	Marseilles	63	8
	Rome	80	17
	Venice	71	13
	Vienna	104	15
	Zurich	49	7½
Rome	Venice	22	6

1st Class tickets cost 50% more than 2nd Class.

There are faster and slower trains — these times are average.

Any journey of 6 hours or longer can be taken overnight.

From this list you should be able to estimate the time and money required for any European train journey. Remember times and costs of journeys per inch on the map are roughly similar at equal latitudes. So to estimate time and cost of a southern journey, compare it to a southern entry on this list. Northern trains are faster and more expensive. Don't worry about more exact information until you get to Europe. Plan with this chart, cocky confidence and a spirit of adventure.

Rhine Cruise

Table 700   KÖLN-DÜSSELDORFER DEUTSCHE RHEINSCHIFFAHRT AG
KD GERMAN RHINE LINE

Tar. km		S	D	Exp O	H	N	R	E	H	P	fast C‡	A	G	J	F	Q	H	M
100	Koblenz {arr.			1100			1120		1335	1355					C		1545	1750	1900
105	dep.		9 00	1105	1030		1130	1130	1340	1400	1400	1400		1430				1905
105	Niederlahnstein dep.		9 24			1055		1155	1155			1425		1455				1930
112	Braubach dep.		9 58		1130			1225	1225		1445	1445	1455		1525				2005
121	Boppard dep.	9 05	1040		1130	1220		1250	1315	1315	d	1525	1525	1544		1615			2045
137	St. Goarshausen dep.	1015	1150			1335	1330	1400	1425	1440		1625	1625	1655		1725		
137	St. Goar dep.	1025	1155			1340	1340	1405	1435	1445		1630	1630	1700		1735		
154	Bacharach dep.	1130	1255		1208	1440	1445	1505	1540	1545		1725	1725	1803		1840		
166	Assmannshausen dep.	1235	1350			1535	1535	1600	1635	1640		1810	1810	1905		1935		
170	Bingen dep.	1305	1420		1228	1605	1602	1630	1705	1710		1835	1835	1930		2000		
172	Rüdesheim arr.	1320	1430		1233	1615	1620	1640	1715	1720		1850	1850	1940		2010		
187	Eltville dep.					1720		1745	1820	1825		1955	1955					
195	Wiesbaden-Biebrich arr.				1300	1805	1800	1835	1910	1910		2040	2040					
200	Mainz arr.				1310	1825	1820	1855	1930	1930		2100	2100					
225	Frankfurt/Main arr.					2130												

Tar. km		A	fast L‡	L	BB	J	F	B	N	T	Q	E	S	P	Exp O
25	Frankfurt/Main dep.							7 15							
0	Mainz dep.		8 45	8 45				1015	1000		1045			1425
5	Wiesbaden-Biebrich dep.		9 05	9 05				1035	1020		1105			1433
13	Eltville dep.		9 25	9 25					1040		1125			
28	Rüdesheim dep.		1015	1015	9 50	9 50		1145	1130		1220		1400		1500
30	Bingen dep.		1030	1030	1015	1015		1200	1145		1235		1415		1505
34	Assmannshausen dep.		1045	1045	1030	1030		1215	1200		1250		1430		
46	Bacharach dep.		1110	1110	1108	1108		1240	1235		1325		1505		
63	St. Goar dep.		1140	1140				1310	1320		1410		1550		
63	St. Goarshausen dep.		1145	1145	1200	1200		1315	1325		1420		1600		1540
79	Boppard dep.		1225	1225	1240	1240					1510		1645	d	1555
88	Braubach dep.		1250		1310						1540		1715		
95	Niederlahnstein dep.				1332						1602		1737		
100	Koblenz {arr.		1330	1320	1350						1620		1755		1720 1618
100	dep.			1330					1550	1625		1800		1725 1620

A— Daily, Apr. 20–30.
B— Suns, May 1–June 2.
C— Daily, May 1–Sept. 18.
D— Daily, April 20–Oct. 30.
E— Daily, June 12–Sept. 18.
F— April 21, 22 and daily April 25–Sept. 18.
G— Daily, Sept. 19–Oct. 30.
H—Daily, Sept. 19–Oct. 2.
J— Daily, Oct. 3–30.
K— Daily, April 20–Oct. 2.
L— Daily, May 1–Oct. 2.
M—Daily, June 12–Sept. 18 (not Koblenz-Boppard on Sats.).
N—Daily except Weds. May 1–Sept. 18.
O—Express service, daily except Mons., May 1–Oct. 2 by hydrofoil *Rheinpfeil*. Also runs Apr. 21, 22, 28, 29,Oct. 8, 9, 15, 16, 22, 23, 29, 30. Special fares apply.
P— Mons., Tues. and Thurs., July 11–Aug. 18 also June 13, 20, 27, July 4, Aug. 22, 29, Sept. 5, 12.

Q—Daily Sept. 19–Oct. 2, also Sats. and Suns. July 10–Aug
R— Daily, Oct. 3–9.
S— Daily, June 12–Sept. 18, except Aug. 27, Sept. 3, 10, 1;
T— Daily, Sept. 19–Oct. 9.
W—Daily, May 8–Oct. 16.
Y— Daily, May 8–Sept. 11.
Z— Daily, Sept. 12–Oct. 15.
AA—Daily, Sept. 12–Oct, 16.
BB—Daily, Oct. 3–30.
b— Daily except Mons., July 10–Aug. 21.
d— Rhine/Moselle excursion to/from Kobern (Moselle).
‡— Fast ship, supplement payable (not applicable between and Köln Sept. 19–Oct. 2).
§— Fast ship, supplement payable applicable only from to Mainz.

European Weather

Here is a list of average temperatures and days of no rain. This can be helpful in planning your itinerary, but I have never found European weather to be particularly predictable.

1st line: ave. daily low; 2nd: ave. daily high; 3rd: days of no rain

	J	F	M	A	M	J	J	A	S	O	N	D
AUSTRIA	26°	28°	34°	41°	50°	56°	59°	58°	52°	44°	36°	30°
Vienna	34°	38°	47°	57°	66°	71°	75°	73°	66°	55°	44°	37°
	23	21	24	21	22	21	22	21	23	23	22	22
BELGIUM	31°	31°	35°	39°	46°	50°	54°	54°	50°	44°	36°	33°
Brussels	42°	43°	49°	56°	65°	70°	73°	72°	67°	58°	47°	42°
	19	18	20	18	21	19	20	20	19	19	18	18
DENMARK	29°	28°	31°	37°	44°	51°	55°	54°	49°	42°	35°	32°
Copenhagen	36*	36°	41°	50°	61°	67°	72°	69°	63°	53°	43°	38°
	22	21	23	21	23	22	22	19	22	22	20	20
EGYPT	42°	44°	50°	59°	69°	70°	73°	73°	71°	65°	54°	45°
Luxor	74°	79°	86°	95°	104°	106°	107°	106°	103°	98°	87°	78°
	31	28	31	30	31	30	31	31	30	31	30	31
FINLAND	17°	15°	22°	31°	41°	49°	58°	55°	46°	37°	30°	22°
Helsinki	27°	26°	32°	43°	55°	63°	71°	66°	57°	45°	37°	31°
	20	20	23	22	23	21	23	19	19	19	19	20
FRANCE	32°	34°	36°	41°	47°	52°	55°	55°	50°	44°	38°	33°
Paris	42°	45°	52°	60°	67°	73°	76°	75°	69°	59°	49°	43°
	16	15	16	16	18	19	19	19	19	17	15	14
	40°	41°	45°	49°	56°	62°	66°	66°	62°	55°	48°	43°
Nice	56°	56°	59°	64°	69°	76°	81°	81°	77°	70°	62°	58°
	23	20	23	23	23	25	29	26	24	22	23	23
GERMANY	29°	31°	35°	41°	48°	53°	56°	55°	51°	43°	36°	31°
Frankfurt	37°	42°	49°	58°	67°	72°	75°	74°	67°	56°	45°	39°
	22	19	22	21	22	21	21	21	21	22	21	20
GREAT BRITAIN	35°	35°	37°	40°	45°	51°	55°	54°	51°	44°	39°	36°
London	44°	45°	51°	56°	63°	69°	73°	72°	67°	58°	49°	45°
	14	15	20	16	18	19	18	18	17	17	14	15
GREECE	42°	43°	46°	52°	60°	67°	72°	72°	66°	60°	52°	46°
Athens	54°	55°	60°	67°	77°	85°	90°	90°	83°	74°	64°	57°
	24	22	26	27	28	28	30	30	28	27	24	24
IRELAND	35°	35°	36°	38°	42°	48°	51°	51°	47°	43°	38°	36°
Dublin	47°	47°	51°	54°	59°	65°	67°	67°	63°	57°	51°	47°
	18	17	21	19	20	19	18	18	18	19	18	18
ITALY	39°	39°	42°	46°	55°	60°	64°	64°	61°	53°	46°	41°
Rome	54°	56°	62°	68°	74°	82°	88°	88°	83°	73°	63°	56°
	23	17	26	24	25	28	29	28	24	22	22	22
PORTUGAL	47°	57°	50°	52°	56°	60°	64°	65°	62°	58°	52°	48°
(Lagos/Algarve)	61°	61°	63°	67°	73°	77°	83°	84°	80°	73°	66°	62°
	22	19	20	24	27	29	31	31	28	26	22	22
	46°	47°	49°	52°	56°	60°	63°	64°	62°	57°	52°	47°
Lisbon	56°	58°	61°	64°	69°	75°	79°	80°	76°	69°	62°	57°
	22	20	21	23	25	28	30	30	26	24	20	21

1st line: ave. daily low; 2nd: ave. daily high; 3rd: days of no rain

	J	F	M	A	M	J	J	A	S	O	N	D
MOROCCO	40°	43°	48°	52°	57°	62°	67°	68°	63°	57°	49°	52°
Marrakesh	65°	68°	74°	79°	84°	92°	101°	100°	92°	83°	3°	66°
	24	23	25	24	29	29	30	30	27	27	27	24
	47°	48°	50°	51°	56°	60°	64°	65°	63°	59°	52°	48°
Tangiers	60°	61°	63°	65°	71°	76°	80°	82°	78°	72°	65°	61°
	21	18	21	22	26	27	31	31	27	23	20	21
NETHERLANDS	34°	34°	37°	43°	50°	55°	59°	59°	56°	48°	41°	35°
Amsterdam	40°	41°	46°	52°	60°	65°	69°	68°	64°	56°	47°	41°
	12	13	18	16	19	18	17	17	15	13	11	12
NORWAY	20°	20°	25°	34°	43°	51°	56°	53°	45°	37°	29°	24°
Oslo	30°	32°	40°	50°	62°	69°	73°	69°	60°	49°	37°	31°
	23	21	24	23	24	22	21	20	22	21	21	21
SPAIN	33°	35°	40°	44°	50°	57°	62°	62°	56°	48°	40°	35°
Madrid	47°	51°	57°	64°	71°	80°	87°	86°	77°	66°	54°	48°
	22	19	20	21	22	24	28	29	24	23	20	22
	42°	44°	47°	51°	57°	63°	69°	69°	65°	58°	50°	44°
Barcelona	56°	57°	61°	64°	71°	77°	81°	82°	67°	61°	62°	57°
	26	21	24	22	23	25	27	26	23	23	23	25
	47°	48°	51°	55°	60°	66°	70°	72°	68°	61°	53°	48°
Malaga	61°	62°	64°	69°	74°	80°	84°	85°	81°	74°	67°	62°
	25	22	23	25	28	29	31	30	28	27	22	25
SWEDEN	23°	22°	26°	32°	41°	49°	55°	53°	46°	39°	31°	26°
Stockholm	31°	31°	37°	45°	57°	65°	70°	66°	58°	48°	38°	33°
	23	21	24	24	23	23	22	21	22	22	21	22
SWITZERLAND	29°	30°	35°	41°	48°	55°	58°	57°	52°	44°	37°	31°
Geneva	39°	43°	51°	58°	66°	73°	77°	76°	69°	58°	47°	40°
	20	19	21	19	19	19	22	21	20	20	19	21
TURKEY	39°	41°	45°	51°	59°	66°	71°	72°	66°	58°	51°	43°
Antakya area	57°	59°	66°	74°	83°	89°	93°	94°	91°	84°	73°	61°
	23	21	25	25	27	28	30	30	29	28	25	24
YUGOSLAVIA	27°	27°	35°	45°	53°	58°	61°	60°	55°	47°	39°	30°
Belgrade	37°	41°	53°	64°	74°	79°	84°	83°	76°	65°	52°	40°
	23	22	24	21	22	21	25	24	24	23	23	22
	42°	43°	47°	51°	58°	64°	69°	69°	65°	58°	51°	46°
Dubrovnik	52°	53°	57°	63°	71°	78°	83°	83°	76°	69°	60°	55°
	23	21	23	23	26	26	28	28	25	23	21	21

Metric Conversion Table
Approximate

1 inch	= 25 millimeters	1 ounce	= 28 grams
1 foot	= 0.3 meter	1 pound	= 0.45 kilogram
1 yard	= 0.9 meter	Temp. (F.)	= 9/5 C + 32
1 mile	= 1.6 kilometers	1 kilogram	= 2.2 lbs.
1 sq. yd.	= 0.8 square meter	1 kilometer	= .62 mile
1 acre	= 0.4 hectare	1 centimeter	= 0.4 inch
1 quart	= 0.95 liter	1 meter	= 39.4 inches

WORLD HUNGER
A CHALLENGE FOR YOU!

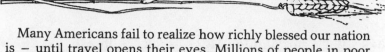

Many Americans fail to realize how richly blessed our nation is — until travel opens their eyes. Millions of people in poor countries will work for twenty years and earn less than what you might spend on this year's vacation ($2,000). As Americans, we are gluttonous kings of the money mountain. We don't have to feel guilty — but we should feel concerned about this inequity. I've found that education cements my commitment to fighting hunger. How's your education? Books like **Bread for the World** by Simon, and **Rich Christians** by Sider are great eye-openers.

World Concern is the most effective and efficient relief organization I've found. Teaching people to be self-sufficient and administering long-term solutions to horrifying immediate problems — with 77 cents out of every dollar contributed actually getting to the workers who are currently working in Asian, African and Latin American trouble spots — I am proud to support them. Their concrete results have proven to me that each one of us, in the comfort of our own comfy world, can make a difference.

So many of us are outraged by the killing and suffering of innocent people we see on the news. Passive outrage. The news doesn't tell us that 15 million children die slow hunger-related deaths each year (40,000 per day) because our society doesn't want to hear that kind of news. It's hopeful, not hopeless. There's more than enough food. With education, compassion and distribution our generation can do to hunger what the people of the 1800s did to slavery — end it.

When I travel I take as much money as I expect to need. If I return with money I give half of it to people who will never see their name on a plane ticket. If this book causes you to bring home some extra money, may I challenge you to do the same? It's a nice way to end a trip. Thanks a million.

For more information write:

 **WORLD CONCERN**®   19303 Fremont Avenue North
Seattle, WA 98133

or call:

800-421-7010

━━━ BACK DOOR CATALOG ━━━

Send Me a Postcard —
Drop Me a Line

Thousands of trips are shaped by this book. I take that as a very heavy responsibility and do my best to keep every page conscientious and up to date. Things do change, however, and travelers are always making new discoveries. I would really appreciate any corrections, additional ideas and discoveries, comments, criticisms and feedback of any kind. All reader correspondence will receive a reply and the latest edition of our Back Door Travel Newsletter.

If you would like to share your discoveries with other "Back Door" readers or help me improve the next edition of ETBD, please send a card to **Europe Through the Back Door,** 111 4th North, Edmonds, WA 98020. Thanks and happy travels!

Index

A

Aiguille du Midi 274
Albania 329
alcohol 98
Alfama 319
alpine huts 48
Alps 210, 267
Alsace 278, 297
American, beautiful 188
American, ugly 186
Amsterdam 219
Andalusia 312
Andorra 348
antiques 249
Aosta 274
APEX 40
art 164
Assisi 224
Aswan 346
Athens 333
Attila 191
Avignon 219

B

backgammon 334, 338
backpackademia 32
Badtowns 348-350
Bagnoregio 229
bargaining 110
Basque 295
Bath 254-255
Bavaria 259
bed and breakfast 78
Belfast 241
Belgrade 349
big city shock 173
Big Mac 50
Black Forest 348
black market 116
books 15
Bordeaux 295, 348
Bregenz, Austria 219
Breton 283
Brittany 283-285, 297
Bucharest 349

budget 103
Bulgaria 307-309
bus tour self-defense 177-181
buses 174
Bygdoy 298

C

Cairo 342
camera 157-158
camping 79
Capuchin Monks 236
car travel 42-44
Carcassonne 286-288
Carmichael, Hoagy 340
carry-on bag 32
Castle Day 263-266
Celtic 283
Chamonix 274
changing money 107
Charlemagne 286
charter 40
CIEE 17
Cinqueterre 231-234
city survival 173-175
Civita de Bagnoregio 228-230
classes 19
clothes, wash 204
clothing 34
Colmar 280-282
communal money 14
complainers 51
contact lenses 144
continental breakfast 96
Copenhagen 219
Cordoba 312
Costa del Sol 312
Cracker Jack boy 45
creative worrier 190
crowds 22

D

Dalmatian Coast 326
Dartmoor 252
dental 143

diarrhea 147
diet 145
Dingle Peninsula 238-240
Dinklesbuhl 259
doctor 143
dollar 64
driving 43-44
Dubrovnik 326

E

Eastern Europe 304-306
Egypt 342-347
Ehrenburg ruins 265
Eiger 268
English Channel 53
Erzurum 337
Estepa 314
Etruscan 226
Eurailpass 25, 48, 259
Europe's Appalachia 327
Europe's magic carousel 192
extrovert 192

F

festivals 30
Fez 324
film 159
first aid 144
flea markets 110
Florence 219, 224
flying 39
folk museums 167
France 292
French cuisine 295-297
Frommer Books 16
Fussen 259

G

Gaeltacht 238
galloping gluttons 87
Gandhi 191
gelati 92
Georges Pompidou Center 172
geriatric globe-trotting 202
Gidleigh 252
Gimmelwald 269-270
Gites Ruraux 285
Granada 312

Gubrovo 308
Gummi Bears 95

H

Hare Krishna approach 62
health 23, 143
Helsinki 302
hiking 47
hitchhiking 44
home-base strategy 218
hostel sheet 35
hostels 73-77
hotels 66-73

I

immunizations 143
Industrial Revolution 167
inflation 64
insurance 292
Interail 52
Interlaken 269
international words 126
Ireland, the troubles 200
Issenheim Alterpiece 281
Italy 210
itinerary 21-30

J

jaded 24
jet lag 30-31
Jungfrau 267

K

Kew Gardens 249
kickbacks 178
Killarney 238
kilo 99
kilometers 44
KISS rule 190
Kleine Scheidegg 267
Kon-Tiki 298
Kurds 200

L

language barrier 120-126
laundry 34, 204
Lauterbrunnen Valley 268
Let's Go: Europe 15

Lisbon   210, 317-320
Loire Valley   263
London   209, 219, 245-251
Lorraine   297
Louvre   170
Luxor   342

M

Mad King Ludwig II   263
Madrid   219
mail stops   29
map   43, 173
Marrakesh   322
McGoo, Mr.   173
men, horney   153
Mensas   95
Michelin   17, 293
Michelin Red Guide   297
money belt   114
Monreale   236
Monterosso   231
Morocco   321-325
Moscow   310-311
Mt. Blanc   274
Munich   219, 259
Murren   269
museums   164
museums, open air folk   166

N

National Tourist Offices   19, 168
Neuschwanstein   263
Nile   344
Normandy   296
North Ireland   241-244
Norway   298
numbers   184
Nurnberg   349
Nutella   95

O

open-jaws   22
orientation   174
Orvieto   225
Oslo   298-300

P

packing light   32-38
Palermo   235-237

Paris   171, 209, 219, 289
pensions   78
phone booth   181
photography   157-163
pick-pockets   113
picnic   98-103
Pileta Caves   315
Plovdiv   307
politics   200
porters   54
portrait   162
Portugal   317
pride   104
pride, swallow   192
Provence   295
public transportation   174-175
pubs   251

R

restaurants   87
Reutte   265
Rhine   278
Rhodes   335
rijstafel   93
Riviera   231
Romantic Road   259-262
Ronda   315
Rothenburg   259
Route du Vin   278
Russians   310

S

Samaria, Gorge of   330-332
Samos   333
San Gimignano   224
Santa's Village   166
Scandinavia   211
Schilthorn   270
Seville   312
shopping   180, 207
showers   72-73
Siena   224
Sigtuna   302
silver spoons   186
sink stopper   205
sleeping bag   35
smorgasbord   94
Sofia   307
souflaki   91

souvenir strategy   206
Spain   210
Spanish hotels   312
Speaker's Corner   249
stand-by   40
Stockholm   301-303
Stonehenge   252
stress   88
subway   174
suitcase   33
Sweden   301
Switzerland   267-273

T

Tangiers   321
Tate Gallery   248
telephoning   181
terrorism   199-202
theater   250
theft   113
Thessaloniki   349
thief   113
things, ugly   95
tip packs   109
tipping   90
toilet paper   149
toilets   149
tour, walking   18, 47, 177
tour, whirlwind   209
tours   11
tours, guided   175
town-hopping, high speed   217
train, most scenic ride   210
train schedules   57
trains   48-63
travel agencies   194
travel agent — quiz   196
travel industry   194
travel partner   75
traveler's checks   106-107
traveling alone   12
tube   245

Turkey   333-341
Turkey, eastern   337-341
Tuscany   224-227
24-hour clock   184

U

Ulster   241
Umbria   224-227
Unterlinden Museum   281
Upsalla   302
USSR   310

V

vagabondage   12
Vernazza   232
Versailles   289
Victoria Station   53
Vikings   298
Visa cards   88
Vosges mountains   278

W

walking gunny sacks   338
Warsaw Pact   305
water   96-97
weather   22
wine festival   91
wine tasting   279
women, single   152

Y

Yankee fetish   72
York Castle Museum   256
youth hostels   73
Yugoslavia   326

Z

zimmer   78
Zurich   348

About the Author

Rick Steves graduated with honors degrees (magna justa barely) in European History and Business Administration from the University of Washington — but that's not where he received his education.

His true education was gained during fifteen years of extensive European travel. From Ireland's Dingle Peninsula to the oasis towns of Saharan Morocco; from Swedish Lapland, lit by the midnight sun, to the ornate subways of Moscow; from the scalps of the Alps to the beaches of Greece, Steves has crisscrossed Europe. With budgets ranging from $3 to $20 a day, he has had no choice but to learn the tricks of budget travel. He travels with finesse. Armed with the philosophy that the less you spend, the closer you get to the real Europe, budget travel has been a joy as well as an education.

Steves has lectured on budget travel throughout the West Coast for ten years. For eight years he has taught "European Travel — Cheap!," a popular five-week course at the University of Washington. He spends a part of each summer leading small "back door" tours through Europe.

His experience as a tour group leader, travel consultant, and travel columnist for several newspapers led him to the logical next step — this book.

Other European Travel Guides by Rick Steves You're Sure to Enjoy!

Europe 101: History, Art and Culture for the Traveler
376 pages, $9.95

Finally, travelers have Europe 101! The first and only travelers guide to Europe's history and art. Full of boiled down, practical information to make your sightseeing more meaningful and enjoyable. Your "passport to culture" in a fun, easy to read manual.

Europe Through the Back Door
1985 Edition, Revised and Expanded, 376 pages, $9.95

The lessons of 14 years of budget European travel packaged into 376 fun to read pages. All the basic skills of budget independent travel, plus 34 special "Back Doors" where you'll find the Europe most tourists miss. Sure to make you a seasoned traveler on your first trip.

Europe in 22 Days: A Step by Step Guide & Travel Itinerary
96 pages, $4.95

Europe's best three weeks — in recipe form. The most efficient mix of famous "must see" sights, intimate "back door" nooks and off-beat crannies. A step by step handbook with city maps, day plans, train schedules, tips on cultural emersion. Ideal for do-it-yourselfers — with or without a tour.

Travel Guides from
John Muir Publications

I'd like to order the terrific travel guides checked below ...

Quantity	Title	Each	Total
	Europe Through the Back Door — *Steves*	$9.95	
	Europe 101: History, Art & Culture for Travelers — *Steves*	$9.95	
	Europe in 22 Days — *Steves*	$4.95	
	Complete Guide to Bed & Breakfasts, Inns & Guesthouses In the U.S. & Canada — *Lanier*	$10.95	
	Free Attractions USA — *VanMeer*	$10.95	
	The People's Guide to Mexico (Revised) — *Franz*	$10.95	
	The People's Guide to Camping in Mexico — *Franz*	$10.00	
	The On & Off the Road Cookbook — *Franz & Havens*	$8.50	

Subtotal $

Shipping $1.50

Total Enclosed $

Send order to:
John Muir Publications
P.O. Box 613
Santa Fe, NM 87504

ALLOW 4 TO 6 WEEKS FOR DELIVERY

Please send my order to:
Name _____
Street _____
City _____ State _____ ZIP _____

☐ I'm not ready to order yet. Send me your FREE descriptive catalog.